Uncle John's

FOURTH BATHROOM READER

by
The Bathroom Readers'
Institute

St. Martin's Press
New York

UNCLE JOHN'S FOURTH BATHROOM READER. Copyright © 1991 by The Bathroom Readers' Institute. All rights reserved. Printed in the United States of America. No part of this book may be used or reproduced in any manner whatsoever without written permission except in the case of brief quotations embodied in critical articles or reviews. For information, address St. Martin's Press, 175 Fifth Avenue, New York, N.Y. 10010.

Library of Congress Cataloging-in-Publication Data

Uncle John's fourth bathroom reader / the Bathroom Readers' Institute.
p.   cm.
ISBN 0-312-06484-5 (pbk.)
1. American wit and humor.   I. Bathroom Readers' Institute
(Berkeley, Calif.)   II. Title: Fourth bathroom reader.
PN6153.U455   1991
818'.02—dc20   91-20579   CIP

10 9 8 7 6 5 4 3

THANK YOU

The Bathroom Readers' Institute sincerely thanks the people whose advice and assistance made this book possible, including:

John Javna	Nenelle Bunnin
John Dollison	Sharilyn Hovind
Jack Mingo	Ann Krueger Spivack
Phil Catalfo	Audrey Baer Johnson
Ross Owens	Gary the proofreader
Eric Lefcowitz	Penelope Houston
Mike Litchfield	Mike Goldberger
Fritz Springmeyer	Gordon Van Gelder
Lyn Speakman	Jay Nitschke
Catherine Dee	Mike Brumsfeld
Lenna Lebovich	Tia Kratter
Melanie Foster	Zoila Zegovia
Dayna Macy	Thomas Crapper
Megan Anderson	Jeff Stafford
Emma Lauriston	The EarthWorks Group
Denise "Hi Ho!" Silver	...and all the bathroom readers

WELCOME BRI
STUDENTS

I f this is your first *Bathroom Reader*, the Bathroom Readers' Institute wants to welcome you to the smallest classroom in the house. It seems like only only yesterday that we plunged in with our first group of satisfied students...and it sewer is grate to see new ones coming down the pipe.

If you're a returning student who has plumbed the depths of our three previous *Readers*, you're entering your senior year of sitting on our commodious Throne of Higher Learning. Plunge in, sink or swim, and you'll probably be able to pass the sit-down exam coming at the end. If you think this stuff 's a whiz, keep straining toward your B.S. degree in Bathological Studies and eventually your PhD (Plumber's Helper Degree). Even if you're drained, washed up, or down the tubes, at least come back next year for our annual homecoming and Big Game, the Ceramic Bowl.

We're overflowing with excitement. This is going to be a watershed year for all of us. So, stop stalling and come out of the water closet—now is the time to sit down and be counted.

And for everything so far, tanks a lot.

**—The In-House and Out-House Staff
of the Bathroom Readers' Institute**

CONTENTS

NOTE
Because the B.R.I. understands your reading needs, we've
divided the contents by length as well as subject.
Short—a quick read
Medium—1 to 3 pages
Long—for those extended visits, when something
a little more involved is required.

UNCLE JOHN'S BATHROOM LEADER

*The Bathroom Reader offers a special "Bowl Me Over" salute to
Lyndon Baines Johnson—probably the only president who
actually conducted affairs of state while seated on the pot.*

GETTING IT BACKWARDS

According to Doris Kearns Goodwin, in her biography, *Lyndon Johnson and the American Dream*, "Few Presidents have permitted the kind of intimacy between themselves and their staffs that Johnson encouraged. When he had to go to the bathroom in the middle of a conversation, it was not unusual for him to move the discussion there. Johnson seemed delighted as he told me of 'one of those delicate Kennedyites who came into the bathroom with me and then found it utterly impossible to look at me while I sat there on the toilet.' "

" 'You'd think he had never seen those parts of the body before. For there he was, standing as far away from me as he possibly could, keeping his back toward me the whole time, trying to carry on a conversation. I could barely hear a word he said. I kept straining my ears and then finally I asked him to come a little closer to me. Then began the most ludicrous scene I had ever witnessed. Instead of simply turning around and walking over to me, he kept his face away from me and walked backward, one rickety step at a time. For a moment I thought he was going to run right into me. It certainly made me wonder how that man had made it so far in the world.' "

THE EARLY DAYS

LBJ's habit of making the most of his "down time" actually began in the 1930s—long before he was elected president. According to biographer Robert Caro, the 24-year-old Johnson, a secretary to a Texas Congressman, bullied the other officeworkers while seated on the pot:

"The toilet in the office was set in a short corridor between its two rooms. Johnson would sit down on it, and there would come a call: "L.E.! [L.E. Jones, Johnson's assistant] L.E.!" L.E. would say,

'Oh, God,' because he hated this. At first, he attempted to stand away from the door, but Johnson insisted he come right into the doorway, so he would be standing over him, and L.E. would stand with his head and nose averted, and take dictation…The tactic was, indeed, 'a method of control'…those who observed it, knew it was being done to humiliate [Jones], and to prove who was boss."

ONE-MAN SHOW

Though a big believer in bathroom business, Johnson would not tolerate it from his staff. According to Caro, he wouldn't allow them to go to the bathroom at all while they worked: 'If he caught you reading a letter from your mother, or if you were taking a crap, he'd say, "Son, can't you *please* try a little harder to learn to do that on your own time?" '

IN THE NEWS

People in Johnson's inner circle weren't his only victims—even members of the press got a taste of his bathroom manner. Steven Bates describes CBS reporter/White House correspondent Robert Pierpont's lunch with LBJ: "After they had eaten…the President told Pierpont to stay for coffee. By about 3:00 p.m. the conversation had become an LBJ monologue. Pierpont tried again to leave. Johnson stood up and said it was time to cross the hall.

"Pierpont followed Johnson into a bedroom. The President started undressing, handing each piece of his clothing to a valet. LBJ stripped naked, continuing his monologue the whole time. He put on a pajama top and walked into a bathroom, 'speaking loudly, over the sound of passing water.' Then LBJ put on the pajama bottoms and got into bed. He talked for another fifteen minutes, then said good-bye—three hours after the conversation had begun."

CONSTITUENT SERVICE

Even *voters* occasionally saw Johnson in the altogether. Caro describes a typical scene during LBJ's 1948 campaign for the U.S. Senate: "Rooms in many small-town hotels had only hand basins, with communal toilets at the end of the hall. These bathrooms were small and hot, and it was cooler if the door was left open, so often Johnson left it open. Not a few voters therefore saw the candidate for the U.S. Senate sitting on the toilet, and described that sight to relatives and friends."

Moses stuttered.

MYTH
CONCEPTIONS

At the BRI, we love "facts" that aren't true.
Here's some info that may surprise you.

M yth: The Great Wall of China is visible from the moon.
Truth: No manmade objects are visible from that far out in
space. According to astronomers, it's about as visible as a
popsicle stick from 240 miles away.

Myth: Alligator shirts have alligators on them.
Truth: They're crocodiles—René Lacoste, a French tennis star known
as *le crocodile*, invented them in the 1920s.

Myth: The sardine is a species of fish.
Truth: The word "sardine" actually refers to any breed of small fish—
including herring and pilchard—that's been stuffed into a sardine can.

Myth: S.O.S. stands for "Save Our Ship."
Truth: It doesn't stand for anything—it was selected as a distress signal because it's easy to transmit in morse code: 3 dots, 3 dashes, 3 dots.

Myth: I.O.U. stands for "I owe you."
Truth: Originally the borrower wrote "I Owe Unto," followed by the
lender's name.

Myth: Thumb sucking causes buck teeth.
Truth: An old wive's tale. Thumb sucking may even be beneficial.
Some researchers believe that it aids the development of facial
muscles and bones.

Myth: Karate is a Japanese martial art.
Truth: It actually started in India and spread to China—before reaching Japan. It first became popular in Okinawa in the 1600s, when officials prohibited Okinawans from possessing weapons.

Poll Results: Only 29% of married couples agree on most political issues.

Myth: Thomas Edison invented the lightbulb in 1879.

Truth: The first incandescent bulb was invented by Sir Humphrey Davy in 1802. But the filaments he used burned out quickly. Edison pioneered the use of carbonized cotton filaments—making the bulbs practical for the first time.

Myth: Your ears are the things you see on the side of your head.

Truth: Technically, the human ear is located inside the skull, and stops at the end of the ear canal. The parts you can see are called the *pinnas*.

Myth: You can judge the nutritional content of an egg by the color of its shell.

Truth: Eggshells don't tell you anything about the egg—but they do tell you about the hen that laid it: white eggs are laid by hens with white earlobes; brown eggs are laid by chickens with red earlobes.

Myth: The Egyptians were master embalmers.

Truth: The dry climate deserves most of the credit. In fact, as Egyptian embalming methods "advanced" over time, corpses began deteriorating more quickly.

Myth: Fortune cookies were invented in China.

Truth: They were invented in the U.S. in 1918 by Charles Jung, a Chinese restaurant owner, to amuse customers while they waited for their food. Only later were they served *after* the meal.

Myth: The French poodle originated in France.

Truth: The breed was created in Germany around the 16th century. Called *puddel,* or "splash" dogs, they were bred to retrieve ducks. They didn't become popular in France until years later.

Myth: According to the Bible, Angels have wings.

Truth: Nowhere in the Bible does it say that angels have wings. The idea didn't become popular until painters and sculptors began adding them.

There are three times as many cows as people in Montana.

THE WHOLE DOUGHNUT

"Doughnuts," says Michael Lasky in his book Junk Food, *"are the ultimate junk food. Fortified with globs of sugar and then fried in oceans of hot grease, they have found a niche in our stomachs."*

Doughnuts originated in 16th-century Holland. They were cooked in oil, and were so greasy that the Dutch called them *oly-koeks*, or "oily cakes."

The Pilgrims, who'd lived in Holland, brought the cakes with them when they came to America. Their version: a round doughy ball about the size of a nut—a *doughnut*.

The origin of the doughnut hole: Captain Hanson Gregory, a 19th-century Maine sea captain, was eating a doughnut while sailing through a storm. Suddenly the ship rocked violently and threw him against the ship's wheel—impaling his cake on one of its spokes. Seeing how well the spoke held his cake, Gregory began ordering all of his cakes with holes in them.

Doughnuts were popularized in the U.S. after the Salvation Army fed doughnuts—cooked in garbage pails and served on bayonets—to troops during World War I. Soldiers got so hooked on them that they were called "doughboys."

The French have a doughnut they call *pet de nonne*,—"Nun's Fart." According to legend, a nun living in the abbey of Marmoutier was preparing food for a religious feast. Suddenly she farted, and the other nuns laughed at her. She was so embarrassed that she dropped the spoonful of dough she was holding into a pot of boiling oil—accidently making a doughnut.

Doughnut-dunking was first popularized at the Roseland Ballroom in the '20s, when actress Mae Murray slipped and accidentally thrust a doughnut into a cup of coffee.

The *glazed* doughnut is almost three times as popular as any other type of doughnut.

WEIRD BOARD GAMES

When you think of board games, you probably think of Monopoly or Risk. But there are plenty of bizarre board games you've never heard of. Here are a few examples. (No kidding—these games were really sold.)

Dr. Ruth Westheimer's Game of Good Sex. Based on her sexual advice talk shows. Couples play the game trying to accumulate Arousal Points in quest of Mutual Pleasure. Two to four couples could play but only consenting adults—over 21—were allowed to buy it.

Mafia. The purpose: to gain control of Sicilian airports, real estate, construction projects, banks, and drug trade. The rules call for each "family," assisted by henchmen, to move around a map of Sicily selling heroin and eluding the police. The Italian-made board game caused considerable controversy in its native country.

Is The Pope Catholic? In 1986, two Boston-based entrepreneurs manufactured this game. Players move around the board trying to attain the rank of pope. Among the obstacles (or temptations) along the way: nipping at holy wine and squandering the church's money on candy. Small miracles help players out. A winner is declared when a cloud of white smoke is sent by the Convocation of Cardinals, signaling the election of a pope.

Twinkies and Trolls. The proprietors of "Buddies," a well-known gay bar in Boston, invented this game, which they described as "a lighthearted reflection of gay life and the gay lifestyle." Players come out of the closet, visit their first gay bar and the "baths" in New York, San Francisco, Provincetown, and Ft. Lauderdale. The object is to amass as many "Twinkies" (gay slang for young, attractive preppies), and avoid "Trolls" (old, ugly gay men).

Class Struggle. Bertell Ollman was a Marxist professor at New York University when he invented this game. The object is to win the revolution, and each player represents a different class of society. Ollman later wrote a book about his experiences in marketing the game. It was called *Class Struggle Is The Name Of The Game: True Confessions Of A Marxist Businessman.*

Gender Bender. Makes players answer questions as if they were members of the opposite sex.

Trump: The Game. Developed by real estate tycoon Donald Trump. Like Monopoly, the object is to make the most money. But unlike Monopoly, the smallest denomination is $10 million…and each bill bears Trump's face. Trump explained: "I wanted to teach business instincts. It's great if they can learn that from a game instead of having to go out and lose your shirt." That, of course, was before Trump lost his own shirt.

NUKE: The Last Game on Earth. Developed by two architects, Chris Corday and Steve Weeks. The game gives players the chance to be world leaders, deciding the fate of the world. If they can't work out their problems, the world is destroyed.

Civil War. In 1989, Naji Tueini, a Lebanese entrepreneur, successful marketed this game based on his country's internal turmoil. It rewards strategy such as "reselling products sent as international assistance" and "taking hostages," but docks points for getting stuck in a fall-out shelter during heavy bombardment. It was translated into English and French.

It's Only Money. In 1989, more than 25 major companies (like Porsche, Seagrams, Revlon and Mastercard) paid $30,000 apiece to have their products promoted in this game. Each company got a storefront" on the board where players (or "shoppers") browsed in a bustling shopping mall, trying to avoid crowds on the escalators. The game's creator, Eric S. Medney, described the game as delivering "corporate messages to the entire family while they're having fun."

Bankruptcy. The object is to acquire as many companies as possible without going bankrupt. If you do declare bankruptcy, however, you have to play Russian roulette with a toy gun included with the set. If the gun pops, you're out. The inspiration for the game? Victor Smith, its creator, explained: "I was on the edge of bankruptcy when the idea hit me."

TAMMY FAYE

Remember when Tammy Faye Bakker was in the news every day?
In case you're feeling nostalgic, here are some of the things she's said.

We were raising money to be missionaries in the Amazon. Can you imagine me in the Amazon! All day long trying to keep my false eyelashes from falling off and my nails from breaking. The only way I would have fit in is that I like jewelry just as much as the natives."

"I'm a good cook. In the evening, I make mostly chicken or tuna sandwiches, or we'll go out for pizza."

"There's times I just have to quit thinking, and the only way I can quit thinking is by shopping."

"We prayed and asked God to give us the money to buy a trailer. We took this meeting in West Virginia, a tiny church up in the mountains. God began to bless and move. We started praying for the trailer in that meeting and people put $100 bills in the offering for us. We were embarrassed because we had been putting $20 and $30 in the bank. Now God was performing a miracle and giving us the most money we had ever had in our lives....The next week, we purchased the most beautiful 30-foot Holiday Rambler trailer."

"I wear wigs all the time, and Jim never knows who I'm going to be."

"One day while eating supper, little Chi Chi, who liked lima beans, ate some and ran into another room....When the dog didn't return, I wondered. Jim had seen the dog fall over on the carpet and not get up. Jim went and checked Chi Chi and then gently said, 'Tammy, Chi Chi is dead.'...I prayed and prayed and prayed. 'O Jesus, please raise Chi Chi from the dead.' I expected Jim to bring Chi Chi home any minute.'"

"No matter what they print, no reporter has ever seen me with black tears running down my face, 'cause I always use waterproof mascara."

"My shoppin' demons are hoppin'."

On average, Nevada gets only 7 1/2 inches of rain per year.

IN THE NEWS

In his book, If No News, Send Rumors, *Stephen Bates tells hundreds of fascinating stories about the news media. It's an excellent bathroom reader. Here are a few excerpts.*

In the early 1700s the price of a newspaper, twopence a copy, was steep. As later gentlemen callers would bring flowers or candy, a man of the era would sometimes bring a newspaper as a gift when calling on a woman, so that she could read of the latest Indian raids, runaway slaves, and pirate attacks.

Early Newspapers were often passed from person to person. Some papers contained one or more blank pages, which a subscriber could fill in with his own news before sending the newspaper on to friends.

A 1987 computer analysis found that these words most frequently appear in the New York Post headlines (in descending order): Cop, Kill, Judge, Wall Street, Death, No, Slay, U.S., Soviet, Court.

The choice for the lead story in *USA Today*'s September 15, 1982 inaugural edition was based on an informal survey undertaken by the newspaper's founder, Al Neuharth. Bashir Gemayel, president-elect of Lebanon had been murdered, and most *USA Today* editors assumed that story would lead the paper, as it did other papers across the country. But Monaco's Princess Grace had died in a car crash, and Neuharth suspected her death was, for most Americans, the more important story.

To find out, he visited a bar and a political gathering. In both places, nearly everyone was talking about Princess Grace. When Neuharth mentioned the Lebanon assassination, people shrugged. The next morning, *USA Today*'s lead story was headlined, "Princess Grace dies in Monaco. Gemayel ended up on an inside page.

When he learned that crucial work on the atom bomb had taken place nearby, the city editor of the *Nashville Tennessean* told a photographer to go out to the research facility and get two pictures—one of a whole atom, and one after it was split.

It's illegal to hunt camels in Arizona.

In the '60s *Rolling Stone* offered a free roach clip to every new subscriber. In the '80s its standard employment contract allowed the magazine to test employees for drug use.

In October, 1967, a major anti-war protest was held in Washington, D.C. Crowd estimates varied widely, in part reflecting the publications' political viewpoints:

Washington Post: 50,000
Time: 35,000
Wall St. Journal: 2,500

On several occasions, William Randolph Hearst's New York *Journal* suggested that President McKinley should be killed. One editorial, for instance, declared that "If bad institutions and bad men can be got rid of only by killing them, then the killing must be done."

For such remarks, the *Journal* was vilified when the president was assassinated in 1901. "The journalism of anarchy," the *Brooklyn Eagle* editorialized, "shares responsibility for the attack on President McKinley." Hearst's enemies spread the false story that McKinley's assassin had been arrested with a copy of the *Journal* in his pocket.

Stung by the criticism, the Journal changed the name of its morning edition to the *American.* Bad feelings remained, though, and five years later the McKinley issue helped defeat Hearst in his campaign for governor of New York.

A *Los Angeles Times* article in 1972 read "70-Car Fog Pileup." In fact, sixty-nine cars had crashed. An editor changed it, reasoning that sixty-nine was a smutty number.

Washington *Post* reporter Carl Bernstein nearly wasn't around to cover the Watergate scandal. Bernstein had asked executive editor Ben Bradlee to make him the full-time rock critic. Bradlee agreed, but the job had ended up going to someone else.

Resentful, Bernstein decided to leave the *Post.* He wrote to *Rolling Stone* and asked if he could replace the departing Hunter S. Thompson as political writer. Bernstein was waiting was waiting for a reply when he was assigned to cover the break-in at the Democratic National Committee's Watergate offices.

POP QUIZ

So you think you know popular culture. Here's a chance to find out.
Some of the answers are in sections of this book and previous
Bathroom Readers—all of them are on page 223.

CLASSIC TOYS

1. On the Japanese Barbie, these are even bigger, rounder and more voluptuous than the on the American Barbie. What are they?

2. What do the inventions of Silly Putty and the Slinky have in common?

3. What gives crayons their distinctive smell?

4. Where was the inventor of the Ant Farm when he came up with the idea?

STYLE

5. Who invented the Hawaiian shirt and why?

6. What animal is on the alligator shirt?

ON THE SCREEN

7. Where did Art Clokey get the idea for the bump on Gumby's little green head?

8. Who almost got the role of Dorothy in the *Wizard of Oz?* Which comic did they write the Wizard's lines for?

9. Who was first choice for the main character in *Casablanca?*

10. Which three of the Stooges were brothers?

11. How much older was Vivian Vance than Lucille Ball?

12. How did *Our Gang's* Alfalfa die?

MUSIC

13. Before it had words, what was the working title of the Beatles' song, *Yesterday?*

14. How many record choices did you get on the first jukebox?

15. The average number of grooves on a 45 RPM record? How does that compare with the number of grooves on a 33 RPM record?

ART VS. REAL LIFE

16. Which are there more of in the world: plastic lawn flamingos or real flamingos?

17. Which lasted longer—the TV show M*A*S*H or the real Korean War?

18. The subject of Andy Warhol's first pop paintings was the thing he loved most. What was it?

MODERN MYTHOLOGY

*A hundred years ago, Americans identified with Uncle Sam,
Paul Bunyan, and Johnny Appleseed. Today, there are a new crop
of cultural heroes, like these characters:*

T he Campbell's Soup Kids. Grace Gebbie Wiederseim grew
up in Philadelphia in the mid-1800s. One morning when
she was a young girl, she stood in front of her parents' mirror and drew a picture of herself. She liked it so much she saved it.
In 1904, Grace was a successful illustrator and the wife of a
Campbell's Soup advertising executive. One afternoon he asked
her to help create an advertising campaign for Campbell's. She
pulled out her childhood self-portrait...and used it to create Dolly
Drake and Bobby Blake—the Campbell's Soup Kids.

Poppin' Fresh (The Pillsbury Doughboy). In 1965 the Pillsbury
Company hired ad exec Rudy Pera to design an advertising campaign for their new refrigerated dough product...But he had trouble
thinking of anything that would make the brand stand out. One
day he began playfully pounding on a container of the dough, hoping to drum up ideas. "I imagined what could pop out," he recalls.
"A dough man? A dough baker? A *dough boy?*" Polls taken more
than 20 years later show that the Pillsbury Doughboy is the most
popular ad character in the U.S.—more popular than Ronald
McDonald, Tony the Tiger, or Morris the Cat.

Mr. Zig Zag. During the 1850s the French army recruited Algeri-
ans to help fight in the Crimean war. One of them is still famous
today—even though his name has been forgotten; his face is on the
cover of Zig Zag rolling papers.

Ronald McDonald. Willard Scott, weatherman on NBC's *Today
Show*, was the first McClown. Here's the story he tells:
"The folks at the NBC television station in Washington—WRC
TV—had signed on a national kiddie show [called "Bozo the

During World War 1, removing straps from corsets saved enough metal to build 2 warships.

Clown"], and they tapped me to star in the thing. That's how I got to be Bozo the Clown…I did a lot of personal appearances as Bozo—at shopping malls, local fairs, that sort of thing. After a while a local McDonald's restaurant asked me to appear at an opening, and before too long my Bozo was a regular fixture at area franchises. When WRC dropped [the show], McDonald's didn't much like the idea of having to drop a successful promotion. They were hooked on clowns…And so—you guessed it—Ronald McDonald was born…Actually, he came very close to being christened Donald McDonald, but Ronald sounded just a touch more natural, so we went with that."

Rudolph the Red-Nosed Reindeer. In 1939, Montgomery Ward hired Robert May to write a Christmas poem for their department store Santas to give away during the holiday season. He came up with one he called *Rollo the Red-Nosed Reindeer.* Executives of the company loved it, but didn't like the name Rollo. So May renamed the reindeer Reginald—the only name he could think of that preserved the poem's rhythm. But Montgomery Ward execs rejected that name, too. Try as he might, May couldn't come up with another name that fit—until his four year-old daughter suggested *Rudolph.*

Teenage Mutant Ninja Turtles. Peter Laird, a 29-year-old artist, was the staff illustrator for the gardening page of a Massachusetts newspaper in 1983. His job didn't pay very well, and he was looking for ways to make extra money on the side…so a local comic magazine editor suggested he work with Kevin Eastman, a 20 year-old short-order cook and amateur cartoonist, to drum up ideas for a new comic book. Laird decided to give it a shot. One night he and Eastman were experimenting with karate themes. Eastman drew a picture of a turtle wearing a Ninja mask. They both liked the idea, and stayed up all night developing a storyline. By morning the one "Ninja Turtle" had expanded to four *Teenage Mutant* Ninja Turtles—Leonardo, Raphael, Michaelangelo, and Donatello.

Why name them after Renaissance artists? Laird explained: "The characters should have have had Japanese names, but we couldn't come up with convincing ones."

AT THE OSCARS

*Here are a few lesser-known stories about
the Academy Awards ceremonies*

THAT LITTLE GOLD STATUE

T•According to legend, the Oscar was named in 1931 when a secretary at the Academy saw the statuette and exclaimed, "Why, he reminds me of my Uncle Oscar!" A reporter overheard the remark and used it in a story, and the name stuck.

• In 1942, gold and bronze were being used in the war, so Oscars were made out of plaster. (Actor Barry Fitzgerald accidentally decapitated his plaster Oscar while practicing his golf swing indoors).

• When Dustin Hoffman accepted his Oscar in 1979, he described the statuette for the audience: "He has no genitalia and he's holding a sword."

HOSTS WITH THE MOST (OR LEAST)

• At the 1947 Oscar ceremony, Ronald Reagan supplied live narration for "Parade of Stars," a silent compilation of Oscar-winning films. Oblivious to the fact that the film was running upside down, backwards, and showing on the ceiling instead of on a screen, Reagan kept reading: "This picture embodies the glories of our past, the memories of our present, and the inspiration of our future."

• Comedian Jerry Lewis was the host in 1958 when the Oscar ceremony actually finished 20 minutes earlier than expected. No one realized the show was ending early until they were well into the closing number, "There's No Business Like Show Business." Lewis shouted "Twenty more times!" and tried to drag out the finale by grabbing a baton and conducting the orchestra. Actors onstage paired up and started dancing. Meanwhile, the audience started to get up and leave. Dean Martin danced by the podium and grabbed a leftover Oscar.

A few minutes later Lewis picked up a trumpet and started trying to play it. That's when NBC turned its cameras off. Eventually, NBC had to plug the hole with a short film on *pistol shooting*.

NO-SHOWS

Not everyone shows up for Oscar night:

• Robert Rich won the Best Screenplay Oscar in 1956 for *The Brave One*, but never claimed his award. That's because there *was* no Robert Rich. The winner was actually Dalton Trumbo, one of the notorious "Hollywood Ten," a group of writers who had been blacklisted for their left-wing views. Trumbo managed to sneak himself onto the nomination list by using "Robert Rich" as a pseudonym.

• In 1970 the Academy decided to give Orson Welles an honorary Oscar—presumably to make up for the fact that they'd snubbed him for *Citizen Kane* in 1941. When he didn't show up to accept it, the Academy announced he was out of the country. Actually, he was just a few miles away, watching the whole thing on television.

• That same year George C. Scott refused a Best Actor Oscar for his title role in the movie *Patton*. Instead of attending the ceremony, he says he watched a hockey game on TV, then went to bed.

• In 1979, 79-year-old Melvyn Douglas was nominated as Best Supporting Actor for *Being There*. His chief competition was child star Justin Henry, who played the contested child in the divorce drama, *Kramer vs. Kramer*. Douglas didn't show up for Oscar night, and told reporters: "The whole thing is absurd, my competing with an 8-year-old." Although Henry did show up, Douglas still won.

AND THE WINNER IS...

• In 1984, F. Murray Abraham won the Oscar for Best Actor. (He played the jealous composer Antonio Salieri in the movie *Amadeus*.) Until then, Abraham's most prominent screen role had been as a leaf in a Fruit of the Loom underwear commercial.

• In 1946, *The Razor's Edge* failed to win the Oscar for Best Picture...But it *was* named the year's best by the National Association of Barbers.

• Humphrey Bogart wasn't thrilled at winning an Oscar for *African Queen*: "Hell," he remarked, "I hope I'm never nominated again. It's meat and potatoes roles for me from now on."

In 16th century Turkey, drinking coffee was punishable by death.

• Playwrite George Bernard Shaw was livid about winning the Best Screenplay Oscar for *Pygmalion*."It's an insult," he railed. "To offer me an award of this sort is an insult, as if they have never heard of me before…and it's very likely they never have."

• The nameplate on Spencer Tracy's first Oscar was mistakenly made out to *Dick* Tracy.

WINNERS, PART II

The ultimate Oscar winner/loser story involved a little-known
Polish director named Zbignew Rybcyznski, who was nominated for Best
Animated Short in 1983:

• Presenter Kristy McNichol tried to pronounce his name as a nominee, but giggled and gave up halfway through. When Rybcyznski won, McNichol tried again. This time she called him "Zbigniewski Sky."

• Rybcyznski made his acceptance speech through an interpreter but they were cut off when the orchestra struck up the theme from "Loony Tunes."

• Co-presenter Matt Dillon tried to ease Rybcyznski off the stage, but the director held his ground by shaking Dillon's hand and kissing McNichol. He added some final words but the interpreter lost them in the translation. They came out, "On the occasion of the film like *Gandhi,* which will portray Lech Walesa and Solidarity."

• Later in the evening, Rybcyznski stepped out for a cigarette. He tried to return to his seat, but a guard wouldn't let him back in. The guard didn't believe that Rybcyznski, who was dressed in a tuxedo and tennis shoes, was a guest. Rybcyznski got angry, kicked the guard, and wound up in jail.

• The director asked for attorney Marvin Mitchelson, who specializes in palimony cases, because he was the only Hollywood lawyer he could think of.

• Mitchelson took the case, but on the following conditions: "First, bring me an interpreter; and then tell me how to pronounce his name." The charges were dropped.

• Rybcyznski's conclusion: "Success and defeat are quite intertwined."

Training a seal to balance a ball on its nose is illegal in Sweden.

PRIME TIME POLITICIANS

You see politicians on TV all the time—but not usually in shows like "The Dukes of Hazard" and "The Beverly Hillbillies." Here are a few actors who followed Ronald Reagan's footsteps into politics.

The Race: U.S. Congress (Virginia), 1984.

Candidate: Nancy Kulp (Democrat). Played Jane Hathaway, the sour-faced bank secretary on *"The Beverly Hillbillies,"* for nine seasons.

Political Background: Worked for Adlai Stevenson in the 1952 presidential race against Eisenhower; elected to the Screen Actor Guild's Board of Directors in 1982. She also worked with the Democratic State Committee of Pennsylvania.

The Race: Kulp ran unopposed in the primary and won the Democratic nomination. But Buddy Ebsen, who played Jed Clampett on "The Beverly Hillbillies," campaigned against her in the general election. He taped a radio ad for Kulp's opponent, Bud Shuster, which said: "I dropped [Nancy] a note to say, 'Hey Nancy, I love you dearly buy you're too liberal for me—I've got to go with Bud Shuster.' " Shuster beat Kulp by 117,203 to 59,449.

The Race: Mayor of Carmel-by-the-Sea, California, 1986.

The Candidate: Clint Eastwood (no party affiliation).

Political Background: Eastwood wanted to expand his Carmel restaurant, the *Hog's Breath Inn*. City Hall refused to let him. So, in true *Dirty Harry* style, he took them on and ran for mayor.

Outcome: He defeated incumbent mayor Charlotte Townshend by 2,166 votes to 799. He held the $200-a-week post for two years.

The Race: U.S. House of Representatives (Iowa), 1986.

The Candidate: Fred Grandy, Republican. Played Burl "Gopher" Smith for nine years on *The Love Boat*.

Political Background: Grandy was David Eisenhower's roommate at Exeter Academy and later was best man at Eisenhower's wedding to Julie Nixon. He also served as a speechwriter for Congressman Wiley Mayne (R-Iowa). A Harvard graduate fluent in both French and Arabic, Grandy wanted to dispel his image as the dimwitted Gopher. Even so, he told *People* magazine, "If there were no Gopher, there would be no Fred Grandy for Congress."

Outcome: Grandy's opponent, Clayton Hodgson, criticized him for not living in Iowa's Sixth district (Grandy had lived in Iowa as an orphan at 12), and aired tapes of Grandy on NBC's "Tonight Show" describing Iowa as the "only place in the world where people still use 'by golly' in a sentence." Still, Grandy won the election in 1986 by 3,000 votes.

The Race: U.S. House of Representatives (Georgia), 1988.

The Candidate: Ben Jones (Democrat). Jones played Cooter, the auto mechanic on *The Dukes of Hazard,* for seven seasons.

Political Background: Worked on Jimmy Carter's 1980 presidential campaign. Lost his first bid for Congressman Pat Swindall's House seat in 1986, but ran again in 1988. Reason for getting involved: "I awoke naked in a tattoo parlor in Talladega, Alabama. I knew it was time to change my lifestyle. So I went into politics."

Outcome: *The Washington Post* described the race as "perhaps the nastiest, most personal congressional campaign in the country." Swindall was facing a perjury indictment for lying about his involvement with an undercover cop posing as a drug money launderer. He tried to portray the four-time married Jones as a wife-beater, alluding to charges of battery against an ex-wife, for which he had been fined $50. Jones' defense: "I'm not your typical political candidate; I've seen the insides of jails." Nevertheless, he captured 60% of the vote and defeated Swindall.

The Race: Mayor of Palm Springs, California, 1988.

The Candidate: Sonny Bono (Republican). Bono and his ex-wife Cher, had a variety T.V. show in the '70s and several hit songs.

Political Background: None.

The Race: Although he faced opposition ("Clint's a big star," commented outgoing Palm Springs mayor, Frank Bogert. "Sonny's a big nothing.") Bono won the election easily. But in 1990 his opponents started a petition drive to recall him after he dropped out of an AIDS walk-a-thon. It failed.

Experts say the best time to study is right before bed.

SURPRISE HITS

Some of pop music's most popular records have become hits through totally unexpected circumstances—discovered by deejays in a 25¢ bin, featured on ads years after their first release, picked as TV themes. These flukes are the equivalent of winning the "pop lottery." Here are a few classic examples:

GET TOGETHER—THE YOUNGBLOODS

Background: The Youngbloods first album was released in 1967 on RCA records. It included the song "Get Together," which was released as a single. Unfortunately, the song only reached #62 on the national charts—a flop, as far as RCA was concerned. The record was quickly forgotten.

The Surprise: To promote Brotherhood Week in 1969, the National Conference of Christians and Jews put together a package of public service messages for TV announcers and radio deejays to read on the air. They decided to include a record for stations to use as background music, and the one they picked—without informing the Youngbloods—was "Get Together."

The Hit: After a week of national radio and TV exposure, the record started becoming popular. Radio stations began playing it…and RCA cashed in by re-releasing it. In the summer of 1969, two years after it was first released, "Get Together" hit #1, sold about 2 million copies, and made the Youngbloods stars.

"HANKY PANKY"—TOMMY JAMES & THE SHONDELLS

Background: In 1963, a Niles, Michigan high school student named Tommy Jackson made a record called "Hanky Panky" with his band, the Shondells. It became a regional hit in parts of Michigan, Illinois, and Indiana. Then it disappeared.

The Surprise: A year and a half later, a Pittsburgh, Pennsylvania, deejay named Bob Livorio found a copy of "Hanky Panky" in a pile of 25¢ records. He began playing it on the air. When it became popular with his audiences, rival deejays dug up their own copies of the record…and a "Hanky Panky" war was on. A local record company bought the rights to the record and distributed it to Pittsburgh record stores. In 3 weeks, "Hanky Panky" was the city's #1 song.

Meanwhile, Tommy Jackson—whose band had broken up when

he graduated from high school the year before—didn't know anything about this. He was at his family's house one evening when he got a phone call from a Pittsburgh deejay named "Mad Mike" Metro. As Tommy recalls it: "He said, 'Your record's #1. Can you come to Pittsburgh?' I said, 'What record? Who is this? What's your name?' I thought it was one of my friends pulling my leg. Finally, the guy started to sound official, and I started hearing radio noises in the background. I said, 'My god! He's telling the truth!' "

The Hit: When Tommy Jackson—now Tommy James—arrived in Pittsburgh, kids went wild. By this time "Hanky Panky" had gotten a lot of publicity in the record industry, and major companies were eager to distribute it nationally. The winner: Roulette Records, which bought it for $10,000. The record repeated its success on a national level, becoming the #1 song in America…and Tommy James became one of pop's biggest stars. "I don't think that kind of stuff can happen anymore," Tommy muses. "We're talking an absolute Cinderella story!"

"HUMAN NATURE"—MICHAEL JACKSON

Background: Steve Porcaro was a studio musician and a member of the group Toto. One day his little daughter came home from school upset about a fight she'd had with some of her playmates. "Why do they do that?" she asked.

"It's just human nature," her father replied.

He realized that phrase might make a good title for a song….So he went into Toto's recording studio and made up a melody—which he put onto a tape cassette, singing nonsense syllables and occasionally throwing in the phrase, "It's just human nature." Then he left the cassette lying around and forgot about it.

The Surprise: About this time, Quincy Jones was looking for songs to use on Michael Jackson's new album, "Thriller." He asked David Paitch—also a member of Toto and one of the most respected songwriters in the music business—to submit material for Jackson. Paitch went into Toto's studio, picked up a used cassette, and recorded three songs. Then he sent the cassette to Quincy Jones.

Jones didn't feel any of Paitch's tunes were right for "Thriller"… but just before he turned off the tape recorder, he realized there was an extra song on the cassette—Steve Porcaro's scratch vocal of "Human Nature." It turned out that without realizing it, Paitch picked up the tape with Porcaro's song on it. Jones decided "Human Nature" was perfect for Jackson. Porcaro, who had no idea anyone had the tape, was astonished.

The Hit: All the song needed now was lyrics. Jones contacted songwriter John Bettis, who wrote the words in two days. Not only was "Human Nature" included on "Thriller," the biggest-selling album in history, it was also released as a single. It reached #7 on *Billboard's* charts, and sold over a million copies.

TIME IN A BOTTLE—JIM CROCE

Background: "Time In a Bottle" was a "throwaway" tune on a Jim Croce album. The producers didn't even bother putting the finishing touches on it because, as one of them said, "No one is ever gonna hear it."

The Surprise: Producers of a 1973 TV movie called "She Lives"—about a woman dying of cancer—heard Croce's album and liked "Time in a Bottle." They decided to make it the movie's theme.

The Hit: "The next day," Croce's record producer recalls,"we got a call from our record company telling us that they had 50,000 orders for the album, just in the Midwest. People had fallen in love with the song. It was just instantaneous. I think they sold something like 200,000 albums in the next two weeks That's why 'Time in a Bottle' was released as a single—because of that show." About three months later, the song hit #1.

"OH HAPPY DAY"—THE EDWIN HAWKINS SINGERS

Background: Edwin Hawkins assembled the 46-member Northern California State Youth Choir in mid-1967. A few months later, he needed to raise funds for the choir's trip to a convention. So he picked out 8 members of the choir and recorded an album (which included "Oh Happy Day") in the basement of his church. He was delighted when the choir sold 600 copies of it.

The Surprise: Two years later, a San Francisco rock promoter happened to find the album in a warehouse while flipping through a stack of gospel records. He gave it to a popular deejay named Abe "Voco" Kesh, who played the record on the air.

The Hit: Kesh played "Oh Happy Day" so often that it became an S.F., then a national hit. Sales jumped from 1,000 to over a million.

PUN FOR THE MONEY

"There's something irresistible about bad puns," notes BRI member Michael McDonald. "For some reason, the worse a pun is the more we like it." Well, here are some real groaners from Get Thee to a Punnery, *by Richard Lederer See if you can fill in the punch lines:*

THE STORY: An ancient jungle king tyrannized his subjects and forced them to build him one elaborate throne after another—first of mud, then bamboo, then tin, then copper, then silver, and so on. When the king became tired of each throne, he would store it in the attic of his grass hut. One day the attic collapsed, and the thrones crashed down upon the chief's head and killed him.

The moral: *"People who live in grass houses _____."*

THE STORY: A congregation decided to paint the walls of the church. They were doing an admirable job until they began to run out of paint, so they decided to thin the stuff in order to complete their task.

Shortly after the job was finished, the rains descended from the heavens, and the paint began to peel from the walls of the church. And a thunderous voice boomed from above:
"Repaint, and _____"

THE STORY: In an ancient kingdom, the castle was surrounded by a treacherous swamp called the Yellow Fingers. Whenever the king would ask his lords and knights to cross the Yellow Fingers, they would reply:
"Let your pages _____"

THE STORY: Mrs. Wong, a Chinese woman, gave birth to a blond-haired, blue-eyed Caucasian baby. When the doctor asked Mr. Wong to explain the astonishing occurrence, he replied:
"It takes two Wongs _____"

Pound for pound, grasshoppers are 3 times as nutritious as beef.

THE STORY: In days of old when knights were bold, people were a lot smaller than they are today, so much smaller, in fact, that many knights rode upon large dogs when they couldn't get horses. One dark and stormy night, as the rain blew about, a squire entered a pet store in order to purchase a large dog for his master, the Black Knight. Unfortunately, all the shopkeeper could offer the squire was one undersized, mangy mutt. Commented the squire: *"I wouldn't send a knight _____"*

THE STORY: In Baghdad, a worthy young man named Abdul found a beautiful urn. When he began to polish the urn, out came a magnificently bearded genie, who introduced himself as Benny. Benny granted Abdul the obligatory three wishes and bid him goodbye. Abdul knew that if he could shave Benny's beard, the genie would have to return to the urn and grant him three more wishes. Wielding a magic razor, Abdul shaved off Benny's beard, and, sure enough, Benny flew back into the enchanted vessel.
The Moral: *"A Benny shaved _____"*

THE STORY: A Frenchman and a Czechoslovakian went out hunting for bear. When the two had not returned after four days, their friends, fearing the worst, went out searching for them. The group came to a clearing, and, sure enough, they saw a mother and father bear each with a bloated belly. Slashing open the belly of the female, the distraught friends found therein the remains of the Frenchman. Their darkest fears confirmed, the group looked at the other bear and guessed:
"The Czech._____."

THE STORY: A witch doctor kept the members of his tribe in subjugation by means of his powerful magic. Whenever one of the tribespeople tried to revolt against the witch doctor, the tyrant uttered a magic incantation and turned the person into an apple. One night a group of the doctor's subjects sneaked into his hut, opened his book of magic recipes, and learned the apple incantation. When the doctor awoke, the people turned him into an apple. But the magic book warned that if the apple ever dried out and changed significantly in weight, it would change back into a doctor, who would take his revenge. So every day they would place the apple on a scale to make sure that its weight remained the same.
Moral: *"A weigh a day _____."*

General George Patton was dyslexic.

THANKS...
BUT NO THANKS

*If you've written a manuscript but can't find a publisher, take heart.
Even the best writers get rejection slips. For example, a newspaper
editor once told Rudyard Kipling: "I'm sorry, Mr. Kipling, but
you just don't know how to use the English language." Here are
some other notable rejection letters from editors to authors.*

Manuscript: *Madame Bovary*, by Gustave Flaubert
Editor's Comment: "You have buried your novel underneath a heap of details which are well done but utterly superfluous."

Manuscript: *Remembrance of Things Past*, by Marcel Proust
Editor's Comment: "My dear fellow, I may perhaps be dead from the neck up, but rack my brains as I may I can't see why a chap should need thirty pages to describe how he turns over in bed before going to sleep."

Manuscript: *The Diary of Anne Frank*, by Anne Frank
Editor's Comment: "The girl doesn't, it seems to me, have a special perception or feeling which would lift that book above the 'curiosity' level."

Manuscript: *Atlas Shrugged*, by Ayn Rand
Editor's Comment: "The book is *much* too long. There are too many long speeches...I regret to say that the book is unsaleable and unpublishable."

Manuscript: *Ulysses*, by James Joyce
Editor's Comment: "We have read the chapters of Mr. Joyce's novel with great interest, and we wish we could offer to print it. But the length is an insuperable difficulty to us at present. We can get no one to help us, and at our rate of progress a book of 300 pages would take at least two years to produce."

The first advertisement to discuss body odor was a 1919 ad for the deodorant Odo-Ro-No.

Manuscript: *The Postman Always Rings Twice*, by James M. Cain
Editor's Comment: "I think it is only a matter of time before you reach out into more substantial efforts that will be capable of making some real money as books."

Manuscript: *Lord of the Flies*, by William Golding
Editor's Comment: "It does not seem to us that you have been wholly successful in working out an admittedly promising idea."

Manuscript: *And to Think That I Saw It On Mulberry Street*, by Dr. Seuss
Editor's Comment: "Too different from other [books for] juveniles on the market to warrant its selling."

Manuscript: *Ironweed*, by William Kennedy
Editor's Comment: "There is much about the novel that is very good and much that I did not like. When I throw in the balance the book's unrelenting lack of commerciality, I am afraid I just have to pass."

Manuscript: *Kon-Tiki*, by Thor Heyerdahl
Editor's Comment: "The idea of men adrift on a raft does have a certain appeal, but for the most part this is a long, solemn and tedious Pacific voyage."

Manuscript: *Lady Chatterly's Lover*, by D.H. Lawrence
Editor's Comment: "For your own good, do not publish this book."

Manuscript: *Animal Farm*, by George Orwell
Editor's Comment: "It is impossible to sell animal stories in the USA."

Manuscript: *The Blessing Way*, by Tony Hillerman
Editor's Comment: "If you insist on rewriting this, get rid of all that Indian stuff."

RANDOM QUOTE: "A man can be happy with any woman as long as he does not love her." —Oscar Wilde.

The Washington Monument is sinking at a rate of 6 inches a year.

THE KING AND I

You may have already seen the famous photos of Elvis Presley and Richard Nixon in the Oval Office. Here's the inside story behind that meeting—taken directly from the memos of the White House staff.

E ven Elvis was a fan. He thought J. Edgar Hoover was "the greatest living American"…and Nixon "wasn't far behind." On December 21, 1970, Elvis dropped by the White House unannounced, asking to see the President. He brought this letter with him:

DEAR MR. PRESIDENT:

First, I would like to introduce myself. I am Elvis Presley and admire you and have great respect for your office. I talked to Vice President Agnew in Palm Springs three weeks ago and expressed my concern for our country. The drug culture, the hippie elements, the SDS, Black Panthers, etc. do not consider me as their enemy or as they call it, the establishment. I call it America and I love it. Sir, I can and will be of any service that I can to help the country out. I have no concerns or motives other than helping the country out. So I wish not to be given a title or an appointed position. I can and will do more good if I were made a Federal Agent at Large and I will help out by doing it my way through my communications with people of all ages. First and foremost, I am an entertainer, but all I need is the Federal credentials. I am on this plane with Senator George Murphy and we have been discussing the problems that our country is faced with.

Sir, I am staying at the Washington Hotel, Room 505-506-507. I have two men who work with me by the name of Jerry Schilling and Sonny West. I am registered under the name of Jon Burrows. I will be here for as long as it takes to get the credentials of a Federal Agent. I have done an in-depth study of drug abuse and Communist brainwashing techniques and I am right in the middle of the whole thing where I can and will do the most good.

I am glad to help just so long as it is kept very private. You can have your staff or whomever call me anytime today, tonight, or to

---

The British pound got its name because it was originally equal to the value of a pound of silver.

morrow. I was nominated this coming year one of America's Ten Most Outstanding Young Men. That will be in January 18 in my home town of Memphis, Tennessee. I am sending you the short autobiography about myself so you can better understand this approach. I would love to meet you just to say hello if you're not too busy.

Respectfully,

Elvis Presley

P.S. I believe that you, Sir, were one of the Top Ten Outstanding Men of America also. I have a personal gift for you which I would like to present to you and you can accept it or I will keep it for you until you can take it.

Dwight Chapin, the White House Appointments Secretary, met with Elvis. He wasn't sure what to do—did Nixon want to speak with the King? Was he a Presley fan? Did he even know who the singer was? Chapin passed the buck and wrote a memo to H.R. Haldeman, White House Chief of Staff:

DEAR H.R.:

Attached you will find a letter to the President from Elvis Presley. As you are aware, Presley showed up here this morning and has requested an appointment with the President. He states that he knows the President is very busy, but he would just like to say hello...I think that it would be wrong to push Presley off on the Vice President since it will take very little of the President's time and it can be extremely beneficial for the President to build some rapport with Presley.

Haldeman approached Nixon about meeting with Elvis, and Nixon agreed. Here are the official White House notes describing the meeting:

DECEMBER 21, 1970

The meeting opened with pictures taken of the President and Elvis Presley. Presley immediately began showing the President his law enforcement paraphernalia including badges from police departments in California, Colorado, and Tennessee. Presley indicated that he had been playing Las Vegas and the President indicated that he was aware of how difficult it is to perform in Las Vegas.

The President mentioned that he thought Presley could reach young people, and that it was important for Presley to retain his credibility. Presley responded that he did his thing by "just singing." He said that he could not get to the kids if he made a speech on the stage, that he had to reach them in his own way. The President nodded in agreement.

Presley indicated that he thought the Beatles had been a real force for anti-American spirit. He said that the Beatles came to this country, made their money, and then returned to England where they promoted an anti-American theme. The President nodded in agreement and expressed some surprise. The President then indicated that those who use drugs are also those in the vanguard of anti-American protest. "Violence, drug usage, dissent, protest all seem to merge in generally the same group of young people."

Presley indicated to the President in a very emotional manner that he was "on your side." Presley kept repeating that he wanted to be helpful, that he wanted to restore some respect for the flag which was being lost. He mentioned that he was just a poor boy from Tennessee who had gotten a lot from his country, which in some way he wanted to repay. He also mentioned that he is studying Communist brainwashing and the drug culture for over ten years. He mentioned that he knew a lot about this and was accepted by the hippies. He said he could go right into a group of young people or hippies and be accepted which he felt could be helpful to him in his drug drive. The President indicated again his concern that Presley retain his credibility.

At the conclusion of the meeting, Presley again told the President how much he supported him, and then, in a surprising, spontaneous gesture, put his left arm around the President and hugged him.

* * *

During a 1958 visit to Venezuela, Vice President Richard Nixon was spit upon by a protester. After Secret Service agents grabbed the man—Nixon kicked him in the shins. He admitted in his book *Six Crises* that "nothing I did all day made me feel better."

It took Leonardo da Vinci four years to paint the Mona Lisa.

OLD NEWS IS GOOD NEWS

Are your newspapers piling up in the garage? Here's some recycling info from The Recycler's Handbook, *written by the EarthWorks Group.*

I f you're one of the millions of Americans who are recycling your newspapers, here's some good news: You're making a big difference.

Not only are you saving natural resources and landfill space, you're helping to change the way the paper industry works.

Until recently, newspaper publishers believed that recycling was just a fad—that we'd "get over it." Now it's clear that Americans are committed...So they're going to give us what we want.

RECYCLING NEWS

• Every day Americans buy about 62 million newspapers...and throw out around 44 million of them. That means the equivalent of about 500,000 trees is dumped into landfills every week.

• If we recycled just half our newsprint every year, we'd need 3,200 fewer garbage trucks to collect our trash.

• If you recycled the *New York Times* every day for a year, you'd prevent 15 pounds of air pollution. That doesn't sound like much, but it adds up. If everyone who subscribes to the *New York Times* recycled, we'd keep over 6,000 *tons* of pollution out of the air.

• According to *Clean Ocean Action*, recycling a 36" tall stack of newspaper saves the equivalent of about 14% of the average household electric bill.

• Top uses for recycled newsprint: More newsprint, paperboard. Also, construction paper, insulation, egg cartons, animal bedding.

PILES OF PAPER

• One of the results of America's new enthusiasm for recycling is a "newspaper glut." More paper on the market means lower prices. This is bad for collection programs, but good for mills.

• Of the 25 newsprint mills in the U.S., only ten of them can recycle. Most of our newsprint is manufactured in Canada, and only two of the 42 newsprint mills there are set up to recycle. However, many have announced plans to recycle; some are beginning.

• It may be a while before mills catch up to the public. It takes about 18 months and $40-80 million to retool a mill to recycle.

• Does this mean we shouldn't bother recycling? No, no, no. Mill-owners and newspapers have been waiting to see if recycling is a legitimate trend before they make major investments. But because we've kept the pressure up, they're making the necessary adjustments.

SIMPLE THINGS YOU CAN DO

1. Find a Recycling Center

• It should be easy. Most recyclers accept newspaper, including curbside programs, recycling centers, charity paper drives, etc.

2. Recycle

• Ask your recycling center or curbside service if newspapers should be tied or left loose.

• If they should be tied, put them in bundles about 10" thick, so they're easy to carry. Tying tip: Lay the string in an empty box with the ends draping out over the sides. Put the paper in the box and make the knot.

• If they should be left loose, store the papers in brown grocery bags or cardboard boxes.

• Don't worry about pulling out all the glossy inserts, but don't *add* any junk mail or magazines to the pile. Try to keep the paper dry.

• If you're taking the newspaper to a recycling center, you may be asked to empty out the bags or cut the strings holding the bundles; some recyclers prefer just the newspaper.

• Don't recycle newspaper you've used for birdcages, for house-breaking your dog, or for painting or art projects.

FOR MORE INFORMATION

"Read, Then Recycle." American Newspaper Publishers Association, The Newspaper Center, 11600 Sunrise Valley Drive, Reston, VA 22091; (703) 648-1125. *A free pamphlet.*

Dog food bags can't be recycled; they have plastic linings inside.

ABOUT JAMES DEAN

What was "The Rebel Without a Cause" really like?

Dean was fascinated with death. He wrote poems about dying, and often drew pictures of himself hanging by a noose from the ceiling of his apartment. During one trip to his home town, he had a local funeral parlor photograph him lying in a casket.

His main body of work consisted of several TV appearances and only three motion pictures—*East of Eden, Rebel Without a Cause*, and *Giant*.

While filming *Giant*, Dean annoyed his coworkers by walking around with unfurled pastries hanging out of each nostril.

Once on the set he even urinated in full view of the public. His explanation: "I figured if I could piss in front of those 2,000 people, man, and I could be cool.…I could get in front of the camera and do just anything, anything at all."

Dean didn't have any front teeth; he had to wear a special bridge to fill in the gap. He liked to startle people by smiling at them with his teeth out.

Dean had several gay roommates while living in Hollywood. When asked whether he was bisexual, he reportedly responded: "Well, I'm certainly not going through life with one hand tied behind my back!" He also avoided the military draft by registering as a homosexual.

In late 1955 Dean filmed a TV commercial on auto safety for teenagers. One of his lines: "Drive safely, the life you save may be mine…" A few weeks later, he was killed in a car wreck.

Dean's last words before he slammed into Donald Gene Turnupseed's 1950 Ford Tudor near Cholame, on California Highway 466: "That guy up there has to stop, he's seen us…"

★

Dean really did say, "Live fast, die young and leave a good-looking corpse."

Two animals—Rin Tin Tin and Lassie—have stars on Hollywood's walk of fame.

STRANGE LAWSUITS

Here are more of the BRI's "worst and weirdest" true-life lawsuits.

THE PLAINTIFF: The Karolinska Institute in Stockholm, Sweden
THE DEFENDENT: Olaf Olavson
THE LAWSUIT: In 1910 Olavson was desperate for cash, so he sold his body to the Karolinska Institute (to be used for medical research after he died). But in 1911 he unexpectedly inherited a fortune and decided to "buy himself back." To his surprise, the institute wouldn't cooperate.

When Olavson flatly refused to donate his body, the institute actually sued for breach of contract.
THE VERDICT: Not only did Olavson owe his body to the Institute...he actually owed them money as well. The judge decided that since he'd had two teeth removed without the Institute's permission, Olavson had illegally tampered with their property.

THE PLAINTIFF: Joyce and David W., of Berlin Heights, Ohio
THE DEFENDENT: Natalina Pizza Co. of Elyria, Ohio
THE LAWSUIT: The couple said a frozen pizza they bought on April 26, 1986 had made them "violently ill," caused "emotional distress," and led to the death of their dog, Fluffy.

Although the expiration date on the pizza was April 18, "it was labeled edible for human consumption seven days after that date"...so the pair ate a few pieces. They claimed it was "spoiled, rotten, rancid, and moldy," and made them so sick they had to seek medical help. Fluffy didn't die from eating pizza; the couple ran him over in the driveway as they headed for the hospital.

They sued the pizza company for $125,000.
THE VERDICT: Not reported.

THE PLAINTIFFS: The Cherry Sisters, an Iowa singing group
THE DEFENDENT: The Des Moines *Register*
THE LAWSUIT: At the turn of the century, the *Register* ran a scathing review of the Cherry Sisters' act. Their reporter wrote that

"Their long, skinny arms, equipped with talons at the extremeties...waved frantically at the suffering audience. The mouths of their rancid features opened like caverns, and sounds like the wailings of damned souls issued therefrom."

Outraged and humiliated, the singers sued for libel.

THE VERDICT: The judge asked the sisters to perform their act for him in court...and then ruled in favor of the newspaper. It was, as one historian says, "a landmark libel case."

THE PLAINTIFF: Sarah, a 27-year-old woman with 46 personalities

THE DEFENDENT: Mark Peterson, of Oshkosh, Wisconsin

THE LAWSUIT: Peterson, who dated Sarah, was accused of deliberately drawing out the personality of Jennifer, described as "a gullible 20-year-old who he thought would have sex with him."

He was charged with rape. During the trial, he took the stand and testified he didn't know Sarah had multiple personalities. "I thought she was talking about her brothers and sisters," he said.

THE VERDICT: After deliberating for six hours, the jury found him guilty.

THE PLAINTIFF: Edith Tyler

THE DEFENDENTS: A restaurant in Flagstaff, Arizona

THE LAWSUIT: Tyler, a patron of the restaurant, ordered stuffed cabbage. She was appalled when she dug into it and found that it "apparently contained a used rubber prophylactic." She sued for $150,000.

THE VERDICT: Settled out of court.

THE PLAINTIFF: Tom H., a 24-year-old resident of Boulder, Colorado

THE DEFENDENTS: His parents

THE LAWSUIT: The young man, who'd spent a lot of time in mental institutions, blamed his parents for screwing him up. He sued them for "psychological malparenting." It was, he explained, a healthy alternative to following through on his "desire to kill his father."

THE VERDICT: He got no money.

THE PLAINTIFFS: Eric Hubert, Jeffrey Stabile, Jr., Christopher Drake

THE DEFENDENT: Disneyland

THE LAWSUIT: In 1988, the men were slow-dancing with each other at a Disneyland concert when a security guard allegedly approached them and told them that "touch dancing is reserved for heterosexual couples only." They sued, claiming their civil rights had been violated.

THE VERDICT: They agreed to drop the suit "in exchange for a pledge from Disneyland that the park would not discriminate based on sexual orientation."

THE PLAINTIFF: Wah-Ja Kim, a 58-year-old acupuncturist from Monterey, California

THE DEFENDENTS: William Hall, her ex-husband, and Jeannie Westall, his friend

THE LAWSUIT: In December 1983 Kim dropped in at Hall's condominium and got into an argument with Westall. During the fight, Westall allegedly bit off Kim's right pinkie. Kim sued for $1 million in damages, claiming that "she could not effectively stick pins in her patients' bodies without her little finger." She also said the loss posed a spiritual problem, since "the Confucianism of her native Korea demands 'that every human being should have a perfect, whole body to join our ancestors and carry on in the next life.' "

THE VERDICT: A jury awarded her $55,000.

THE PLAINTIFF: Relatives of a recently deceased man

THE DEFENDENT: A Vallejo, California cemetary

THE LAWSUIT: At the end of a funeral, cemetary employees realized the coffin they were about to lower into the ground was too wide for the hole. They tried turning the coffin on its side, but mourners stopped them. Then the employees tried breaking off the handles; it didn't work. Finally, "they tried to force it by jumping up and down on the lid." The coffin broke, and the funeral had to be stopped. Relatives sued for $500,000.

THE VERDICT: Settled out of court.

The film *Total Recall* contained 55 paid references to 31 products.

WHAT'S THE WORD?

Here are some unusual origins of common words,
provided by BRI member John Dollison.

Addict. Slaves known as *addicts* were given to Roman soldiers to reward performance in battle. Eventually, a person who was a slave to anything became known as an addict.

Appendix. In Latin it means "the part that hangs." A human appendix hangs at the end of the large intestine; appendices come at the end of books.

Bistro. In the 1812 campaign against Napoleon's armies, Russian soldiers pushed all the way into the outskirts of Paris. They became known for shouting "bistro"—"hurry up"—at slow-moving waiters in sidewalk cafes.

Quakers. During a run-in with the law, George Fox, founder of the Society of Friends, told the British judges hearing his case to "tremble at the word of God." One of them laughed back at Fox, calling him a "quaker." The nickname stuck.

Atlas. It was once a tradition for map-makers to include a scene of the Greek god Atlas carrying the Earth on his shoulders in their map books. In time the books themselves came to be known as *atlases*.

Avocado. A South American Indian word for testicle.

Escape. In Latin, *escape* means "out of cape." The ancient Romans would often avoid capture by throwing off their capes when fleeing.

Oklahoma Sooners. Before opening the Oklahoma Territory to settlers, the United States government sealed the borders temporarily to allow everyone a fair chance to claim the free land. Some settlers broke the law and entered before the deadline—getting there *sooner* than anyone else.

People removed at the last minute from the Sgt. Pepper cover: actor Leo Gorcey, Gandhi, and Hitler.

Posh. Originally stood for "Port-outbound, Starbord-home." Clever passengers traveling through the Suez canal in the 1800s ordered cabins on the left side of the ship for the trip out and cabins on the right side for the return voyage. This kept their staterooms in the shade both ways. The desirable accommodations were recorded as "P.O.S.H." in ship records.

Kangaroo. During a trip to Australia Captain Cook, the British explorer, asked a tribesman the name of the large animals he saw hopping about. The tribesman replied "kangaroo"…which means "I don't know."

Pandemonium. Coined in the 1600s by the English author John Milton in his book *Paradise Lost.* Pandemonium is the capital of Hell, where Satan and other demons plan their adventures.

Noon. Derived from the Latin word for ninth. The word "noon" originally meant the 9th hour after sunrise, or 3:00 pm.

Best Man. It was traditional in Scotland for a prospective groom to kidnap the woman he wanted for his wife. His friends would help him. The largest and strongest was called "the best man."

Sincere. *Sine Cera* means "without wax" in Latin. Legend has it that Roman stone carvers would pass off hollow columns (used for building) as solid by filling them with wax. In time *sine cera* came to refer to anything that was authentic or pure.

Coconut. Portugese explorers thought the three holes on the shell made the coconut resemble a human. They named it *coco*—"smiling face."

• • •

BAD JOKE DEPARTMENT:

Q: How many psychiatrists does it take to change a lightbulb?

A: One…But the lightbulb has to want to change.

Glass is considered a liquid, not a solid.

CHEWING GUM

Does your chewing gum lose its flavor on the bedpost overnight? Not if it's in a glass of water, according to The Whole Pop Catalog. *Here are some other bits of gum trivia from the book.*

"Every year, nearly two billion dollars worth of chewing gum is sold in America alone. That's enough to give 300 pieces a year to every American over the age of three."

"Even our most primitive ancestors engaged in recreational chewing. Along with human bones and other prehistoric artifacts, archaeologists at some sites have discovered well-chewed wads of tree resin."

"The first mass-produced gum (made of spruce resin) was manufactured by John Curtis in 1848."

"Clove gum was one of America's most popular flavors during Prohibition; patrons of speakeasies used it to hide the smell of alcohol on their breath. Today the most popular flavor is mint."

"The first bubble gum was invented by Frank Fleer in 1906—but never made it to market. It was so sticky that the only way to remove it from skin was with vigorous scrubbing and turpentine."

"It took Fleer more than twenty years to fix the recipe. In 1928 the 'new improved' gum was introduced as Dubble Bubble gum. It became the largest selling penny candy within just a few years."

"Why is bubble gum pink? Pink was the only food coloring on the shelf the day the first commercial batch of Dubble Bubble was made."

"New York Central Railroad once employed a full-time gum removal man to clean discarded gum from Grand Central Station. He harvested an average of seven pounds a night. The wad grew to fourteen pounds on holiday weekends."

"On June 3, 1965, the Gemini IV astronauts chewed gum in outer space. And according to NASA, when the astronauts were finished with the gum they swallowed it."

There are an estimated 4,000 sunken ships off the coast of New England.

MYTH AMERICA

Here's a batch of historical "truths" that aren't true.

TORY, TORY, TORY

The Myth: The vast majority of American colonists supported the rebellion during the Revolutionary War.

The Truth: According to President John Adams, at the beginning of the war only about a third of the people were on the side of the revolution. Another third were on the side of the British, and the rest didn't care either way. After a while, the ratio changed as British supporters were terrorized, publicly humiliated and finally attacked. Many fled to Canada.

FOOLED AGAIN

The Myth: Abraham Lincoln said: "You can fool all the people some of the time and some of the people all of the time, but you can't fool all of the people all of the time."

Background: Claims that Lincoln said it did not surface until more than 50 years after he was supposed to have said it. The remark was not recorded in any newspapers in Lincoln's time.

The Truth: Some researchers attribute the remark to circus showman P.T. Barnum.

ASLEEP AT THE WHEEL

The Myth: John F. Kennedy was a hero in World War II; when his tiny PT-109 patrol boat was rammed and sunk by a destroyer, he singlehandedly saved three members of his own crew.

Background: In his (ghost-written) book *PT-109*, Kennedy presented this version of the events that night. Yet, while he apparently showed great endurance and courage after his boat sank, there's some question as to whether the incident might have been avoidable in the first place.

The Truth: At least one Kennedy biographer argues that Kennedy's own negligence may have doomed his boat. According to a number of the ship's crew members, Kennedy and most of the crew were sleeping when PT-109 was rammed—not attacking the destroyer as Kennedy later claimed. Naval experts point out that it is unlikely for a ship as small and quick as PT-109 to be out-maneuvered by a ship as large as a destroyer, unless the crew is caught off guard.

SWAN SONG

The Myth: General Douglas MacArthur coined the saying "Old soldiers never die; they just fade away."

The Truth: He was just quoting a British Army song from World War I.

SO HIGH, SOLO

The Myth: Charles Lindbergh was the first person to fly nonstop across the Atlantic Ocean.

The Truth: He was the *67th* person to fly nonstop across the Atlantic. The first nonstop flight was made by William Alcock and Arthur Brown in 1919, eight years before Lindbergh's flight. Lindbergh's was famous because he did it *alone*.

IN THE GROOVE

The Myth: Thomas Edison invented the phonograph to bring music to the masses.

Background: When Edison first played "Mary Had a Little Lamb" on his crude recording device, he knew he was onto something commercially significant. But he didn't have a clue what it was.

The Truth: He was actually trying to create the first telephone answering machine. The problem he saw with the phone was that, unlike the telegraph, you couldn't leave messages for people. Edison came up with an idea and—to his shock—it worked the first time he tried it. Still, it became clear that the machine wasn't suited for telephones. So Edison began marketing phonographs to businesses, believing that it was only suitable as a dictating machine. It took fifteen years and the successes of other manufacturers for him to be convinced that people would buy the machines for home music.

KISSING

*This won't help you kiss any better, but it will give
you something to talk about afterwards.*

H OW KISSING EVOLVED
• One theory: it evolved from sniffing, a form of greeting
still used by animals. In some languages "kiss me" translates literally as "smell me."
• Another theory: it's a holdover from breast feeding.

PROCEED WITH CAUTION
• Europeans of the Dark Ages took kissing very seriously. French women who kissed men other than their husbands were considered guilty of adultery, and Italian men who kissed women in public had to marry them.
• The Great Plague that struck London in 1665 killed thousands—and put kissing out of style. The "substitute" kisses Londoners developed to avoid actually kissing someone—tipping hats, waving hands, and bowing—are still used as greetings today.
• Concerned about the moral and hygienic dangers of kissing, a group of Kansas men founded the Anti-Kissing League in 1909. Members took vows never to kiss their wives again.

SCREEN KISSES
• Thomas Edison filmed the first movie featuring an onscreen kiss in 1896. The "film"—called *The Kiss*—was a 30-second clip starring May Irwin and John C. Rice. It played in nickelodeons.

• Ronald Reagan's ex-wife gets the credit for the longest kiss in Hollywood history. In the 1940 film *You're in the Army Now*, Jane Wyman's kiss with Regis Toomey lasts more than 3 minutes.

• In the mid-1980s Rock Hudson kissed Linda Evans on TV's "Dynasty." Soon afterward he died of AIDS, setting off a nationwide debate on the safety of kissing. Today the Screen Actor's Guild requires film companies to notify actors in advance if their roles require "deep kissing."

The average homebuyer looks at eight houses before finding the right one.

KISSING FACTS

• According to Dr. Joyce Brothers, American women kiss an average of 79 men before marrying.

• Longest kiss on record, according to the *Guiness Book of World Records:* 130 hours, 2 minutes. Bobbie Sherlock and Ray Blazina set the record at a charity "Smoochathon" held in Pittsburgh, Pennsylvania in 1979.

• The Japanese did not kiss at all before coming in contact with Westerners.

• Do you kiss your wife goodbye in the morning? Some studies have shown that you'll outlive people who don't by as much as five years.

• In the Middle Ages, where you kissed someone depended on their social status. You kissed equals on the mouth, and superiors on the hand, knee, or feet (the more "superior" they were, the lower you kissed). You didn't have to kiss inferior people at all; they kissed you.

• Studies conducted in the 1950s showed that more than 250 colonies of bacteria are transmitted from one person to another during an average kiss. The good news: most are harmless.

• • •

FROM OUR WRONG # DEPARTMENT:

In 1940 A. Douglass Thompson, a Tennessee paper boy, was delivering his papers when he was attacked and bitten by a neighborhood dog. Thompson had it taken to the pound. It was released to its owner a few days later.

But the owner of the dog, Gertrude Jamieson, was so upset at Thompson for impounding her pet that she began harassing him with obscene phone calls several times a day. She kept it up—for 43 years. Finally in 1983, at the age of 85, she stopped calling Thompson (who by now was age 59)—but not because she had forgiven him. The only reason she stopped calling was because she had suffered a minor stroke and was confined to a hospital room without a telephone.

Horses use 17 muscles to twitch their ears. Humans use only 9.

RUTH'S TRUTHS

Babe Ruth did more than hit home runs.
He gave a few interviews, too.

(Responding to a comment that he made more money than President Hoover): "I had a better year than he did."

"I have only one superstition. I make sure to touch all the bases when I hit a home run."

"A man ought to get all he can earn. A man who knows he's making money for other people ought to get some of the profit he brings in. Don't make any difference if it's baseball or a bank or a vaudeville show. It's business, I tell you. There ain't no sentiment to it. Forget that stuff."

"Don't quit until every base is uphill."

"Gee, it's lonesome in the outfield. It's hard keeping awake with nothing to do."

"Hot as hell, ain't it, Prez?" (His greeting to President Calvin Coolidge, during a game at the Washington ball park.)

" I hit big or I miss big. I like to live as big as I can."

"If I'd just tried for them dinky singles, I could've batted around six hundred."

"It's hell to get older."

"I've heard people say that the trouble with the world is that we haven't enough great leaders. I think we haven't enough great followers. I have stood side by side with great thinkers—surgeons, engineers, economists; men who deserve a great following—and have heard the crowd cheer me instead…I'm proud of my profession. I like to play baseball. I like fans, too…But I think they yelled too loudly and yelled for the wrong man."

"What I am, what I have, what I am going to leave behind me—all this I owe to the game of baseball, without which I would have come out of St. Mary's Industrial School in Baltimore a tailor, and a pretty bad one, at that."

"You need a certain number of breaks in baseball…and every other calling."

In 1991 General Motors was #1 on the Fortune 500 list—but 485th in profitablilty.

THE SOUND OF MUZAK

You hear it in the elevator, in your dentist's office, at the supermarket—even in the reptile house of the Bronx Zoo. Here's the inside story on the music you love to hate:

ORIGIN

General George Squier was the head of the U.S. Signal Corps in World War I. During the war he discovered a way to transmit music over electrical lines. When the war was over, he showed his discovery to a Cleveland, Ohio utility. The company liked his invention, and in 1922 helped Squier set up the Wired Radio Company.

• Their plan: provide an alternative to radio by broadcasting music to households through their power lines (for a fee).

• Squier changed his company's name to *Muzak* in 1934. Why? He liked Kodak's name, and wanted something that sounded similar.

MUZAK AT WAR:

Squier overlooked one thing when he started his business: households receiving radio broadcasts free of charge would not see any reason to pay a monthly fee for Muzak's wire broadcasts. This made it tough to attract customers. However, events during World War II helped keep the company in business:

• To combat assembly line fatigue, the British government began broadcasting the BBC in defense factories.

• When production at these plants increased as much as 6%, the U.S. government hired Muzak to pipe sound into U.S. plants. Their productivity rose 11%.

• Studies showed that even cows and chickens increased productivity when "functional" music played in the background.

• Seeing this, the company switched its focus to increasing productivity for business customers. Today it broadcasts via satellite to

---

Only 41% of Americans say they like the way they look in the nude.

180 different Muzak "stations" around the country—and into the ears of more than 100 *million* "listeners" worldwide.

MIND CONTROL

If you thought Muzak just played songs at random, think again:

At Work

• To maximize Muzak's uplifting potential, the company gives each of its songs a "mood rating" that ranges from "Gloomy" (minus three) to "Ecstatic" (plus eight). An overall "stimulus value" is determined for each song.

• Broadcasts are divided into 15 minute "segments": 14 minutes of songs with 1 minute of silence at the end. The "stimulus value" of a segment increases with each song.

• To revive sluggish workers, Muzak plays speedier segments between 10:00 and 11:00 am.

• The songs slow down again at 1:00 pm. Why? To calm employees after lunch.

• By 3:00 pm the music picks up pace—to energize workers at the end of the day.

At the Supermarket

The broadcasts Muzak provides to supermarkets are *always* slow-paced—studies have shown that shoppers who listen to slow music spend more time shopping…and as much as 35% more money.

MUZAK FACTS

• President Dwight D. Eisenhower played Muzak in the White House—and Lyndon Johnson liked it so much he bought a local Texas franchise. He even had Muzak speakers installed in the trees of the LBJ ranch.

• Neil Armstrong listened to Muzak during the Apollo XI voyage to the moon.

• During the fall of Saigon in 1975, State Department staffers evacuated the American embassy compound with Muzak playing in the background.

• No surprise: 90% of Muzak "listeners" say they like the stuff. Andy Warhol claimed it was his favorite music.

There are enough stones in the Great Wall of China to build an 8 ft. wall around the equator.

FAMILIAR NAMES

Some people achieve immortality because their names are associated with common items or activities. You already know the names—now here are the people

Atoine de la Mothe Cadillac. A French explorer, Cadillac founded Detroit in 1701.

Ernesto Miranda. Miranda was arrested in 1963 for stealing $8 from a Phoenix, Arizona bank employee. He confessed, but the U.S. Supreme Court threw out his conviction—the police had not advised him of his rights. To avoid the same mistake, police now read the *Miranda Warning* to people they arrest.

Alexander Garden. A South Carolina botanist born in 1730. The Royal Society of Botany in London named a newly discovered tropical plant, the *gardenia*, in his honor in 1755.

Captain William Lynch. A Virginia farmer during the Revolutionary War, Lynch organized bands of townspeople to dispense justice to outlaws and British collaborators. These bands became known as "Lynch Mobs," and hanging someone without a trial became known as "Lynching."

Ludwig Doberman. A German dog breeder in the late 1800s. He is the "father" of Doberman Pinschers.

Henry Deringer. An American gunsmith of the 1840s, Deringer invented a tiny pistol that he named after himself. Imitators copied his guns—and misspelled his name. Today derringer is still spelled with two r's.

Thomas and William Bowler. The Bowlers, English hatmakers in the 1860s, made a brimmed hunting hat for one of their customers. It became known as a "bowler" hat.

Thomas Derrick. A notorious hangman in England during the 17th century, Derrick designed a hoisting apparatus for the gallows—which he used to execute more than 3,000 people. The apparatus—and the crane that resembles it—are both called derricks.

Annual event: About 650,000 Americans invite dogs to birthday parties thrown for their own dogs.

Charles Henry Dow and Edward D. Jones. Journalists at the turn of the century, Dow and Jones created the first index of U.S. stock prices—the Dow-Jones Average. It later appeared in the newspaper they founded, *The Wall St. Journal*.

Captain Fudge. Though his first name has been forgotten, Captain Fudge was a captain in the British Navy in the 1600s. His wild tales about his seafaring adventures earned him the nickname "Lying Fudge." Sailors of the day referred to his storytelling as "fudging it."

Dr. Thomas Lushington. Lushington was a heavy-drinking English chaplain in the 1600s. His reputation as a drunk was so great that the *City of Lushington*, a London drinking club, was named in his honor more than 200 years after his death. The club's inebriated clientele inspired the word *lush*.

Mr. Scheuster. Like Captain Fudge, Scheuster's first name has been forgotten. He was a crooked criminal lawyer in New York in the 1840s, whose name inspired the term *shyster*.

Admiral Edward "Old Grog" Vernon. Old Grog was famous for pacing his ship's deck in a grogram cloak—that's how he got his nickname. But he was also famously cheap. When he began watering down the rum he served to his sailors, they christened the weakened spirit "Grog."

E.A. Murphy, Jr. Murphy was not an optimist. An American engineer in the 1940s, he was the first to utter the words "Anything that can go wrong *will* go wrong"— Murphy's Law.

John Taliaferro Thompson. A general in the U.S. Army in the 1920s. He was one of the inventors of the Thompson sub-machine gun in 1921. Though the "Tommy Gun" never really caught on with the military as Thompson had hoped, by the late 1920s it was a big hit with the mob.

Antionette Perry. A popular stage actress whose career spanned from 1905 to 1949. The Tony awards are named in her honor.

Sequoya. Sequoya—who also used the name George Guess—was an Indian scholar who developed a system of writing for his native Cherokee language. Sequoia redwood trees are named after him.

IFS AND BUTTS

Warning: The Surgeon General has determined that reading about cigarettes is not harmful to your health.

Richard Joshua (R.J.) Reynolds—one of the fathers of the cigarette industry—hated cigarettes. He preferred chewing tobacco and would not allow smokes in his house.

Though Turkish tobacco is popular all over the world, 7th century Turks hated smokers. One punishment: smokers were led through town on muleback—with their pipes shoved up their noses.

In 1989, Reynolds introduced Uptown, a menthol brand designed specifically for blacks. Within days of its introduction, civil rights groups and anti-smoking organizations lit into Reynolds. Two months later, Uptown was dumped.

Who's the camel on the package of Camel cigarettes? Old Joe, a camel in Barnum and Bailey's circus. R.J. Reynolds had his personal secretary photograph him in 1913. The package is an exact copy of the photo.

Unlucky promotion: R.J. Reynolds paid Amelia Earhart to take Lucky Strikes with her on her ill-fated trip across the Atlantic.

Kent cigarette filters were originally made from the same material as WW II gas masks.

In the late 1980s, R.J. Reynolds spent $300 million developing Premier, a high-tech "smokeless cigarette" that came with a 4-page set of instructions. Smokers were supposed to light the "carbon heat source" at the tip and suck flavorings out of the "flavor capsule." It flopped.

If you were a tobacco farmer in the 1930s and 40s, you wouldn't have had to fight in World War II. Pres. Roosevelt declared tobacco "an essential crop" at the outbreak of the war—exempting tobacco growers from the draft.

Mafia means "beauty, excellence, bravery" in Italian.

THE DUSTBIN OF HISTORY

They were VIPs in their time…but they're forgotten now.
They've been swept into the Dustbin of History.

FORGOTTEN FIGURE: Lord Cornbury (Edward Hyde), colonial governor of New York from 1702 to 1708.

CLAIM TO FAME: Edward Hyde, a cousin of Queen Anne, was appointed governor of New York in 1702. When colonists went to welcome him, they found him rocking on his porch, knitting a doily and wearing one of his wife's dresses.

Things got weirder when he threw his first dress ball. Not only was he decked out in a formal gown; he also charged an admission fee, and insisted that his guests all feel his wife's ears…which he had described in a long poem as "conch shells."

For many years, he was the was the talk of New York—especially when it turned out he had taken the governorship to escape creditors in England. Then in 1708 he was caught embezzling public funds.

INTO THE DUSTBIN: Cornbury was confined to debtor's prison until his father died, when he inherited a title and returned to England. No monuments to his rule were built, but he did leave his family name on land along the Hudson: Hyde Park.

FORGOTTEN FIGURE: Lucy Page Gaston, 1860-1924, American anti-tobacco reformer.

CLAIM TO FAME: After legendary prohibitionist Carrie Nation, she was the most famous American female reformer of her time. In 1899 she founded the Chicago Anti-Cigarette League, which became the National Anti-Cigarette League two years later. For a while the movement she inspired was a real threat to the tobacco industry, as cigarette sales dipped by 25%.

By 1920 she was so well-known that she became a candidate in the Republican presidential race, vowing to "emancipate" the country from smoking. But she won few votes, and Warren

---

The golden eagle can spot a rabbit from almost 2 miles away.

Harding, a smoker, was nominated.

INTO THE DUSTBIN: In June, 1924, Gaston was hit by a trolley while crossing a street. She was taken to a hospital, but did not respond well to treatment. That's when doctors discovered she was terminally ill. She died two months later—of throat cancer.

FORGOTTEN FIGURE: Luise Rainer, a film star of the '30s.

CLAIM TO FAME: She was the first person ever to win two consecutive Academy Awards—for Best Actress in 1936 (for *The Great Ziegfeld*) *and* in 1937 (for *The Good Earth*).

In 1936, nominations were still carefully controlled by movie studios. Rainer's first nomination was engineered by MGM to help develop her career. (It was only her second film, and it was a relatively small part.) No one thought she would actually *win* the Oscar. That's why everyone voted for her.

The following year, voting was opened up for the first time to thousands of actors, writers, etc. Rainer, who was well-liked for not acting like a "star," beat out Greta Garbo and Barbara Stanwyck.

INTO THE DUSTBIN: For some reason, MGM forced Ranier into a quick series of throwaway roles; two years and five insignificant pictures later, she was a has-been. Her downfall led gossip columnist Louella Parsons to coin the term "Oscar jinx."

FORGOTTEN FIGURE: Smedley Butler, America's most famous soldier—a U.S. Marine and two-time Medal of Honor winner, nicknamed "Old Gimlet Eye."

CLAIM TO FAME: Once called "the finest fighting man in the armed forces" by Teddy Roosevelt, Butler was renowned for personal bravery, tactical brilliance, and the ability to inspire his fellow soldiers. He joined a Marine force in China during the Boxer rebellion, and helped carry a wounded comrade 17 miles through enemy fire back to their camp. He was promoted to captain—at age 18. He later served in Cuba, Nicaragua, Panama, Honduras, and Haiti.

Butler served in France during World War I—not at the front, but as commander of a troop depot, Camp Pontanezen. Ironically, his greatest fame came from this post. The camp was practically buried in mud; and the troops were short of food and blankets. But somehow, Butler scrounged a huge supply of slats used for trench floors and created walkways and tent floors to keep the troops out

---

The letters "J" and "V" are the youngest letters of the alphabet. They're about 350 years old.

of the mud.

The grateful soldiers never forgot him; as one said, "I'd cross hell on a slat if Butler gave the word."

After the war, Butler was regarded as presidential material (he didn't run). He was also a popular figure on the lecture circuit.

In the early '30s, he was approached by men claiming to be associated with the American Legion. They wanted him to organize a fighting force to overthrow Franklin Roosevelt—and said there was $300 million available to fund the insurrection. Butler played along and eventually learned he was being courted by the American fascist movement. He divulged the plot before the Un-American Activities Committee in 1934, but nothing much came of it; the story was hushed up because several prominent figures were involved.

INTO THE DUSTBIN: Butler retired from the Corps in 1931, but continued to speak out on military and foreign-policy issues. He died in 1940.

FORGOTTEN FIGURE: William Walker, American journalist, physician, lawyer, and soldier of fortune.

CLAIM TO FAME: Walker is the only native-born American ever to become president of a foreign nation. From July 1856, to May 1857, he was self-appointed dictator of Nicaragua, a nation he took over with a hand-picked force of mercenaries who called themselves "The Immortals."

Walker's success made him a hero throughout the U.S., where the notion of "Manifest Destiny" was gaining wide acceptance. Crowds cheered his exploits, newspapers hailed his triumphs. But a coalition of Central American nations, financed in part by Cornelius Vanderbilt, overthrew Walker. On May 1, 1857, he and his troops fled back to the U.S.

Walker made three more attempts to win control in Central America. Finally, in the fall of 1859, he and his men attacked Honduras and were captured by British and Honduran troops.

INTO THE DUSTBIN: Walker surrendered to the British, expecting he would again be returned to the States. But he was turned over to the Hondurans instead, and was executed by a firing squad on September 12, 1860.

He was so hated by Nicaraguans that he became a symbol of "Yankee Imperialism." He is still remembered there.

HOW LONG?

*See if you can guess the average lifespan of the following things
(answers on page 223):*

1. The American male in 1900: A. 32.4 years B. 46.3 years C. 66.3 years

2. American male in 1990: A. 67.3 years B. 72.1 years C. 78.6 years

3. The American female in 1900: A. 48.3 years B. 52.8 years C. 60.1 years

4. American female in 1990: A. 68.4 years B. 74.8 years C. 79.0 years

5. Beer: A. 3-5 weeks B. 12-18 months C. 3 months

6. Freeze-dried fish squares (Stored at 70° F): A. 25 years B. 12 months C. 72 months

7. Facelifts: A. 1-3 years B. 6-10 years C. 10-18 years

8. U.S. Patents: A. 17 years B. 70 years C. Unlimited

9. Lightning Bolts: A. 1-7 microseconds B. 45-55 microseconds C. 11 seconds

10. Cockroaches: A. 40 days B. 6 months C. 7 years

11. Bras: A. Up to 9 months B. Up to 2 years C. Up to 5 years

12. Ballistic missiles: A. 10-15 months B. 10 - 15 years C. 100-150 years

13. Snowflakes: A. From 7 minutes to several centuries B. From 30 seconds to 4 days C. From 1 minute to 9 months

14. Televisions: A. 7-10 years B. 10-15 years C. 15-18 years

15. Skywriting: A. 45-60 seconds B. 5-7 minutes C. 45 minutes

16. A professional football (when used in an NFL game): A. 6 minutes B. 30 minutes C. One hour

17. Moonbeams: A. 1.3 Seconds B. 12 minutes C. 1 hour

18. A dollar bill (in circulation): A. 3.8 months, or 900 folds B. 18 months, or 4,000 folds C. 2.5 years, or 10,000 folds

---

Three million cars are abandoned every year in the U.S.

JOIN THE CLUB

*Every time you drive into a town, you see signs with info on Rotary,
Kiwanis, or Elk's club chapters. How did they come up
with those names? Here are some answers.*

The Benevolent and Protective Order of Elks: The group
started out in the 1860s as "The Jolly Corks," a drinking
club for vaudevillians. Members changed the name to the
Elks after they saw a stuffed elk in Barnum's Museum in New York
City.

Kiwanis International: Founded as The Benevolent Order of
Brothers in 1914 by Allen S. Browne, a Detroit businessman. A
year later the group changed its name to Kiwanis, borrowing from
the Canadian Indian expression "nun keewanis." They believed
that it meant "we trade." Actual translation: "we have good time/
we make noise."

The Rotarians: When a group of Chicago businessmen founded a
service organization in 1905, they decided to make the meetings
convenient for everyone by *rotating* the meeting place from one
member's office to another. They couldn't think of a name for it—
so they just named it the *Rotary* Club.

The Shriners: During a visit to France in 1867, Walter M. Fleming, a New York doctor, went to see an Arabian musical comedy.
At the end of the performance, the cast initiated the audience into
a "secret society." Fleming liked the idea—and in 1872 he formed
the Ancient Arabic Order of the Nobles of the Mystic Shrine…
commonly known as the *Shriners.*

The Freemasons: The group traces its roots back to 17th century
guilds of English "freestone mason" guilds of highly skilled crafts-
men who carved the ornate stonework used to build monasteries,
palaces and cathedrals.

The Lion's Club: Adopted when the group was founded in 1917.
It stands for what members consider "the true meaning of citizen-
ship: **L**iberty, **I**ntelligence, and **O**ur **N**ation's **S**afety."

Vital stats: 42% of U.S. men and 31% of U.S. women say they clean their belly buttons every day.

CLASSIC MOVIES: BEHIND THE SCENES

You've seen the films—now here are the stories.

P RIDE OF THE YANKEES (1942). The film biography of New York Yankee first baseman Lou Gehrig starred Gary Cooper...who'd never played baseball in his life. He couldn't run, couldn't field, and couldn't throw.

• The studio hired an expert to teach him baseball fundamentals, but it didn't do any good. Doubles still had to be used whenever Gehrig was supposed to be out in the field.

• Cooper had a knack for batting, though; he was able to meet the ball solidly, with a fairly convincing swing. Unfortunately, he was right-handed and Gehrig had been left-handed.

• Director Sam Woods's solution: He filmed Cooper hitting right-handed and flipped the film so the actor appeared to be batting from the left side.

• That meant other details had to be reversed. For example: Special mirror-image Yankee uniforms had to be designed. And new ballpark billboards that were printed backwards were erected, so the signs would be readable.

• After all that trouble, Wood wouldn't take any chances casting an actor as Babe Ruth. He signed the Babe to play himself.

SINGIN' IN THE RAIN (1952). For years Arthur Freed, the producer of this classic musical, wanted to name a film—any film— "Singin' in the Rain" (after the popular 1920's song)...and this was his chance. It didn't matter to him that there were no rain scenes originally planned for the movie...or that its star and director, Gene Kelly, thought he was nuts.

• When Freed insisted, Kelly gave in and choreographed the film's main dance sequence around the song.

• But the splashing footsteps that audiences heard in the "Rain"

The Ringling Brothers were originally a family orchestra, not a circus.

dance routine weren't all Kelly's. To enhance the "puddle" effect, a young dancer sloshed through a series of water-filled buckets off-screen. (The dancer was Gwen Verdon, who later starred in *Damn Yankees*.)

• During the dance, Kelly looked joyful. Actually, he was miserable. He had a terrible cold and was afraid that prancing around in all that water would give him pneumonia.

• He was also unhappy about his 19-year-old female co-star, Debbie Reynolds. She'd never sung or danced before, and he had to tutor her for every number.

KING KONG (1933). Merian C. Cooper, the film's producer, wanted to include a scene audiences would never forget. As Paul Boller reports in his excellent book, *Hollywood Anecdotes*: "Late one afternoon in February 1930, as he was leaving his office in midtown Manhattan, Cooper heard the sound of an airplane, glanced out of the window, and saw a plane flying close to the New York Life Insurance Building, then the city's tallest building. At once it flashed into his mind: 'If I can get that gorilla logically on top of the mightiest building in the world, and then have him shot down by the most modern of weapons, the airplane, then no matter how giant he was in size, and how fierce, that gorilla was doomed by civilization.' "

• "By the time RKO came to make the picture, Cooper had had to move Kong, first to the new Chrysler Building, and then, finally, to the Empire State Building, which, when completed in 1931, was the tallest structure in the world."

• King Kong, of course, was a model. He was actually 18" tall.

HIGH NOON (1952). Gary Cooper starred as a sheriff who had to face a band of outlaws by himself. Cooper, who was 50 years old, was praised for the convincing way he made his character seem pained and worried. Actually, it wasn't all acting. Right before filming began, Cooper was hospitalized for a hernia. During the filming, he was troubled by a hip injury. After the film was finished, he went right back to the hospital—this time to have a duodenal ulcer removed.

• He had other reasons to look worried: He thought his co-star, Grace Kelly, was too inexperienced, and that the movie was dull.

• Kelly *was* inexperienced—*High Noon* was only her second movie—but that's why the director had hired her. He wanted the character to seem innocent and naive.

• The movie *was* dull, too. It bombed in its first preview and had to be completely re-edited. Editor Elmo Williams shortened it, sped up the pace, and transformed it from a turkey to a classic. Cooper won an Oscar for Best Actor.

THE GRAPES OF WRATH (1940). The film that made Henry Fonda a star was adapted from one of the most controversial novels in America's history. The book was denounced—and even banned —in many communities as "subversive."

• Author John Steinbeck insisted that 20th Century Fox guarantee the studio would "retain the main action and social intent" of his book.

• Before agreeing, Fox hired detectives to check the accuracy of Steinbeck's portrayal of life in migrant camps. The report: conditions were even worse than Steinbeck had suggested.

• Fox was worried the film's pro-labor message might provoke a response from banks and agri-business (the novel's two villains). So they filmed it under tight security, with unusual secrecy.

• They posted armed guards at the studio door. None of the actors was given a complete script; they had to read from mimeographed sheets instead. The sheets were collected at the end of each day; no one was allowed to leave the set with a script. During shooting, the film was given a false title—*Highway 66*—so the crew could film wherever they pleased without creating a controversy.

• The cast and director John Ford went out of their way to make sure the public knew the film was "apolitical," and it won two Oscars.

AND NOW A SHORT FEATURE FROM THE BOOK,
Hollywood Anecdotes, **by Paul Boller:**
"For the opening of Pinocchio (1940) Walt Disney's publicity department decided to hire eleven midgets, dress them in Pinocchio outfits, and have them frisk about on top of the theater marquee on

---

Annie Oakley was so good with a gun that Sitting Bull called her "Little Sure Shot."

opening day. At lunchtime, food and refreshments were passed up to the marquee, including a couple of quarts of liquor. By three o'clock that afternoon things had gotten out of hand and an amused crowd in Times Square was regaled by the spectacle of eleven stark-naked midgets belching noisily and enjoying a crap game atop the Broadway marquee. Police with ladders removed the gamblers in pillowcases. "

CLASSIC BLOOPERS

• In *The Invisible Man*, the title character is supposed to be naked, but the footprints he leaves are of shoes instead of bare feet.

• If you look closely in the famous chariot race scene in *Ben Hur* (1959), you'll see a red sports car driving by the Coliseum in the distance.

• In *El Cid*, a 1961 movie extravaganza about an 11th century Spanish hero, a costly crowd scene was spoiled by an extra wearing sunglasses.

• *The Green Berets* features a dramatic shot of the sun...setting in the east.

• In another crowd scene, this time from the 1982 epic *Gandhi*, one of the peasants is sporting Adidas tennis shoes.

MOVIE NOTES

• A South Korean movie theater owner decided that *The Sound of Music* was too long, so he shortened the movie himself—by cutting out all of the songs.

• Why was the computer in *2001* named HAL? The director claimed the name is a hybrid of the two principal learning systems Heuristic and Algorithmic. However, a number of critics have pointed out that if you replace each initial in HAL with the letter that succeeds it, you wind up with the well-known name of a real-life computer...IBM.

• The shortest shooting schedule for a full-length, commercial film was two days...for Roger Corman's 1959 classic, *Little Shop of Horrors*.

George Reeves, TV's Superman, needed three people to help him out of his costume.

THE COMPASS IN YOUR NOSE

What do you know about your body? Here's some fascinating info from a book called, The Compass in Your Nose, *by Marc McCutcheon*

THE COMPASS IN YOUR NOSE

Magnetic Attraction

• All humans have a trace amount of iron in their noses, a rudimentary compass found in the ethmoid bone (between the eyes) to help in directional finding relative to the earth's magnetic field.

• Studies show that many people have the ability to use these magnetic deposits to orient themselves—even when blindfolded and removed from such external clues as sunlight—to within a few degrees of the North Pole, exactly as a compass does.

• Though no one knows how this "sixth" sense is processed by the brain, more than two dozen animals, including the dolphin, tuna, salmon, salamander, pigeon, and honeybee, have been found to have similar magnetic deposits in their brains to help them in navigation and migration.

The Off-Duty Nostril

• Nostrils switch on and off every three to four hours, so that one is always smelling and breathing while the other closes down and rests.

Whose Nose?

•Women have a better sense of smell than men due to higher levels of the female hormone estrogen.

• Interestingly, a woman can detect the odor of musk—a scent associated with male bodies—better than any other odor.

Scent-sational

• The sex/scent connection is a powerful one. About 25 percent of people with smell disorders—due to either head injuries, viral infections, allergies, or aging—lose interest in sex.

The comic strip "Dick Tracy" was originally called "Plainclothes Tracy."

HAIR TODAY, GONE TOMORROW

Get Growing

• On the scalp, each hair grows continuously for 3 to 5 years, then enters a resting phase. After about 3 months of "resting," the hair falls out; a new hair starts growing 3 to 4 months later. Ninety per-cent of the scalp is always in the growing phase.

• Eyebrow hairs stay short because their growing phase only lasts for 10 weeks. Eyelashes are replaced every 3 months. A person will grow about 600 complete eyelashes in a lifetime.

• "Beards grow faster than any other hair on the body, and blond beards grow fastest of all. The average beard grows about 5-1/2 inches in a year—or about 30 feet in a lifetime. The longest beard on record was grown by Hans Langseth of Kensett, Iowa." When he died in 1927 his beard measured 17-1/2 feet.

Baldness

• One out of every five men begin balding rapidly in their 20s. An-other one out of five will always keep their hair. The others will slowly bald over time.

• As a general rule, the more hair a man has on his chest at age 30 the less hair he'll have on his head at age 40.

• Women typically lose as much as 50 percent of their hair within 3 months of childbirth. This partial and temporary balding is caused by severe fluctuations of hormones.

Hair Growth and Loss

• The average hair grows half an inch per month, with the fastest growth generally occurring in the morning hours. Hair sprouts fast-est of all when you're in love, which may also be due to fluctua-tions of hormones.

• A loss of about 70 hairs per day is typical, but emotional stress (including falling out of love), illness, malnourishment, and anemia can more than double this amount.

Goosebumps

• The goosebumps that break out on our skin when we're cold rep-resent little more than the body's effort to erect the coat of fur our ancestors lost over 100,000 years ago. Raised body hair provides added insulation.

80% of Americans have never eaten breakfast in bed. 68% say it's a bad idea.

ONLY SKIN DEEP

Sags, Lines, and Wrinkles

• Collagen—the skin's network of protein fibers—breaks down and becomes less pliable with age, causing sags, lines, and wrinkles to form on the face, neck, and hands. Any expression that manipulates the skin deeply and consistently will promote wrinkling (it takes about 200,000 frowns to create one permanent brow line), but exposure to sunlight and cigarette smoke hastens the process.

Dead Skin and Where It Goes

• The body constantly sheds dead skin cells and replaces them with new ones. Thousands of these cells are lost, for example, every time we shake hands or swing a baseball bat. By the time we reach age 70, we'll have shed 40 pounds of dead skin.

• Of the dust floating around in the average house, 75 percent is made up of dead skin cells.

HEAR, HEAR

Human versus Animal Hearing

• Vampire and fruit bats can hear pitch as high as 210,000 hertz, ten times higher than humans. The dolphin's hearing is even more sensitive, with an acuity of 280,000 hertz.

• The best overall long-distance hearing, on the other hand, belongs to the fennec, a small African fox. Its oversized ears enable it to hear the movements of another animal up to one mile away.

The Future of Ear Wiggling

• The ability to wiggle the ears is a vestige of evolution, a throwback to a time when our ancestors could "cock," or adjust, the ears to aid in hearing. The musculature for ear cocking has gradually diminished over the eons through genetic reprogramming. Most of us have lost the ability to move the ears at all in such a manner.

ON ANOTHER SUBJECT...

Doo-wop Mysteries Of Life:

How can you tell if a singer is singing "Bom-Bom," or "Bomp-bomp"? And is there any way to be sure that it's "Dip-dip" rather than "Dit-dit"?

Alibi means "elsewhere" in Latin.

ABE LINCOLN, WARTS AND ALL

We've all heard so much about Abraham Lincoln that it's easy to assume we know everything important about him. Actually, most of us know almost nothing. For example, did you know...

THE REAL ABE
• Some photographs of Lincoln show him with a mole on the right side of his face—but other photos show it on the left. The reason: few full-length pictures of Lincoln existed when he was running for president. So when photographers needed one, they put Lincoln's head onto other people's bodies. Sometimes the head needed to be reversed to fit the body they were using—and the mole on his right cheek ended up on his left.

• Although Lincoln's voice is often portrayed in movies as being deep and booming, his actual voice was high-pitched, piercing and shrill. Though unusual, it payed off politically: It carried for hundreds of yards—a distinct advantage in open-air speeches and debates.

TRY, TRY AGAIN

Lincoln wasn't always a success:

• He lost a race for the state legislature in 1832. He also lost his job.

• His grocery business failed the following year. It took him 15 years to pay off the debt.

• He was elected to the state legislature in 1834, but he lost races for speaker of the house in 1836 and 1838.

• He was elected to Congress in 1846 but was defeated after only two years, and in 1849 lost the race for a land-office seat.

• He lost the U.S. Senate race in 1854 and again in 1858. In between, he lost the Vice Presidential nomination.

• It makes you wonder why he even bothered to run for president in 1860—but he did...and won. He was reelected in 1864.

HONEST ABE?

• Lincoln's presidential campaigns used dirty tricks to get ahead:
During the 1860 Republican National Convention, his campaign
managers forged convention passes in order to pack the galleries
with Lincoln supporters, shutting out hundreds of his opponent's
supporters in the process. Lincoln won the nomination.

• Lincoln wasn't always that honest: After one trip to Springfield,
Illinois, he filed for compensation for the 3,252 miles he claimed
to have traveled. The actual length of the trip was 1,800 miles.

ABE FACTS

• Lincoln hated being called "Abe"—friends called him Lincoln.

• He really did carry important documents in his stovepipe hat.

• He was the first President to support womens' suffrage. In 1832,
while running for the state legislature, he provided a newspaper
with a prepared statement that supported the idea.

• Though the Gettysburg Address is considered the most eloquent
oration in American history, the *Chicago Times* hated it. The day
after Lincoln delivered it, the *Times* wrote: "The cheek of every
American must tingle with shame as he reads the silly, flat and
dish-watery utterances of the man who has been pointed out to in-
telligent foreigners as the President of the United States."

STRANGE BUT TRUE

Lincoln took his dreams seriously, and believed that strange events
foretold the future. According to some accounts, he may even have
"predicted" his own assassination.

• On one occasion, he looked into an old mirror and saw two re-
flections of himself. His interpretation: he would serve a second
term as President—but would die in office.

• About a week before his assassination, Lincoln had a dream in
which he "awoke" to the sound of sobbing and went to the East
Room of the White House—which had been prepared for a funeral.
When he asked a guard who had died, he replied: "The President."

• The morning of the assassination, Lincoln told his aides that he
had had another dream, one in which he was sailing "in an inde-
scribable vessel and moving rapidly toward an indistinct shore."

Dr. Seuss designed the first animated color TV commercial in 1949, for Ford.

BATTLE OF THE SEXES

*Looking for words of wisdom about love and life? Try TV quotes
from the book* Primetime Proverbs, *by Jack Mingo and John Javna.*

ALL ABOUT MEN

"Men are nothing but lazy
lumps of drunken flesh. They
crowd you in bed, get you all
worked up, and then before you
can say 'Is that all there is?'
that's all there is."
>**—Mrs. Gravas
(Latka's mom), *Taxi***

Cosmetic Clerk: "You know
what the fastest way to a man's
heart is?"
Rosanne: "Yeah. Through his
chest."
>**—*Roseanne***

ALL ABOUT WOMEN

"It's not the frivolity of women
that makes them so intolerable.
It's their ghastly enthusiasm."
>**—Horace Rumpole,
*Rumpole of the Bailey***

"There she was—dejected, des-
perate, and stoned. Everything
I could hope for in a woman."
>**—Louie DePalma,
*Taxi***

"It's been proven through history that wimmin's a mystery."
>**—*Popeye***

ON MARRIAGE

"In my town, we didn't have
datin.' You washed your hair
every Saturday night and
when you were fourteen, you
married your cousin."
>**Nurse Laverne,
*Empty Nest***

"Well, well, well...So you're
going to get married, ha, ha,
ha. Welcome to the ranks of
the living dead."
>**—Kingfish,
*Amos & Andy***

"Men are such idiots, and I
married their King."
>**—Peg Bundy,
*Married with Children***

ABOUT SEX

"With my first husband, it was
like a news bulletin: brief, unexpected, and usually a
disaster."
>**—Mary Campbell,
*Soap***

"You can point out any item in
the Sears catalog and somebody wants to sleep with it."
>**—Det. Stanley Wojohoicz,
*Barney Miller***

More than 44 million Americans say they want to quit smoking. Only 1.3 million will.

BREAKFAST SERIALS

You're not supposed to read this book at breakfast, of course. But you can read it after breakfast. Here's the perfect reading fiber.

RAISIN' DOUBTS

Everybody knows a raisin is heavier than a cereal flake. So how come all the raisins in Kellogg's Raisin Bran don't end up at the bottom of the box?

The raisins are mixed evenly with the cereal as the boxes are filled. Since the flat flakes pack so densely together, the raisins can't move around much during shipping.

GETTING FLAKY?

According to one researcher, large doses of cereal may contain enough natural LSD to induce mild euphoria. Dr. David Conning, director of the British Nutritional Foundation, suggests that eating a large bowl of shredded wheat or bran flakes in one sitting may be enough to set you off. This is because LSD is produced by ergot, a common fungal infestation of wheat that may, in some cases, survive food processing. A high-bran diet could result in a daily consumption of 100 micrograms of LSD, four times the minimum dose needed to produce an effect on an inexperienced user of the drug. Eight to ten slices of whole wheat bread, the doctor said, could have the same effect. Turn On, Tune In, Snap, Crackle Pop?

SO SWEET

Are cereals ashamed of their sugary roots? Three that have been renamed to appeal to the new nutrition-conscious consumer are: Super Sugar Crisp (has become Super Golden Crisp), Sugar Pops (now called simply Corn Pops); and Sugar Smacks (changed to the healthy-sounding but still tooth-aching sweet Honey Smacks). But that doesn't mean they're less sugary—Honey Smacks and Super Golden Crisp are right up there with Froot Loops and Apple Jacks on the list of "high sugar content" cereals, some of which contain more than half their weight in sugar.

George Washington's false teeth were made of Hippopotomus ivory.

SOMETHING USEFUL, FOR A CHANGE

A notorious "Phone Phreak" (a pre-computer hackers of the late 1960s who developed elaborate strategies for getting free phone calls through guerrilla technology), called himself Cap'n Crunch. This was in honor of a "free-inside" premium whistle from the cereal of the same name which, according to legend, was exactly the right frequency for triggering free long distance calls if blown into the phone right after dialing the number.

STATISTICS:

• Nielsen Marketing Research tells us that last year nearly 2.5 billion boxes of hot and cold cereal were sold in the US.

• The manufacturers of Post cereals use a staggering 75,000,000 pounds of corn, 1,550,000 bushels of wheat and 7,500,000 pounds of rice each year, which they sweeten with 36,000,000 pounds of liquid sugar.

• Kellogg's reports that the average American child consumes 15 pounds of cereal in a year.

• A Cheerios box with a Lone Ranger Frontier Town premium on the box sold for 18¢ in 1948. The price today for this vintage box? $165 to $350 (cereal not included). A full set of the Frontier Town (four maps and 72 models) sells for $7,200 on the collectibles market.

• Potato chips: the new breakfast of champions? A bowlful of Wheaties contains twice as much sodium as a similar size serving of potato chips, according to researchers at *Consumer Reports* Magazine.

AMERICA'S BEST-SELLING CEREALS

1. Kellogg's Corn Flakes
2. Kellogg's Frosted Flakes
3 General Mills Cheerios
4. Kellogg's Raisin Bran
5. Kellogg's Rice Krispies

CR_ _ SW_ _ D
P_ ZZL_ S

What's an 8-letter word for the smallest library in the house? While you're pondering the answer, here's some crossword puzzle trivia.

The first crossword puzzle appeared on December 21, 1913, in the pages of the *New York World* newspaper. It was created by a reporter named Arthur Wynn.

Dick Simon, a struggling publisher, was visiting his aunt one afternoon in 1924. She wanted to give her daughter a book of crossword puzzles, but none existed. So Simon and his partner, Lincoln Schuster, published one themselves. It became a bestseller overnight—and made enough money to keep the fledgling Simon and Schuster company afloat.

Crosswords were so popular in the twenties that in 1925 the B & O Railroad put dictionaries on all its mainline trains for its many crossword-solving passengers.

During the Roaring '20s, crossword puzzles even influenced fashions: Clothes made with black and white checked fabric were the rage.

In December, 1925 Theodore Koerner, a 27-year-old employee of the New York Telephone Co., shot and wounded his wife after she refused to help him solve a crossword puzzle.

In 1926, a waiter living in Budapest, Hungary commited suicide. He left behind a note—in the form of a crossword puzzle—explaining why he killed himself. His motive: unknown. The police couldn't solve the puzzle.

Today crossword puzzles are the most popular hobby on Earth. The Bible is the most popular Crossword puzzle subject.

What's a 14-1etter word for a crossword maniac? CRUCI-VERBALIST.

More than 28 million Americans buy Christmas presents for their dogs every year.

1ST-CLASS COACH

It seems as though Vince Lombardi is quoted more often than other football coaches. Here's an example of what he had to say.

"To play this game, you must have that fire in you, and there is nothing that stokes that fire like hate."

"Pro football...is a violent, dangerous sport. To play it other than violently would be imbecile."

"Winning isn't everything. It's the only thing."

(On his "Winning is everything" quote): "I wish to hell I'd never said the damn thing...I meant the effort...I meant having a goal...I sure as hell don't mean for people to crush human values and morality."

"I think the rights of the individual have been put above everything else...The individual has to have every respect for authority regardless of what authority is."

"The harder you work, the harder it is to surrender."

"Run to daylight."

"A real executive goes around with a worried look on his assistants."

"No one is ever hurt. Hurt is in the mind."

"If you aren't fired with enthusiasm, you'll be fired with enthusiasm."

"If you can't accept losing, you can't win."

"The greatest accomplishment is not in never falling, but in rising again after you fall."

"A school without football is in danger of deteriorating into a medieval study hall."

"There are three important things in life: family, religion, and the Green Bay Packers."

"Football isn't a contact sport. It's a collision sport. Dancing is a contact sport."

"Football is a game of clichés, and I believe in every one of them."

Sea lions can swim at speeds of up to 25 miles per hour.

THE PONY EXPRESS

Remember those dramatic scenes in TV westerns where everyone's waiting for the Pony Express to arrive with the mail? It turns out that didn't happen very often...or for very long.

THE MYTH

The Pony Express was one of the most important links connecting the gold rush towns of the West and large cities in the East. For years, it was the fastest way to send a letter to California; without it the western states might never have developed.

THE TRUTH

In its short lifetime (18 months—1860-61), the Pony Express *was* the fastest way to send a letter to California. Riders could deliver a letter in 10 days—half the time to send it by sea. But it had its problems:

• Hardly anyone could afford to use it. A single letter initially cost $5.00 to mail, and never dropped below a dollar. The largest customers were newspapers that depended on late-breaking news to keep readers up to date.

• The shipping firm of Russell, Majors & Waddell—founders of the Pony Express—knew their enterprise could never make money with normal business; they counted on winning a contract with the federal government to help cover its enormous costs ($70,000 up front and $4,000 per month). They never got one. The government was more interested in Samuel Morse's telegraph.

• By 1861 the nation's first transcontinental telegraph line was completed—making the Pony Express obsolete overnight. It folded less than two years after its introduction, over $500,000 in debt.

EXPRESS FACTS

• There wasn't a single pony in the Pony Express. Ponies didn't have the stamina to carry large loads of mail over long distances.

• Few of the riders were adults. Most were teenagers, hired through newspaper advertisements that read: "Wanted: Young skinny wiry fellows, not over 18. Must be expert riders willing to risk death daily. Orphans preferred."

What state has the highest percentage of literate citizens? Iowa.

DON'T CAN IT

Here are some recycling tips from The Recycler's Handbook, *by the EarthWorks Group.*

For the recycling novice—in other words, almost all of us—aluminum cans are as close to perfect as you can get: No matter how many of them you have, they're still light enough to carry; you don't need any fancy storage containers—you can even pile them into a paper bag. And you don't have to hunt very far to find someplace to take them—cans are worth so much that there's always someone around who collects them.

The secret is that it's a lot cheaper to recycle aluminum cans than it is to make them out of new metal. So years ago, the aluminum industry set up collection services, and they've been paying top dollar to get cans back ever since.

So if you're wondering where to start recycling, put aluminum cans at the top of your list.

ALUMINATING FACTS

• Aluminum was worth more than gold when it was discovered. It was first used to make a rattle for Napoleon's son.

• In 1989, Americans used 80 billion aluminum cans. That's the equivalent of about 16 cans for every person on the planet.

• We recycled a record 60% of them that same year.

• Making cans from recycled aluminum cuts related air pollution (for example, sulfur dioxides, which create acid rain) by 95%.

• Recycling aluminum saves 95% of the energy used to make the material from scratch. That means you can make *20* cans out of recycled material with the same energy it takes to make *one* can out of new material.

• Americans throw away enough aluminum every three months to rebuild our entire commercial air fleet.

WHAT YOU CAN DO

1. Find a Place to Take Them

• Virtually all recycling programs accept aluminum cans.

Call recycling centers in your area for more details.

• If you're having trouble finding a recycling center, try the toll-free Reynolds Aluminum hotline: (800) 228-2525. If there's a Reynolds recycling center in your area, they'll tell you where it is.

• Check phone listings under "Scrap Metal." Many scrap dealers aren't interested in small loads, but aluminum is valuable—so they may take it.

• Contact your state recycling office.

2. Recycle

Cans

• Crushing cans makes storing and transporting them easier. But before recycling, check with your recycler to find out if crushing them is okay. In some states with deposit laws, recyclers prefer to get the cans intact; they need to see the brand and the name of the factory the can came from.

• In most places, it's not necessary to rinse cans...but a large batch of unwashed cans may attract bees and ants.

Foiled Again

• Aluminum foil, pie plates, TV dinner trays, etc. are all reusable and recyclable. Lightly rinse them off first if they're dirty (you don't have to waste water—use dishwater).

• Some places request that you keep foil and cans separate. Check with your local recycling center.

Other Items

• Containers aren't the only source of aluminum scrap. Other common items include window frames, screen doors and lawn furniture. However, check with your recycling center before including these.

• Is your scrap aluminum? Check it with a magnet; aluminum isn't magnetic. Check small pieces like screws, rivets, etc.

• Remove everything that's not aluminum.

FOR MORE INFORMATION

"Aluminum Recycling: America's Environmental Success Story." The Aluminum Association, 900 19th St., N.W., Washington, D.C. 20006. (202) 862-5100.

UNCLES & ANT FARMS

*Ever had an ant farm? It's one of those toys people buy you when they're
trying to get something "educational" instead of something you can
actually play with. Even when you're a kid, you can't help but
wonder: Who could have come up with an idea like this?...
And where did they get the ants? Here's the answer.*

THE BEGINNING

It was Independence Day, 1956, when the idea struck. "It
just came to me in a flash," "Uncle" Milton Levine says. He
was a 32-year-old entrepreneur looking for new products to help
expand his line of mail order novelties. "I was at a Fourth of July
picnic at my sister's house in the Valley [California's San Fernando
Valley]. I saw a bunch of ants around the pool. I saw a bunch of
kids, and they were interested in the ants. And it came to me."

• Levine's first ant farms were six inches by nine inches, and sold
for $1.98. They consisted of a solid-colored plastic frame that sand-
wiched a layer of sand between two sheets of transparent plastic.
There was a plastic farm scene—barn, silo, farmhouse, and wind-
mill.

• To attract customers, Levine bought a 2-inch ad in the *Los An-
gles Times*, inviting the curious to "Watch the ants dig tunnels and
build bridges" in their own Ant Farm. "I got so many orders, you
wouldn't believe it," he says.

•Uncle Milton ran into an unexpected problem, though. The ants
in his first farms kept dying—the result of either glue fumes (Levine's former partner's theory) or the booze the assembler used to
drink (Levine's theory). Whatever the cause, the problem was
eventually solved.

DOWN ON THE FARM

• The Ant Farm is an enduring product; Over 12 million farms—
containing more than 360 million ants—have been sold so far.
Most customers are satisfied: the company receives about 12,000

Idi Amin was Uganda's heavyweight boxing champ from 1951-1960.

letters each year from happy Ant Farm owners. But not all the letters are positive: one child wrote in complaining that his ants weren't wearing top hats like it showed on the box.

• How do the ants survive weeks on toy store shelves? They don't—the farms are sold empty, with a certificate the owner sends to Uncle Milton Industries for a shipment of free ants.

• Every farm comes with *Uncle Milton's Ant Watchers' Manual*, which tells you how to care for your ants, and gives you information about your new livestock (Do ants talk? Yes. Do ants take baths? Yes).

• One improvement on the Ant Farms of yesteryear: Newer models have connectors for plastic tubes—so you can connect any number of ant farms together and watch the ants crawl back and forth.

THE ORIGINAL ANT FARMER

• Kenneth Gidney started digging ants in 1959 after answering an ad Uncle Milton had placed in the *Los Angeles Times*. One of his children, Robin Brenner, is still doing it today—she's one of only three diggers that supply the 15 million ants the company sends out each year.

• Not that it's an easy job, according to Brenner. You get bitten a lot. "Sometimes when I'm sitting up late at night, I think 'People don't know how hard this is. They don't know where these ants come from. They don't know how much sleep I'm missing.' "

• Every ant catcher has his or her own technique. Some take straws and blow into antholes, catching the ants as they run out. Brenner's father carefully sliced the tunnels and the kids gathered the ants into coffee cans. Brenner herself digs up the ant tunnels and then sucks up the ants using a car vacuum fixed to a Tupperware container.

• It takes about 10 hours to gather 50,000 ants, for which you can earn about $550. Afterward a half-dozen workers tediously fill little plastic vials with exactly 30 ants each, and these are mailed out to Ant Farm owners.

ANT FARM FACTS

• All the ants supplied for the Ant Farm are female. In the ant world, there aren't many males, and all they do is mate and die (an anty-climax, if you will). And since the company can't legally ship queen ants, Ant Farm colonies can't reproduce and will eventually dwindle to nothing.

• Out of thousands of varieties of ants, the harvester ant was chosen for the Ant Farm because it's big and is one of the few varieties that will dig in daylight.

• The leading cause of barnyard death is overfeeding. If you exceed the recommended ration of one birdseed or a single corn flake every two days, the food gets moldy, and your ants "buy the farm."

• The next leading dangers are too much sunlight (baked ants). Shaking the farm has been known to cause mass death by shock.

• At a funeral, the live ants always carry the dead ant to the northeastern corner of the farm. If the farm is rotated to a new direction, the pallbearers march into action again, digging up the dead ants and reburying them in the northeast. Why? Nobody knows.

• The technical name for an ant farm (or any ant habitat) is a formicarium.

• Why is Levine called "Uncle Milton"? "Everyone always said, 'You've got the ants, but where's the uncles?' So I became Uncle Milton."

• Ant farms aren't the only culturally significant product Uncle Milton Industries makes. Some others:

    —the plastic shrunken heads that hang from rear-view mirrors.

    —the Spud Gun, which fires potato pellets

    —the once-popular insecticides Fly Cake and Roach Cake

    —"100 Toy Soldiers for a Buck"

ANT FACTS

• In medieval times, it was thought that ants in the house were a sign of good luck and abundance.

• Chinese farmers use ants against pests. A large colony can capture several million insects a year.

AD NAUSEUM

*Here's a horrible thought: Every day the average American is
exposed to 3,000 ads. Today you get to read about them, too.*

In a 1985 Procter & Gamble poll, 93% of the people questioned recognized Mr. Clean, but only 56% of the same group could identify Vice President George Bush.

More American kids age 3-5 recognize Ronald McDonald than Santa Claus or any other entity, real or mythical.

The typical 30-second prime-time TV ad costs about the same to produce as the half-hour program it interrupts.

Advertisers spend about $400 a year on each newspaper subscriber and $300 a year on each television household.

The first advertisement to discuss body odor was a 1919 ad for the deodorant Odo-Ro-No.

The infamous "this is your brain on drugs" ad had an unintentional side effect: Small kids all over the country refused to eat fried eggs, believing they were somehow laced with drugs.

In early cuts of *Die Hard II*, Bruce Willis clearly used a Black & Decker drill in a key scene. When the scene was cut, Black & Decker—which paid for the scene and had planned an expensive promotion campaign around it—sued for damages.

The first recorded singing commercial was for Moxie, the most popular soft drink of the '20s; it was released on disc (on the Moxie label) in 1921.

Michael Jackson's hair-burning Pepsi ads in the mid-1980s boosted Pepsi drinking among 12-20 year olds, the elderly and Japanese. They actually hurt sales among 25-40 year-old blacks, who saw Jackson's plastic surgery and cosmetic touches as a repudiation of his roots.

If you're an average American, you'll spend a year and a half of your life watching TV commercials.

MORE MYTH CONCEPTIONS

Here are two more pages of "facts"
that everyone knows—but aren't true.

Myth: The song "Chopsticks" was named after the Chinese eating utensils with the same name.

Truth: The song was written by Euphemia Allen, a 16-year-old British girl in 1877. She advised pianists to play it with their hands turned sideways, using chopping motions.

Myth: Alan Shepard coined the phrase "A-OK" during his first spaceflight in May, 1961. Reason: "OK" by itself could not be heard over the static.

Truth: Even *we* thought he said it—we mentioned it in our *Third Bathroom Reader*. But he never did. Colonel "Shorty" Powers—NASA's public relations officer at the time—came up with the phrase himself and attributed it to Shepard, hoping it would catch on. It did—even though most astronauts hated it.

Myth: Chinese checkers were invented in China.

Truth: The game was invented in England in the 1800s. It was originally called *Halma*.

Myth: The Guinea pig originated on the island of Guinea.

Truth: It's actually from South America. And it's not a pig—it's a rodent.

Myth: Goats can eat anything—even tin cans.

Truth: Even if their jaws were strong enough to crunch metal, goats hate the taste of tin cans.

Myth: Switching from butter to margarine will help you lose weight.

Truth: Margerine may be lower in cholesterol than butter, but it has the same number of calories—so it won't help you lose weight.

Alaska is closer to the USSR than it is to the 48 contiguous United States.

Myth: The Romans used chariots in battle.

Truth: Chariots weren't effective on the battlefield—soldiers couldn't fight while holding onto the reins. The Romans used them only in sports and as transportation.

Myth: Dogs sweat through their tongues.

Truth: Dogs cool off by breathing rapidly; not by sticking their tongues out. Their tongues don't have sweat glands—and the only large sweat glands they have are in their feet.

Myth: Having so many ships in Pearl Harbor when the Japanese attacked in 1941 was one of the worst disasters of World War II.

Truth: It may actually have been *lucky*: the ships in port had better air cover, didn't sink as deep, and were much closer to repair facilities than if they had been out at sea.

Myth: If too many pores in your skin clog up, you can get sick—even die.

Truth: The pores in your skin don't breathe—and you don't need to keep them "open." It is possible to clog all the pores in your body for an extended period of time without suffering any ill effects.

Myth: You can tell the age of a rattlesnake by counting the number of rattles it has.

Truth: The number of rattles a snake has does increase with age, but not at a uniform rate. Snakes shed their skins more than once a year—and the interval varies with each individual snake.

Myth: In high winds, skyscrapers can sway as much as eight feet in any direction.

Truth: Even the most limber buildings won't move more than a few inches.

Myth: Cold-blooded animals have cold blood.

Truth: A "cold-blooded" animal's body temperature changes with the surrounding air temperature. Many cold-blooded animals have body temperatures that are higher than "warm-blooded" animals.

Given a second chance, 18% of Americans say they would not remarry their spouses.

THE GOSPEL ACCORDING TO BOB

You've heard his songs. Here are a few of his comments.

"Colleges are like old-age homes; except for the fact that more people die in colleges.

"Just because you like my stuff doesn't mean I owe you anything."

"Art is the perpetual motion of illusion."

"Rock and roll ended with Little Anthony & the Imperials."

"I'd like to see Thomas Jefferson, Benjamin Franklin and a few of those other guys come back. If they did I'd go out and vote. They knew what was happening."

"I'm just as good a singer as Caruso…I hit all those notes and I can hold my breath three times as long if I want to."

"It's always lonely where I am."

"They're just songs. Songs are transparent so you can see every bit through them."

"You can get sex anywhere. If you're looking for someone to *love* you, now that's different. I guess you have to stay in college for that."

"I sometimes dream of running the country and putting all my friends in office. That's the way it works now, anyway."

"I have no message for anyone, my songs are only me talking to myself.."

"On some of my earlier records, I sounded cross because I was poor. Lived on less than 10 cents a day in those times. Now I'm cross because I'm rich."

"Death don't come knocking at the door. It's there in the morning when you wake up. Did you ever clip your fingernails, cut your hair? Then you experience death."

"Money doesn't talk—It swears."

White House meals were cooked over a fireplace until 1850.

THE PIGMENT OF YOUR IMAGINATION

Do you remember your first box of Crayola Crayons?
Here's some info you probably never knew about them:

BACKGROUND

In 1885, Joseph W. Binney founded the Peekskill Chemical Company in Peekskill, NY and began producing lampblack, charcoal and red iron oxide barn paint. In 1900 his son and nephew, Edwin Binney and C. Harold Smith, took over, renamed the company "Binney and Smith," and added schoolroom slate pencils to their line of goods.

• In selling to schools, they learned that teachers were dissatisfied with the classroom chalk and crayons available at the time. The chalk was too crumbly and dusty, the European-made crayons too expensive and their colors too anemic.

• Binney and Smith went to work, developing first a "dustless" chalk and then a better-quality crayon. Further research went into finding non-toxic pigments when they discovered that many kids then, as now, thought the colors look good enough to eat.

WHAT'S YOUR NUMBER?

In 1903 the first boxes of Crayolas rolled off the line, priced at five cents and offering eight colors: red, blue, green, yellow, orange, brown, violet and black. The number of colors available has changed several times since then: By 1949, Crayolas were up to 48 colors; by 1958, 64; and in 1972 eight fluorescent colors were added. The company has stuck with 72 colors ever since. To introduce new ones they have to retire some, most recently in 1990.

RED SCARE

Crayons, although ageless, are not exempt from the changing world. Consider these examples:

• In 1958, with Cold War xenophobia in full bloom, the company

---

In 1991, there were 16 people on the FBI's ten most wanted list.

changed the name of "Prussian Blue" to "Midnight Blue."

• In 1962, heightened consciousness brought on by the civil rights movement led Binney and Smith to change the name of "Flesh" to "Peach," recognizing, as the company put it, "that not everyone's flesh is the same shade." On the other hand, the color "Indian Red" still exists.

• In 1990, with much ballyhoo, Binney and Smith discontinued eight of their less-popular colors (Blue Gray, Green Blue, Lemon Yellow, Maize, Orange Red, Orange Yellow, Raw Umber, and Violet Blue) in order to replace them with the brighter colors (Cerulean, Dandelion, Fuchsia, Jungle Green, Royal Purple, Teal Blue, Vivid Tangerine, and Wild Strawberry) that their marketing research indicated that kids wanted.

• The problem: parents. When the colors were introduced, a small knot of protesters picketed the Binney and Smith headquarters, carrying signs with slogans like "We Take Umber-age" and "Save Lemon Yellow." The company refused to back down. But it did make one concession; it promised to ensconce a five foot replica of each color in its "Crayon Hall of Fame," a new feature of its guided tours.

CRAYON FACTS

• The name *Crayola* comes from combining the French word "craie" meaning a stick of color with "ola" from the word "oleaginous," referring to the oily paraffin wax in the crayons. It was Binney's wife Alice (a schoolteacher, incidentally) who coined the term.

• Surveys have shown that the smell of crayons is one of the most recognized smells in America. Its source: stearic acid, also known as beef fat.

• Four out of five crayons sold in the U.S. are Crayolas. Each year Binney and Smith manufactures more than 2 billion of them. That's enough to produce a giant crayon 35 feet in diameter and 410 feet tall, towering 100 feet taller than the Statue of Liberty.

• 65% of all American children between the ages of 2 and 7 will pick up a crayon at least once today. American kids will spend 6.3 billion hours coloring this year—that's 27 minutes a coloring session, longer if the crayons are brand new.

James Smithson, founder of the Smithsonian Institution, never visited the U.S.

THE PHRASE IS FAMILIAR

Here are some well-known phrases and the stories behind them.

WHEN MY SHIP COMES IN

Meaning: When financial luck improves.

Background: Before steamships, cargo ships depended on wind, luck and weather. Investors who had a large financial stake in a ship's cargo often waited anxiously, hoping the ship would arrive before they ran out of money.

PULL OUT ALL THE STOPS

Meaning: To use every means at your disposal.

Background: Each pipe in an organ contains a "stop" which blocks the flow of air; pulling out specific stops allows sets of pipes to sound. An organist wanting the loudest sound possible "pulls out all the stops."

THE LION'S SHARE

Meaning: A greedily large portion.

Background: Taken from an Aesop's fable in which a lion goes hunting with a cow, a goat and a sheep. When the animals catch a deer, the lion divides it into four portions—then takes them all.

THE BOONDOCKS

Meaning: A very remote area.

Background: *Bundok* is the Philipino word for mountain. U.S. soldiers brought the term back from the Spanish-American War.

TO THE HILT

Meaning: All the way.

Background: A hilt is a handle of a sword or dagger. When you stab as far as you can, it's "to the hilt."

Researchers say that more than 90% of all Americans bite their fingernails.

IN CAHOOTS WITH

Meaning: To conspire with.

Background: Thieves in medieval Germany's Black Forest often shared cabins known as *kajuetes*. They were literally "in kajuetes" with each other.

NOT WORTH HIS SALT

Meaning: Overpaid.

Background: Before the invention of money, the Romans paid their soldiers in portions of salt, then a very valuable commodity. It was believed to have magical properties. They'd throw it over their shoulder for luck or sprinkle it on food they suspected might be spoiled or poisoned, which explains another salt phrase—"Take it with a grain of salt."

A DOG EAT DOG WORLD

Meaning: A brutishly hostile world.

Background: An old English saying goes: "dog does not eat dog"— another way of saying "birds of a feather stick together." In a "dog eat dog world" life is so brutal that even natural law is overturned.

EXAMINE WITH A FINE-TOOTH COMB

Meaning: Look at thoroughly.

Background: The phrase comes from the days before chemical treatment, when the only cure for head and body lice was using a special comb with spaces small enough to trap the tiny bugs. The same device comes up in the old song *Won't You Come Home, Bill Bailey?* in which the singer says she was abandoned with "nothing but a fine-tooth comb"—in other words, a case of the crabs.

PUT A SOCK IN IT

Meaning: Shut up!

Background: In early days, handwound Victrolas didn't come with a volume control, and in a small room they could be pretty loud. People discovered that you could lower the sound level by jamming a heavy woolen stocking into the phonograph's horn.

This year, 300,000 school-age children will be educated entirely at home.

PIRATE LEGENDS

*Captain Kidd, Blackbeard…their exploits are legendary.
But did you know they were real people, too?*

EUSTACE THE MONK

Background: No one knows for sure who inspired the legend of Robin Hood, but Eustace is a strong candidate. He was born in the late 1100s, and really was a priest at one time. He lived in a monastery near Nottingham…until his father was murdered. Then Eustace left religious life forever.

His Exploits: At first, he lived as a hermit in Sherwood Forest. But gradually he developed new interests—killing and looting. He built a reputation as a soldier of fortune, and even delved into piracy. His attacks on ships in the English Channel were so effective that King Philip II warned English ships: "if you fall into the hands of Eustace the Monk…do not put the blame on us." Eustace's career as a pirate spanned nearly twenty years. It ended on August 24, 1217, when King Henry III defeated him in the battle of Sandwich and had him beheaded.

Note: Eustace stole from the rich, but he probably never gave to the poor. That part of the legend didn't surface until the 1300s.

CAPTAIN KIDD

Background: William Kidd was born in Greenock, Scotland in 1645. He had an unusual background for a pirate; he was a respectable ship owner in New York, and the son of a Presbyterian minister. He never even wanted to be a pirate—he seized only two ships; and only because he had no other choice.

His Exploits: The English East India Company hired him in 1695 to work as a *privateer*—a "bounty hunter" who attacks pirate ships in exchange for a share of the recovered loot. But after more than a year at sea, he hadn't caught a single pirate; he had nothing to pay his men with. So in 1697 he let his crew plunder a single ship. But they insisted on raiding another. Kidd refused; he flew into a rage and hit one of his crew members over the head with a bucket. The

The elephant tree sprays a foul smelling spray at animals that try to eat its leaves.

man died the next day. Fearing mutiny, Kidd backed down and let his crew seize a second ship.

Soon after the second adventure, Kidd and his men finally found a real pirate ship to plunder—the *Resolution,* sailing in the Indian Ocean. Kidd gave the order to attack the ship, but his men refused—and most of them jumped ship to join the pirate crew. Exasperated, Kidd gave up and sailed home.

Though he had committed acts of piracy and murder, Kidd didn't expect to be arrested when he landed in New York. He was friends with the governor, and the East India Company stood to profit enormously from his plunder. Nevertheless, he was seized as soon as he pulled into port, and extradited to England for trial. He was found guilty and was hanged on May 23, 1701.

Note: Eleven days before he was scheduled to be executed, Kidd petitioned the House of Commons with a deal: in exchange for a delay in his execution, he would lead a fleet to the spot where he claimed to have buried his treasure. His offer was denied. Searches for Kidd's "lost treasure" have been conducted all over the Northeastern United States and other parts of the world, but nothing has been found. One possibility: it's buried on Oak Island.

BLACKBEARD

Background: Edward Teach was born in Bristol, England in the late 1600s. Like Captain Kidd, he got his start on a privateering ship. But unlike Kidd, he was good at it—so good that in 1713 his captain gave him command of one of the captured ships. That was a mistake—he turned to piracy almost immediately and began plundering English ships.

His Exploits: Though his pirate career spanned only five years, Teach came about as close as anyone to living up to pirate lore—even in appearance. According to one historian: "he wore a sling over his shoulders, with three brace of pistols hanging in holsters like bandoleers; he stuck lighted matches under his hat...and his eyes looked fierce and wild...Imagination cannot form an idea of a fury from Hell to look more frightful." He tied his enormous black beard into braids, which he threw back over both ears. He had at least 14 wives—each one in a different port.

Teach operated out of several bases off the coast of South Caroli-

The TV soap opera "General Hospital" has been on the air for 27 years

na, which he set up with the help of the state's corrupt governor. But in 1717 his numerous attacks on ships off the New England coast prodded Virginia's *un*corrupt governor into action. Using his own money, he hired Lieutenant Robert Maynard, a privateer, to hunt Teach down.

On November 21, 1718 Maynard found Teach's ship anchored off the coast of the Carolinas. He pulled within shooting distance and opened fire. Teach weighed anchor and tried to flee, but his ship ran aground. He fired back with his cannon, forcing Maynard to send his crew below decks. Seeing so few people on Maynard's ship, Teach assumed that he had killed most of the crew. But when his men tried to board the ship, Maynard's men reemerged from below decks and attacked. Within minutes they had overwhelmed the pirate crew.

While this was going on, Teach and Maynard fought man-to-man—first with pistols, then with cutlasses. Teach came very close to winning. He broke Maynard's blade off at the hilt and knocked him to the ground, but as he was moving in for the kill, one of Maynard's men rushed up and slashed Teach's throat. He kept on fighting, but collapsed and died a few minutes later. Maynard cut off his head and hung it from the ship's bow. The pirates who survived the fight didn't fare any better: all but two were tried for piracy, convicted, and hanged.

ROBINSON CRUSOE

Background: Alexander Selkirk—who inspired the tale of Robinson Crusoe—was born in Largo, Scotland, in 1676.

His Exploits: In his early teens he signed up with a privateering expedition, and remained a privateer until 1704. That year he had an argument with his captain—and as punishment, was dumped on an island in the South Seas. He lived there for more than five years, off the wild goats that roamed the island.

Selkirk was rescued in 1709 after a passing ship noticed his signal fire. He returned to Scotland, but never really recovered from his isolation. He remained a recluse, spending much of his time in a cave in his father's garden. He died in 1721. By that time his story had been immortalized in *Robinson Crusoe*, a novel Daniel Defoe had written two years earlier.

SECTS SCANDALS

Sex scandals involving famous preachers? Jimmy Swaggert and Jim Bakker were only following a pulpit tradition. As the Bible says, there is nothing new under the sun.

THE SINNER: **Horatio Alger.** Before becoming one of the most successful American writers of the 19th century, Alger was a preacher. In 1864, at the age of 32, he became pastor of the First Unitarian Parish in Brewster, Massachusetts.

THE SCANDAL: More than a few people noticed that he "was always with the boys"—at first this seemed liked commendable interest in their spiritual development, though parishioners began wondering why the eligible bachelor didn't pay attention to any the congregation's single women. An 1866 investigation concluded that he and several of his young charges had committed acts "too revolting to relate."

JUDGMENT DAY: Alger didn't deny the charges, but admitted only that he was "imprudent." He resigned and left town. Church officials warned other parishes of his dismissal (without getting specific), and some families threatened legal action. But Alger had promised to abandon his clerical career, and the matter was allowed to die quietly. Resettling in New York, he became a literary success, writing more than 100 books about poverty-stricken boys whose hard work and diligence earned them the attention of rich older men who helped them earn fortune and honor. The shocked parish concealed its findings for more than a century, until the 1970s, when its records were finally made public.

THE SINNER: Henry Ward Beecher. The famous Congregational preacher of the 1860s and 1870s (and brother of *Uncle Tom's Cabin* author Harriet Beecher Stowe) was a skilled orator—some called him "the greatest preacher since St. Paul." Pastor of Brooklyn's prestigious Plymouth Congregational Church, where 2,500 people came to hear him weekly, Stowe's eloquent advocacy of abolition, women's rights and Darwinism brought him both fame and an enormous salary of $40,000 a year.

THE SCANDAL: In 1874, his close friend and protege, Thomas Tilton, filed suit against Beecher, charging that he had been having an affair with Tilton's wife over several years. Noted feminist writer Victoria Woodhull (with whom Tilton was also suspected of having an affair) dared Beecher to admit his adultery. Beecher would not make a forthright admission of guilt, and the suit went to trial.

The trial itself became a sensation. Ticket scalpers charged $5 for admission passes they had gotten for free; up to 3,000 people were turned away every day; vendors made a killing selling refreshments and binoculars before and after trial sessions. Up against the testimony of 95 witnesses, Beecher declared he was "unable to remember" nearly 900 times.

JUDGMENT DAY: The trial ended in a hung jury, and Beecher, free and unabashed, expelled Tilton from Plymouth Church. He continued to enjoy great popularity and influence until his death in 1887.

THE SINNER: Aimee Semple McPherson. Pentecostal evangelist, "Queen of Heaven" and founder of the International Church of the Foursquare Gospel, McPherson seemed to have it all: youth, good looks, a large following, and part ownership in the Angelus Temple, the 5,000-seat, $1.5 million Los Angeles church where she preached to the accompaniment of choirs, bell ringers, and an 80-piece xylophone band.

THE SCANDAL: On May 18, 1926, the 36-year-old McPherson vanished while swimming in the Pacific Ocean. It was feared she was drowned. Her congregation took to walking into the sea where she was last seen, looking for clues and signs, resulting in the drowning death of one. A few days later, the first of several ransom notes arrived, and police received reports of sightings in Santa Barbara, Denver, El Paso, and Tucson. On June 23, Sister Aimee staggered across the U.S.-Mexican border into Douglas, Arizona with a tale of harrowing escape from kidnapers.

But details of her story failed to check out—for one thing, her arduous trek across the Mexican desert somehow left her shoes un-scuffed. Things got sticky for Sister Aimee. Reporters turned up accounts that McPherson and a married former employee had rented a cottage in Carmel-by-the-Sea, a few hundred miles north of Los Angeles, for ten days in May. Newspapers had a field day, calling it a "honeymoon cottage" and "love nest." A Temple worker told police the kidnaping tale was merely a cover-up for the Carmel tryst. In September, McPherson and others were arrested on charges including "conspiracy to commit acts injurious to public morals."

JUDGMENT DAY: During the trial the key prosecution witness—the Temple worker who had blown the cover story—was arrested on a bad-check charge, and it was revealed she had previously been committed to a mental hospital because of a tendency to create elaborate lies. The district attorney dropped the charges against McPherson without explanation. Sister Aimee, who fainted when she heard the news, left the next day for a "Vindication Tour" of the East Coast, but the bad publicity had its effect. She was finished as an influential evangelist. She died at the age of 53 from an accidental overdose of barbiturates.

• • •

FROM OUR "HEROES OF LITERATURE" DEPARTMENT

A few tales of Mark Twain:

• He got hundreds of photos from people who claimed they were "his exact double." After a while, he got so sick of answering them that he had a form letter printed up: "My dear Sir, I thank you very much for your letter and your photograph. In my opinion, you are more like me than any other of my numerous doubles. I may even say that you resemble me more closely than I do myself. I fact, I intend to use your picture to shave by. Yours thankfully, S. Clemens

• A ruthless businessman he knew announced that "Before I die, I'm going to make a pilgrimage to the Holy Land. I will climb Mount Sinai and read the Ten Commandments aloud at the top."

Twain's reply: "I have a better idea. Stay home in Boston and keep them."

PRODUCT NAMES

*You probably have some of these products in your house...
But do you know how they got their names?*

AVON PRODUCTS. Founder D.H. McConnell lived in a small New York town called Suffern on the Ramapo in the 1880s. The name reminded him of Shakespeare's Stratford-upon-Avon.

TONI HOME PERMANENTS. Richard Harris began selling "Roll-Wav" home permanent kits through the mail in 1943. For the first time, women could do at home for 25¢ what cost them $10 or more in a beauty salon. But he ran into a problem; the curling chemicals he used were too harsh. "Roll-Wav" flopped. Harris fixed the problem by using a milder curling agent, but something still wasn't right—customers weren't buying. Finally, one of his distributors gave him the advice he needed: "What you need is a *tony* name—one with class." Harris took the advice—literally.

NOXZEMA. After more than ten years of mixing up batches of skin cream in his coffeepot, Dr. Avery Bunting, a Maryland pharmacist, hit on a formula he felt was perfect in 1914. But he couldn't find the perfect name—after hundreds of tries he gave up. Then one of his customers walked into the store and said "Doc, you know your sunburn cream has sure knocked out my eczema." Bunding was inspired: The cream that "knocked eczema" became known as *Noxzema*.

SHELL OIL COMPANY. Believe it or not, the Shell Oil company got its name because it started out as a *shell shop*. Marcus Samuel owned a London novelty store in the mid-1800s; he began selling shells after getting the idea while on vacation by the sea. Over time his business grew into a large trading company and began selling things other than shells—including *kerosene*.

There are an estimated 1,000,000,000,000,000 ants on earth.

MURINE. Otis Hall, a banker recovering from a serious eye infection in the 1890s, was so impressed with the eye lotion his doctors made for him that he spent years trying to get them to sell it directly to the public. They finally consented—on the condition that its name be derived from its chemical formula: *mur*iate of berber*ine*.

DIXIE CUPS. Hugh Moore founded the American Water Supply Company in 1908...but decided that there was more money to be made in supplying paper cups. He changed the company's name to the Individual Drinking Cup Company, then to the Health Kup Co. But his business still wasn't successful. The company next door, The Dixie Doll Company, was doing well at the time. He thought some of their luck might rub off on him if he used their name.

PRINCE MATCHABELLI. Georges Matchabelli had it made— or so he thought. A prince with enormous land holdings in southern Russia, Matchabelli was vacationing in Europe when the Bolsheviks seized power in 1919. He lost his entire fortune overnight. But he still had his title—and when he opened an antique shop on New York's Madison Avenue, the well-to-do from all over the world flocked to his store. To maintain their interest, he began making perfumes for individual clients—perfumes he claimed matched their personalities. His customers began ignoring his antiques altogether, asking only about his perfumes. He took the hint.

PYREX GLASS. Dr. Jesse Littleton was a scientist who worked for the Corning Glass Works in New York. One morning in 1913, he brought a chocolate cake to work and shared it with the office. After his coworkers finished eating, he told them he had baked the cake in a *glass* pan he'd made out of a battery jar—something they had insisted was impossible. It wasn't. Though heat-resistant glass had been used in industry for more than 20 years, no one had thought of using it to make cooking utensils. Within three years, Corning introduced Pyrex glassware—naming it after the first product they manufactured: a glass *pie* pan.

RANDOM FACT: What do electric eels use their electricity for? To detect and kill their prey.

UNCLE JOHN'S BATHROOM NEWS

Bits and pieces of bathroom trivia we've flushed out in the past year.

T AKE A STAND
According to a 1991 survey by the Scott Paper Company:
• "You can gauge a person's education by whether they read in the bathroom. More than two-thirds of people with master's degrees and doctorates read in the stall, the survey shows. Only one in two high school grads read while in the bathroom, and 56 percent of those with college degrees do."

• "Fifty-four percent of Americans fold their toilet tissue neatly while 35 percent wad it into a ball before using it."

• "7% steal rolls of toilet paper."

• "More than 60 percent prefer that their toilet paper roll over the top, 29 percent from the bottom. The rest don't care."

LEFT OUT
• According to *Why Do Clocks Run Clockwise, and Other Imponderables*, here's why toilet flush handles are on the left side:

"Most early flush toilets were operated by a chain above the tank that had to be pulled down by hand. Almost all of the chains were located on the left side of the toilet, for the user had more leverage when pulling with the right hand while seated.

"When the smaller handles near the top of the tank were popularized in the 1940s and 1950s, many were fitted onto existing toilets then equipped with pull-chains. Therefore, it was cheaper and more convenient to place the new handles where they fitted standard plumbing and fixtures."

STRONGER THAN DIRT
According to a book called *Bigger Secrets*, by William Poundstone, here's a bit of bathroom science you should know about:

Nearly half of all psychatrists have been attacked by one of their patients.

- "The combination of Sani-Flush and Comet cleansers can explode. Comet (sodium hypochlorite and grit) is a common all-purpose abrasive, and Sani-Flush (a.k.a. sodium bisulfate) is designed to keep toilet bowls clean. Many think that the combination ought to work all the better.

"The Sani-Flush label warns consumers not to mix it with a chlorine-containing cleanser lest hazardous fumes be released. But few people know which other cleansers contain chlorine, and in any case the label says nothing about explosions. In 1985 Hilton Martin of Satellite Beach, Florida, cleaned the bowl of his toilet with Comet and then hung a Sani-Flush dispenser inside the tank. He noticed the water starting to bubble when the phone rang. While he was in another room on the phone, the toilet detonated. American Home Products has denied that Sani-Flush poses an explosion hazard."

LIFE-STALLS OF THE RICH AND FAMOUS

If you're *really* famous, you can't even go to the bathroom in peace. Example: In February, 1979, Jacqueline Kennedy was on her way to her nephew's wedding in Gladwyne, Pennsylvania. She pulled into an Arco gas station to answer the call of nature. The owner of the gas station commemorated the event by mounting a plaque in the ladies room: "This room was honored by the presence of Jacqueline Bovier Kennedy Onassis on the occasion of the wedding of Joseph P. Kennedy II and Sheila B. Rauch, February 3, 1989."

ALL TOGETHER NOW

During a showing of the movie *Airport* on television, the Lafayette, Louisiana Waterworks Department recorded changes in water pressure during the show. Their findings: "At approximately 8:30, a bomb exploded in the airplane, and from then until nine p.m., when the pilot landed safely and the movie ended, almost nobody left his television to do anything—then there was a twenty-six pound drop in water pressure." The department estimates that as many as 20,000 Lafayette residents used the john at the same time. Ratings for other films: *The Good, the Bad, and the Ugly*: a 19 lb. drop in pressure; *Patton*: 22 lbs.

The energy produced by chewing bubble gum every day could light a city the size of L.A.

HERE'S LOOKING AT YOU, KID

*Humphrey Bogart is one of the most popular movie stars of all time.
Here are some inside facts about two of his most popular films.*

THE MALTESE FALCON (1941)

The film that made Bogart a star was adapted from a 1929 novel by Dashiell Hammett (who also wrote *The Thin Man*). Warner Brothers bought the screen rights in 1930 and milked the story for all it was worth; they made three different versions of *Falcon* in 10 years.

Bogart's film, the third version, was regarded as a minor picture by Warner Brothers...so they let a screenwriter named John Huston make his directing debut with it.

• George Raft, a popular personality who played slick gangsters, was Warners' first choice for Sam Spade. He turned it down because he didn't like the idea of working for a first-time director. "I feel strongly that *The Maltese Falcon* is not an important picture," he explained.

• It was the fifth time in five years that Bogart (a minor star who specialized in tough gangster roles) was forced to take a part Raft didn't want. Earlier in 1941 Raft even refused to appear in a film if Bogart was cast in a supporting role. He once protested to Jack Warner: "You told me I would never have to play Humphrey Bogart part." After *Falcon*, he never had the chance again.

• Sydney Greenstreet, "the Fatman," had never acted in a movie before *Falcon*. He was an English stage actor who specialized in comedy. He earned an Oscar nomination for his movie debut... and was typecast as a film heavy.

• Mary Astor prepared for her scenes as conniving, unstable Brigid Wonderly, by hyperventilating almost to the point of dizziness. "It gives me the heady feeling of thinking at cross purposes," she said.

It takes at least 60 chinchillas to make a chinchilla coat.

• Real life imitates art: In 1975, one of the seven Falcons used in the movie was stolen from its exhibit in a Los Angeles art museum.

CASABLANCA (1943)

The Oscar winner for Best Film in 1943 started out as an unproduced play called *Everybody Comes to Rick's*. It was written by a New York City school teacher whose inspiration was a visit to a nightclub in southern France in 1938. The club's mix of refugees, Nazis, and French made it, he remarked to his wife, "a marvelous setting for a play."

The rights to the play were purchased by Warner Brothers the day after Pearl Harbor was attacked.

• Legend has it that George Raft was offered the leading role of Rick and, as usual, turned it down. Actually, Raft *wanted* the part...but by this time Bogart was a bigger star and got first choice.

• Ronald Reagan was one of the actors initially considered for Rick.

• *Casablanca's* famous theme, "As Time Goes By," was included in the original play because the author had been fond of it in college. It first appeared in a 1931 Broadway show called *Everybody's Welcome*.

• Believe it or not, that classic song was nearly cut out of the movie. After *Casablanca* had been shot, the composer who'd scored it decided to write his own tune, because theme songs are worth a lot of money in royalties. But that would have meant reshooting several scenes—and Ingrid Bergman had already cut her hair for her next role (in *For Whom the Bell Tolls*). So reshooting was impossible, the song was left in.

• Dooley Wilson (Sam) didn't really know how to play the piano. He just pretended to finger the keys as he sang, while a studio musician did the playing offstage.

• *Casablanca* won the Oscar for best screenplay, yet the actors never had the luxury of a complete script. In fact, Bogart and Bergman were sometimes handed their lines just before a scene was to be shot. Other times Bogart and the screenwriters would sit around with a bottle of whiskey and argue what should happen next. Ingrid Bergman didn't even know which of the story's main characters

---

Thomas Edison attended school for less than three months in his entire life.

she was supposed to love more. She found out when everyone else did—in the final scene.

• Humphrey Bogart's agents took out a $100,000 insurance policy on the actor (a huge amount in those days) during the filming. Bogart's wife was convinced that Bogie was having an affair with Ingrid Bergman and had threatened to kill him if she found them together. The agents decided they'd better not take any chances.

.• Good timing may have been what turned *Casablanca* into a hit. In November 1942, Allied forces launched a successful assault on occupied cities in North Africa, including Casablanca. Less than three weeks later the movie premiered in New York. It opened throughout the rest of the country in January of '43, just as Franklin Roosevelt, Josef Stalin, and Winston Churchill were holding a secret conference—in Casablanca.

• The Germans considered *Casablanca* a propaganda film, and banned it. Even after the war, only a censored version was allowed to be shown; all references to Nazis were cut out.

• After the success of *Casablanca*, Bogart signed a contract that made him the world's highest-paid actor.

AND NOW...Some Miscellaneous Movie Trivia

• Actress Jane Wyman broke up with husband Ronald Reagan because, she said, "He talked too much."

• Spencer Tracy and Humphrey Bogart never appeared in a film together because they could never agree on who'd get top billing.

• Actor Peter Lorre specialized in psychotic characters. But in his native Germany he was a student—not a patient—of Sigmund Freud and Alfred Adler.

• Garbo actually said, "I want to be *let* alone."

• Bogart got his distinctive lisp as the result of a childhood accident. A tiny piece of wood lodged in his lip, and the operation to remove it was botched. It left him with a partially paralyzed lip and a permanent speech impediment.

• *Casablanca* was turned into an ABC TV show in 1955. It flopped, and was cancelled after only a few months.

THE 7 WONDERS OF THE ANCIENT WORLD

Here's some more useless info you can use to drive your friends and family crazy, contributed by BRI member Phil Catalfo.

THE ORIGIN OF THE "7 WONDERS"

Today we think nothing of 100-story skyscrapers. But in the earliest days of civilization, huge structures were considered superhuman feats. The most impressive of these came to be known as "The Seven Wonders of the World."

• How they got that name is a pretty interesting story in itself. (After all, there were no intercontinental broadcasts to tell people about them.). It turns out that in the timewhen Greece and Rome dominated the course of history in Europe, North Africa and the Middle East, private fleets made money ferrying passengers to "exotic" lands. To tout these destinations, the world's first tourist guidebooks were created.

• Among their most popular attractions were...The Seven Wonders of the World. The earliest list of them on record was compiled by Antipater of Sidonin in the Second Century B.C.

THE EGYPTIAN PYRAMIDS AT GIZA

Built: Between 2600 and 2500 B.C.

History: Three enormous pyramids were erected as burial tombs for Egyptian pharaohs thousands of years before the golden ages of Greece and Rome. The largest, called the Great Pyramid, stands some 450 feet high at its peak; its base takes up 13 acres. The Greeks and Romans were impressed by their size, but, unaware of their religious significance, considered them extravagant.

Fate: Still standing. And they still attract millions visitors from around the globe every year.

THE HANGING GARDENS OF BABYLON

Built: Sometime in the late Seventh or early Sixth Century B.C.

History: King Nebuchadnezzar II, who ruled Babylon (near the modern city of Baghdad) between 605 and 562 B.C., built the hanging gardens for his queen, the daughter of the Median king Cyaxares. She was supposedly uncomfortable on the hot Mesopotamian flatlands, and longed for the cool, lofty heights of her mountainous homeland. So Nebuchadnezzar had the enormous garden structure designed and built with elevated terraces containing groves of trees, lush vegetation, fountains and exotic birds. According to contemporary accounts, the gardens were laid out on a brick terrace about 400 feet square and 75 feet above the ground; irrigation was provided by slaves turning screws to lift water from the nearby Euphrates River. The stone used in the construction is not found anywhere on the Mesopotamian plane; historians believe it was ferried down the Tigris River from a far-off mountain quarry.

Fate: Destroyed. Archaeologists have been unable to discover and positively identify the remains of the gardens.

THE TEMPLE OF ARTEMIS (DIANA) AT EPHESUS

Built: Circa 550 B.C.

History: One of the grandest and most architecturally advanced of ancient temples, the temple of Artemis (whom the Romans called Diana) was located in the Greek city of Ephesus, across the Aegean from modern Greece, on the west coast of what is now Turkey. According to Pliny, it took 120 years to build. It was made entirely of marble, except for its tile-covered wooden roof. It rested on a foundation measuring 377 by 180 feet, and featured 106 columns—each represented by a different king—about 40 feet high.

The Ephesians (the same ones St. Paul preached to) used an especially clever technique for lifting the giant marble stones: They built an inclined plane of sandbags up to the apex of the columns, and dragged the stones up the plane to be laid atop the columns. Then they slit the bags so the sand would empty out, leaving the marble slabs resting in place.

Fate: The original temple was destroyed by an arsonist (who said he did it to achieve immortality for his name) in 356 B.C. A replacement of similar design was erected on the same foundation. The replacement was burned by the Goths in 262 A.D. Today only the foundation and parts of the second temple remain. Sculptures from the second temple can be found in the British Museum.

THE STATUE OF ZEUS, OLYMPIA, GREECE

Built: Circa 435 B.C.

History: Built by the Greek sculptor Phidias, this depiction of the Greek king of the gods may have been the ancient world's most famous statue. It stood 40 feet high and depicted Zeus—symbol of power, thrower of thunderbolts—on his throne. His robe and ornaments were made of gold, his body of ivory. He wore a wreath on his head and held a figure of his messenger Nike in his right hand, and a scepter in his left.

Fate: Destroyed (No one is sure how or when).

THE MAUSOLEUM AT HALICARNASSUS, IN ASIA MINOR (Southwestern Turkey)

Built: About 353 B.C.

History: Originally built as a burial tomb for Mausolus, a local ruler in part of the Persian Empire, this huge, white marble edifice stood about 135 feet high, and measured 440 feet around its rectangular base. Above the base was a colonnade formed by 36 columns, and, above them, a stepped pyramid, which, historians believe, held a statue of Mausolus in a chariot.

Fate: The top part was destroyed by an earthquake. Only pieces of the building, and its decorations (called friezes) remain; the British Museum holdings include some sculptures from the site. King Mausolus has been immortalized in the word used to name any large tomb.

THE COLOSSUS OF RHODES

Built: Early Third Century B.C.

History: According to historians of the time, this huge bronze statue stood astride the harbor at Rhodes, an island in the Aegean. It took the Greek sculptor Chares twelve years to build. Created in honor of the sun god Helios, it stood 120 feet high—roughly the height of the Statue of Liberty—and was made of hollow stone blocks held together by iron bars, a construction technique still used today.

Fate: Destroyed by an earthquake in 224 B.C. The iron bars were sold for scrap some 800 years later, in 653 A.D.

THE PHAROS LIGHTHOUSE AT ALEXANDRIA

Built: Sometime during the reign of Ptolemy II (283-246 B.C.)

History: Designed by the Greek architect Sostratos, the 400-feet-high lighthouse stood on the island of Pharos in Alexandria's harbor. It achieved such renown that the word *pharos* came to mean "lighthouse." The structure's design was particularly striking: the bottom section, resting on a stone platform, was square; the middle section was eight-sided; and the top section was circular. A fire at the apex provided light.

Fate: After helping mariners enter the harbor for *1,500 years*, the lighthouse collapsed in an earthquake.

SO WHAT ELSE IS NEW?

Johnny B. Goode, by Chuck Berry

Berry says: "It sounds like it's autobiographical, but it's not. I never lived in Louisiana.... I just improvised the story, typical of what I thought a young, enthusiastic guitar-player from the South would go through. As for the log cabin, I don't think I've actually seen a real log cabin, much less lived in one."

Etch A Sketch

It was invented in France by Arthur Granjean, who called it "L'Ecran Magique" (The Magic Screen). Representatives of the Ohio Art Company saw it at the Nuremberg Toy Fair in 1959 and decided the toy had possibilities. They purchased the rights to it.

• Ohio Art management decided to introduce their version of it at the New York Toy Fair in February, 1960. They had no idea the toy would become a big success, but they got an inkling on the plane flight to the New York show when company officials started bickering about who would get to play with the prototypes next.

• The toy was officially released to the public on July 12, 1960. More than 60 million of them have been sold to date.

CARNIVAL LINGO

Next time you wander through a carnival, listen to the hucksters chatting with each other. Here are a few things you might hear them saying, from the marvelous book, Carnival Secrets, *by Matthew Gryczan.*

Carny: Carnival employee.

Jointee: A carny who works in one of the booths.

Ride Monkey: A carny who operates a ride.

Kootch: Strippers.

Alibi agent: A game operator who uses undisclosed "rules" (player touched the rail, leaned over the foul line, etc.) to avoid giving out prizes to winners.

Fixer: The person who handles complaints about rigged games and payoffs to local police.

Marks, Tips: Players

Chumps: Naive players.

Sharpies: Practiced players who are skilled at winning games.

Lot lice: Carnival-goers who don't spend money.

Patch Money, Ice, Juice: Money that's used to pay off the police.

Hey Rube: A call for help when carnies are in trouble.

Mitt camp: Palm readers.

Circus candy: Cheap candy in an impressive box.

Floss: Cotton Candy.

Plaster, Slum: Cheap prizes.

Donniker: A toilet.

Flat stores: Games set up solely to cheat players as soon as possible.

Gaff: Rig a game so that players have absolutely no chance of winning.

Gig: Take all of a player's money in one try.

Two Way Joint: A game that quickly converts from a dishonest to an honest one in case the police come by.

Ikey Heyman, G-wheel: A wheel of fortune with brakes—so the operator can control which number it lands on.

Burn the lot: Cheat contestants outrageously because you don't expect to return to the same location again.

Build up: Excite a player into spending more money.

If you floss your teeth, you'll probably use about 5 miles worth of floss in your lifetime.

POP CULTURE

*These pages on the history of soda are brought to you
by the BRI's Snack Food Division.*

P**OPPING OFF**
In the early 1800s, the closest thing to soft drinks on the
market was "impregnated water," a corked bottle of carbo-
nated water that was sold as a "health tonic." By 1860 makers were
adding sugar and flavoring—with mixed success: The corks in the
bottles (metal caps hadn't been invented yet) often blew off under
the extra pressure created by sugar fermenting in the bottles. This
made a popping sound—and the drinks became known as "Soda
Pop."

A CURE FOR WHAT ALES YOU

Selling soda pop to an unitiated public wasn't easy...so most manufacturers tried to boost sales by promoting their concoctions as
cures for fever, nausea, dehydration, indigestion, and so on. If the
government hadn't passed the Pure Food and Drug Act in 1906,
they'd probably be making similar claims today.

Some examples:

Dr. Pepper: "Brightens the mind and clears the brain"; an "anti-
dote" to cigarette smoking; and "alone on the bridge defending
your children against an army of caffeine doped beverages." (Note:
Today's version contains caffeine).

Hires Root beer: "Soothing to the nerves, vitalizing to the blood,
refreshing to the brain...helps even a cynic see the brighter side of
life."

Moxie "Nerve Food": "Can recover brain and nervous exhaustion;
loss of manhood, imbecility and helplessness. It has recovered par-
alysis, softening of the brain...and insanity."

Seven Up: "Tunes tiny tummies," "For Home and Hospital Use,"
"Cures Seven Hangovers."

HIRES ROOT BEER: Recipes for drinks made from boiled roots date back to the colonial days. But most people didn't want to bother collecting their own roots, so in 1870 Charles F. Hires, a Pennsylvania pharmacist, began selling premixed ingredients through the mail. He originally called his drink "Root Tea," but changed its name to "Root *Beer*" after a friend suggested it would sell better with a stronger name.

Hires' mix sold well, but he realized that bottled soft drinks were the wave of the future. So in 1882 he began bottling his creation— and by 1885 was selling 3 million bottles a year.

The Sober Truth: The company ran into trouble in 1895, when the Woman's Christian Temperance Union called for a nationwide boycott of Hires. Reason: the WCTU assumed that, like regular beer, root beer contained enough alcohol to get people drunk. The boycott remained in effect (and devastated sales) until 1898, when an independent laboratory decided to finally *test* Hires' root beer and see how much alcohol it actually contained. Its finding: a bottle of Hires had as much alcohol as half a loaf of bread. The WCTU backed off, and sales returned to normal.

DR. PEPPER: In the 1880s, a Virginia pharmacist's assistant named Wade Morrison fell in love with his boss's daughter. The pharmacist "decided the assistant was too old for his daughter" and encouraged Morrison to move on. He did, moving to Waco, Texas, where he bought his own drug store. When one of his employees developed a new soft drink syrup, Morrison named it after the man who got him started in the pharmacy business—his old flame's father, Dr. Kenneth Pepper.

THE MOXIE GENERATION: You've probably heard the expression "He has plenty of moxie." But have you heard of the soft drink that inspired it? It was the most popular soda in the U.S. during the '20s—even outselling Coca-Cola.

• What went wrong? The problem wasn't that it started out as a "medicine;" so did Coke. The problem was that it *tasted* like one. It contained gentian root, which has a very bitter aftertaste. Americans wanted a sweeter drink.

ON JINGLES

• "Things go better with Coke" was the first slogan that appeared on everything Coke did. They worked on it for two and a half years, and spent millions of dollars figuring out how to present it to the public. The first "things go better" jingle was sung by the Kingston Trio. This jingle was also the first in which Coke experimented with rock music. They used the Shirelles for it.

• The "You've got a lot to live . . ." campaign of the mid-1960s was a smashing success for Pepsi.

   Pepsi received over ten thousand letters congratulating them. Some people even said they were on the verge of suicide until they heard the ad. The lyrics were written by the songwriter who composed "You Light Up My Life."

SODA FACTS

• During World War II caffeine was so scarce that Coca-Cola chemists experimented with a substitute made from bat guano. Executives dumped the idea. They thought that if the public identified their drink with bat "droppings," it would doom the company.

• In 1900, Americans were drinking an average of twelve bottles and glasses of soft drink a piece. Today, it's 556 cans each.

• According to the *University of California Wellness Letter*, "If you drink only sugared soft drinks, those 566 cans (at an average of 150 calories each) would add up to about 83,400 empty calories per year."

• Only about five percent of all soft drink caffeine is taken from cola nuts. The other 95% is added during the manufacturing. Where does it come from? Usually the leftovers processed out of decaffeinated coffee.

• Which soda has the most caffeine per serving? Jolt Cola is #1, with 72 milligrams, followed by Mountain Dew (54), Coke (46), Dr. Pepper (40) and Pepsi (38). A cup of coffee contains 50-200 milligrams.

•Research suggests that as many as 950,000 Americans drink Coca-Cola for breakfast.

Listen closely: On at least one episode, George Burns was the voice of Mr. Ed (the horse).

INSTANT HITS

It usually takes work to write a hit song. But now and then a performer creates one spontaneously. Here are a few of the better-known examples.

THE SONG: "Sweet Dreams" by the Eurythmics (1983)

THE SITUATION: Annie Lenox and Dave Stewart, the Eurythmics, had never had a hit. One day they were quarreling so bitterly that it felt like the end of their partnership. Annie was lying on the floor of their studio, curled up in the fetal position. Dave was at the opposite end of the huge room, angrily playing with the recording equipment.

INSTANT HIT: As they glared at each other, Stewart fiddled around with his drum machine for a while. He came up with a catchy rhythm...then added a bass line. "It sounded so good," Annie recalls, "that I couldn't resist getting up and playing the synthesizer." Off the top of her head, Lenox began singing: "Sweet dreams are made of this." In thirty minutes the entire song was finished.

They recorded it on their eight-track as a demo tape, but when Stewart took it in to a record company, incredulous record execs told him it was "already perfect." So the "demo" was released; it sold millions of records and established them as major pop celebrities of the early '80s.

THE SONG: "What'd I Say," by Ray Charles (1959)

THE SITUATION: It was almost 1:00 AM. Ray Charles and his band were playing at a Midwestern night club; they were almost through for the night, but still had about fifteen minutes to go when they played the last song in their repertoire. So Ray just started "noodling."

INSTANT HIT: "I couldn't think of nothin' else to play," Ray says. " So I told the guys...'Look, I'm just gonna start this rhythm pattern and just follow me." He also told his back-up singers to repeat whatever he said (which is where the title "What'd I Say" came from). Charles made up the words as he went along. "People went crazy," he recalls, "and so the next night we did the same thing and got the same reaction, in a different town. Somebody came up to me and asked me, 'Listen, where can I buy this record?'

The all-aluminum can was introduced in 1964.

I said, 'Record? What record?' He said, 'But that's a great [song]!' So Charles called up his record producers and said, "Listen, I got a song and I want to record it." He went into the studio on Feb., 18, 1959 and recorded a long version ("because it was for dancing, see?") that was split into Part I and Part II. It became his first record to reach the Top 10 on the pop charts.

THE SONG: "Satisfaction," by The Rolling Stones (1965)

THE SITUATION: During their tour of North America in 1965, the Rolling Stones spent a night in a Clearwater, Florida, motel.

INSTANT HIT: In the middle of the night, Keith Richard woke up with some music running through his head. He got out of bed, recorded it on his tape recorder, and went back to sleep. "In the morning," Richard says, "I still thought it sounded pretty good. I played it to Mick and said the words that go with this are, 'I can't get no satisfaction.' That was just a working title. It could have been, 'Aunt Millie's Caught Her Left Tit in the Mangle,' I thought of it as just a little riff, an album filler. I never thought it was commercial enough to be a single." Jagger wrote lyrics as he sat by the motel swimming pool. But Richard didn't like them; he said the song "sounded too much like a folk song." The song was actually recorded over Keith Richard's objections; he thought it was too corny. It became the band's unofficial anthem, and the #1 song of 1965.

THE SONG: "When a Man Loves a Woman," by Percy Sledge (1966)

THE SITUATION: Percy Sledge worked as an orderly at Colbert County Hospital in Alabama during the day, and sang with a band called The Esquires Combo at night.

INSTANT HIT: One evening the Esquires Combo was playing at a club in Sheffield, Alabama, and Percy just couldn't keep his mind on the songs he was supposed to sing. He was upset about a woman. Overcome by emotion, he turned to bass player Cameron Lewis and organ player Andrew Wright, and begged them to play something he could sing to—anything—it didn't matter what. The musicians looked at each other, shrugged, and just started playing. Percy made up "When a Man Loves a Woman," one of the prettiest soul ballads ever written, on the spot.

The sperm whale can hold its breath for 82 minutes.

W.C. FIELDS FOREVER

Little-known facts about one of America's classic comedians.

Fields didn't get his legendary bulbous nose from drinking; he got it as a kid in street fights with neighborhood toughs.

His raspy voice, another trademark, was the result of a long series of colds brought on by exposure; a circus hand, he slept outdoors year-round from age 11 till age 15.

According to Groucho Marx, Fields had about $50,000 worth of booze stored in his attic. Groucho: "Don't you know that Prohibition is over?" Fields: "Well, it may come back!"

Fields' misanthropy was legendary. He liked to hide in the bushes of his San Fernando Valley home and shoot spitballs at passing tourists.

He left his mistress, Carlotta Monti, $25,000—to be paid out in 1,000 weekly installments of $25 each.

On his deathbed, Fields supposedly said: "I've been thinking about those poor little newsboys out there peddling their papers in cold and rain, working to support their mothers. I want to do something for them." But after a few minutes he sat up in bed and said "On second thought, f--- 'em."

Fields had a lifelong fear of returning to the crushing poverty of his youth. He opened hundreds of bank accounts as he traveled, under scores of aliases. Most of the money is still unclaimed.

In his 31-year acting career, Fields appeared in 42 films, many of which he wrote and directed as well. Of these, almost a third have vanished or are otherwise not available for viewing.

The title "Mr." originally applied only to ministers, schoolmasters, and property owners.

THE NUMBERS GAME

You're in the supermarket checkout line and have a few dollars to spare. Should you buy some lottery tickets, or a copy of the National Enquirer? Here's some info to help you decide.

THE EARLY DAYS

Lotteries in the U.S. may seem like a recent fad, but they date back at least as far as the 1700s. The original 13 colonies were financed with the help of lottery dollars, and the U.S. government used them to help pay for the Revolutionary and Civil Wars. Even the Ivy League universities—Harvard, Yale and Princeton—used them to get started.

State lotteries didn't begin until the 1960s. The first, a $100,000 sweepstakes tied to a horse race, was held in New Hampshire in 1964. Today at least 30 states have lotteries, which generate $17 billion a year in revenues.

LOTTERY FACTS

• According to *Consumer's Research* magazine, lotteries have the worst odds of any form of legalized gambling. In terms of average payouts, highest percentage is craps (98%), followed by roulette (95%), slots (75-95%), jai alai (85-87%), the race track (83-87%) and, last, the lottery (49%). Only 0.000008% of the 97 million people who play the lottery annually win a million dollars.

• Lotteries with the best odds: Delaware, Maryland, Michigan, Pennsylvania and Washington, DC. The odds of winning their jackpots are 1 in 1000. Worst odds: California and Florida. Their odds are 1 in 14 million.

WINNERS AND LOSERS

• In 1983, Joseph R. Wyatt, 29, of Union, New Jersey ripped up his lottery ticket—which read "Void if torn or altered" on the back—before realizing it was worth $1,600,000. In tears, he taped his ticket back together and presented it to New Jersey lottery officials, begging them to overlook the rule. They did—he got his money.

An estimated 79% of all Americans have bought lottery tickets.

• In 1983, Don Temple accidentally threw away a lottery ticket worth $10,000 in a trash can outside a Seattle convenience store. When he realized his mistake, he talked the store into dumping that week's garbage onto the driveway of his father-in-law's home. Temple sifted through the trash for four days, but never found his ticket. The booby prize: he had to pay haulers $200 to take the garbage away.

• In 1985, Donna Lee Sobb won $100 in the California lottery, which qualified her for a $2,000,000 jackpot. But when her photograph appeared in a local paper, a local law officer recognized her—and arrested her on an eight-month-old shoplifting warrant.

• In 1986, California lottery winner Terry Garrett of San Diego was arrested only months after winning $1,000,000—for selling cocaine out of the sports car he had bought with his winnings.

• In 1988, Henry Rich, a computer expert from Harrisburg, Pennsylvania, used a computer at work to forge a winning ticket for a $15,200,000 lottery prize that hadn't been claimed. He had a friend come forward with the fake ticket and explain that he had been using it as a bookmark without realizing that it was the winner. The scheme almost worked: the friend was actually issued a first installment check for $469,989. But lottery officials arrested Rich and his friend when they realized the real ticket had been issued in another part of the state.

• In 1984, Hai Vo, a Vietnamese refugee, spent more than $200 of spare change he had saved up from food stamp purchases to buy California lottery tickets. One ticket won $2,000,000. A week later a couple from Mill Valley, California sued Vo to recover $616.26—the amount they paid in state income taxes that year—claiming Vo had used some of their earnings (in the form of state-subsidized food stamps) to buy the ticket. They lost; Vo kept his winnings.

THE SAD TRUTH

How much is a $1 million prize *really* worth? The IRS deducts 20% automatically—and state and local taxes are also taken out, leaving about $560,000. The state pays the first $50,000 in cash, but pays out the rest over twenty years, saving another $100,000. Conclusion: the $1 million prize is worth about $468,000.

A *moment* used to be defined as lasting exactly 1 1/2 minutes.

DEFINITIONS

How's your vocabulary? Here's another batch of unusual words you can use to impress your friends and neighbors.

Deosculate: To kiss passionately.

Pap-hawk: A child who's breast fed.

Moirologist: A person hired to mourn at a funeral.

Philematophobe: A woman who hates to be kissed.

Hippocampine: Having to do with seahorses.

Sneckdraw: A sneaky or mean person.

Hircine: Something that smells like a goat.

Eruciform: Something that resembles a caterpillar.

Snoach: Talk through your nose.

Fripperer: A person who sells old clothes.

Clipster: A woman barber.

Girn: Bare your teeth in anger.

Snollygoster: A politician with no interest in issues or principles.

Butyric: Having to do with butter.

Cacogen: A hostile, unfriendly person.

Coprology: The study of pornographic art and writing.

Napiform: Shaped like a turnip.

Natiform: Shaped like a buttock.

Hippopotomonstrosesquipedalian: Having to do with a very long word.

Phaneromania: An obsession with picking at your skin.

Pussock: An old maid.

Smell-Feast: An uninvited guest at a feast.

Mastodont: Having teeth that look like a mastadon's.

Powsowdy: A broth made from sheep's heads.

Wallydrag: A completely useless person.

Onygophagist: A person who bites his or her nails.

Eirmonger: Someone who sells eggs.

Fagotist: A person who plays the bassoon.

There is only one diamond mine in the entire continent of North America. It's in Arkansas.

THE MYSTERY OF OAK ISLAND

The romance of searching for pirates' treasure has been celebrated in dozens of stories since Robert Louis Stevenson's Treasure Island. *But is there* _really_ *any buried treasure to be found? Maybe so...on Oak Island.*

TREASURE ISLAND

In 1795, a teenager named Daniel McGuinnis discovered an unusual, saucer-shaped depression on Oak Island, a tiny island off the coast of Nova Scotia. Next to the hole was an ancient oak tree with sawed-off limbs. And according to legend, a ship's tackle hung from the tree directly over the depression—as if it had been used to lower something very heavy into the hole.

McGuinnis was certain he had found buried pirates' treasure, and with the help of two friends began digging for it. Within minutes they hit rock—which turned out to be a flagstone buried two feet below the surface. They hit another barrier made of oak logs at 10 feet deep; another at 20 feet, and a third at 30 feet. McGuinnis and his friends kept digging—but they never found any treasure and eventually gave up. Still, word of their discovery spread.

SECOND TRY

In 1803 a wealthy man named Simeon Lynds took up the search. The diggers he hired found another platform at 40 feet, and found several more deeper down. Finally, at 90 feet, the workers found a large stone with strange symbols carved into it. No one could decipher what the stone said, but the workers were convinced they were close to the treasure and kept digging. (The stone was later stolen.) At 98 feet deep, their shovels struck what felt like a wooden chest. But the sun was going down so they stopped for the night.

By the time the workers got back the next morning, the hole had flooded to the top with seawater. And it somehow kept refilling, even as the workers tried to bail it out. They never were able to drain the pit enough to finish digging.

Like McGuinnis, Lynds had hit a dead end.

There are 44 million ways to make Bingo on a single bingo card.

AMAZING DISCOVERIES

Lynds wasn't the last person to dig for treasure on Oak Island. In fact, so many excavations have been attempted that the precise location of the original hole—known as the "Money Pit" because so much money has been spent trying to solve its mysteries—has been lost because so many other holes have been dug nearby. Even young Franklin D. Roosevelt supervised a dig in 1909; he followed Oak Island's progress even as president. And the search continues today. Some findings:

• There's at least *some* gold down there. In 1849 treasure hunters sank a drill to the 98 ft. level. Like Lynds, they hit what felt like a wooden chest. They dug through the top into what felt like "22 inches of metal in pieces (possibly gold coins)," through more wood, and into another 22 inches of metal. When they pulled the drill back up to the surface, three links of a gold chain were stuck to it. In nearly 200 years of digging, that's all the treasure that's been found.

• In 1897 another group of drillers dug down to 155 feet. They pulled up a half-inch-square piece of parchment—but that was all. They also hit what they thought was a heavy iron plate at 126 feet, but couldn't pull it up.

• In 1987, an IBM cryptologist finally deciphered an engraving of Lynds' lost stone. The message read: "Forty feet below, two million pounds are buried."

HIGH SECURITY

• Whoever dug the original pit went to a great deal of trouble to do it. In 1850 explorers resting on a nearby beach noticed that the beach "gulched forth water like a sponge being squeezed." So they dug it up—and discovered it was a *fake*. The beach was actually a manmade network of stone drains that filtered seawater and fed it into the Money Pit. The drains—designed to flood the pit whenever treasure hunters got close to the treasure—had been buried in sand to avoid detection.

• The Money Pit may even be protected by poison gas. On August 17, 1965, treasure hunter Bob Restall blacked out and fell into the pit he had dug. His son and four others tried to rescue him, but

---

In 1952, Albert Einstein was offered the presidency of Israel.

they also blacked out and fell in. Restall, his son, and two of the workers were killed. The autopsy finding: death by "marsh-gas poisoning and/or drowning."

TODAY

In 1977 the Montreal-based Triton Alliance Ltd., a consortium of 49 investors headed by David Tobias, bought the 128-acre Oak Island for $125,000. They have spent more than $3 million digging for treasure.

• During one drill, Triton's workers found bits of china, glass, wood, charcoal—even cement. But no treasure.

• Perhaps the strangest incident associated with Oak Island occurred in 1971 when Tobias' partner Dan Blankenship lowered an underwater video camera into a water-filled cavity at the bottom of a shaft. On the monitor, Blankenship suddenly saw what looked like a human hand. Horrified, he called over three crew members, who later verified his story. Asked by *Smithsonian* magazine about the legitimacy of his hand-sighting, he answered, "There's no question about it."

WHAT'S DOWN THERE?

Oak Island's "treasure," if there is one, could be worth over $100,000,000. Among the many theories of what the Money Pit could be hiding:

1) The missing crown jewels of France. The Nova Scotia area was frequented by pirates in the 16th and 17th centuries—when the jewels were stolen. The local Mahone Bay takes its name from the French word *mahonne*, a craft used by Mediterranean pirates.

2) Inca gold plundered by Spanish galleons and later pirated by Sir Francis Drake. A carbon analysis of wood samples recovered from the area dated back to 1575, around the time of Drake's explorations. However, there is no record of Drake ever having been to Nova Scotia.

3) Captain Kidd's buried treasure. Some believe Kidd buried his treasure there before being extradited and later hanged by the British. Before Kidd was executed in 1701, he offered a deal: "He would lead a fleet to the spot where he had hidden his East Indian

treasure, if the authorities would put off his execution. The deal was refused—and Kidd's treasure has never been found." There is, however, no evidence that Kidd was ever near Oak Island.

• Others have their doubts. Some feel that the Money Pit is merely an elaborate decoy, and that the treasure is actually buried in a nearby swamp. Others think it is just a sinkhole. Many doubt whether pirates had the resources and engineering know-how to construct such an elaborate trap.

POST SCRIPT

Similar Money Pits are rumored to have been found in Haiti and Madagascar, although these discoveries have not been confirmed by archaeologists.

• • •

...AND NOW A LITTLE MOOD READING

Here's a brief quote from Treasure Island, *by Robert Louis Stevenson. Appropriately, it's the part where they find the spot the treasure should be...and see that it's already been dug up.*

"We were now at the margin of the thicket.

" 'Huzza, mates, altogether?' shouted Merry; and the foremost broke into a run.

"And suddenly, not ten yards further, we beheld them stop. A low cry arose. Long John Silver doubled his pace, digging away with the foot of his crutch like one possessed; and next moment he and I had come also to a dead halt.

"Before us was a great excavation, not very recent, for the sides had fallen in and grass had sprouted on the bottom. In this were the shaft of a pick broken in two and the boards of several packing-cases strewn around. On one of these boards I saw, branded with a hot iron, the name *Walrus*—the name of Flint's ship.

"All was clear to probation. The *cache* had been found and rifled: the seven hundred thousand pounds were gone!"

If you're into classic books and buried treasure, Treasure Island *could be a good bathroom reader. The chapters are all about six pages long, and a new copy shouldn't cost more than $3.*

The White House didn't have running water until 1833.

ZZZ-Z-Z-Z-ZZZ

According to author Marc McCutcheon, your heart can stop beating for as long as 9 seconds while you're asleep. Here's some more information on sleep from his book, The Compass in Your Nose.

S leep deprivation lasting more than 48 hours typically causes hallucinations and psychosis.

The world record for going without sleep is 11 days (264 hours and 12 minutes), a feat considered extremely dangerous by sleep researchers.

30 million Americans suffer from sleep disorders. Most men begin having problems falling asleep in their mid-twenties; women have the same difficulty during their mid-forties.

While normal sleepers change body positions about 30 times per night, insomniacs may toss and turn more than 100 times.

Dream sleep has been observed in all animals studied except the spiny anteater.

Sleep studies show that if your sleeping partner is absent in your sleep, you'll almost always move over to the side of the bed normally occupied by him or her.

An aftenoon nap is healthy. One study indicates that afternoon nappers are 30 percent less likely to suffer coronary artery disease, although the reasons behind this are not yet known.

Humans stay awake far longer than many animals. Bats, cats, porcupines, lions, gorillas, and opossums sleep 18 to 20 hours a day, and some woodchucks snooze for as long as 22 hours.

Pigeons frequently open their eyes during sleep to watch for predators. The dolphin, remarkably, only "half" sleeps: its brain shuts down only one hemisphere at a time.

Horses and rats dream 20 percent or the time during sleep. Cows kept in barns dream 40 minutes per night, while cows sleeping in meadows dream only half as much.

OFF TO SEE
THE WIZARD

The Wizard of Oz is one of our most enduring modern fairy tales. In the first Bathroom Reader, we explained it as a political allegory. Here are some some other interesting facts about the book and film.

T HE BIRTH OF THE BOOK
According to some accounts, the land of Oz was created when Lyman Frank Baum, the author, was weaving a tale of fantastical creatures for some neighborhood kids. When one child asked where the imaginary people lived, Baum glanced around. His eyes fell on the labels on his file cabinet; the top was labeled A-N and the bottom, O-Z.

• He didn't write the story down for some time after. But suddenly it took over and demanded to be written: "I was sitting," he wrote later, "in the hall telling the kids a [different] story and suddenly this one moved right in and took possession. I shooed the children away and grabbed a piece of paper and began to write. It really seemed to write itself. Then I couldn't find any regular paper, so I took anything at all, even a bunch of old envelopes." His pencil-written longhand manuscript went right to the typesetter.

• He called his story *The Emerald City*. But his publisher wouldn't release it under that title, citing a long-standing publishers' superstition that any book with a jewel named in its title was doomed to failure.

• So he changed it to *From Kansas to Fairyland*, then *The Fairyland of Oz*, then *The Land of Oz*. They filed for a copyright under this last name, but Baum was still looking for something more colorful and eye-catching. Right before the book was supposed to go to press, illustrator W. W. Denslow pasted a new title over the old one: *The Wonderful Wizard of Oz*.

FILM FACTS
• Panned by many critics when it was first released in 1939, the

film version of the book was considered a flop. It didn't earn back its initial investment until 1959—twenty years later. Cult status only came as a result of annual TV showings, starting in 1956.

• The cast consisted of 9,200 actors and actresses, including dancing trees, flying monkeys, and 124 midgets as Munchkins. Ray Bolger and Jack Haley were paid $3000 a week; Judy Garland, only $500 a week.

• Dorothy's dog Toto was paid $125 a week, more than twice the wage of each of the 122 midgets hired to play munchkins. Although the little people of Oz were paid $100 a week, their benevolent manager, Leo Singer (Papa), pocketed half. Clearly the Lollipop Guild and Lullaby League were ineffective unions.

• *Oz* was nominated for five Academy Awards. But the competition was fierce and *Gone With the Wind* dominated the event, *Oz* did win for Original Score and Best Song—"Over the Rainbow," written in a car parked outside Schwab's drugstore.

• Ironically, "Rainbow" was the song studio execs wanted to cut out when the finished film was too long. "Why is she singing in a barnyard?" one of the producers had asked. But the director and others complained. Instead, MGM removed a scene (and song) in the Haunted Forest, where Dorothy and crew were attacked by Jitter Bugs (a kind of oversized pink and blue mosquito). The scene, which took five weeks and $80,000 to shoot, has never been found.

MEET LITTLE DOROTHY

• When the MGM movie was first planned, Shirley Temple was the unanimous choice to play Dorothy. (Likewise, Frank Morgan was the third choice for the Wizard. The lines were written with W.C. Fields in mind. Ed Wynn turned down the part, too.)

• But Shirley Temple wasn't available. While searching for another Dorothy, L.B. Mayer viewed a short called *Every Sunday* and was taken by its star, Deanna Durbin. He told his assistant: "Sign up that singer— the flat one." (He might have been referring to the pitch of Durbin's voice). What the assistant heard was, "Sign up the fat one." He thought Mayer was talking about a different girl in the short, who had a bit of baby fat...so he called Francis Gumm

---

The tornado in the "The Wizard of Oz" was a custom-built spinning 35 foot muslin "miniature."

(quickly renamed "Judy Garland"). But don't cry for Deanna Durbin—she went on to Universal where her movies brought in $100 million in the next 10 years.

• Judy Garland was 16, but she was playing an 11-year-old. So the studio put her on a diet to make her look younger; she was only allowed to eat four days a week. And every morning before filming, her breasts were taped flat so she'd look more like an adolescent.

• MGM's constant attempts at keeping Garland thin with pills and diets may have ultimately cost her life—Garland died in June, 1969 of a drug overdose.

INSULTS AND INJURIES
• While the Tin Man bemoaned his heartless condition, it was another vital organ that caused him the biggest problems during the filming of Oz. Buddy Ebsen, the original tin man, had an extreme allergic reaction when his lungs were coated by the aluminum powder dusted onto his tin makeup. Seriously ill, he spent several weeks in the hospital. He was replaced by Jack Haley.

• The Wicked Witch, Margaret Hamilton, was badly burned on face and hand while filming her dramatic exit from Munchkinland and was off the set for a month. The fire effect went off before she was safely below the trap door. Ironically, a little water thrown her way might have helped.

• She wasn't the only injury: Her double, Betty Danko, was injured when her broom exploded during a stunt shot. Two winged monkeys crashed to the stage floor when their support wires snapped. And Toto too? Yes, Toto too—out of action for a week after being stepped on by one of the witch's huge "O-EE-O"-chanting Winkie guards.

SHOE FETISH
Although 50 years have passed, at least four pairs of Dorothy's ruby slippers have survived and they bring out-of-sight auction prices (top price so far—$165,000). One pair is on exhibit at the Smithsonian, another at Walt Disney World-MGM Studios. The rest are in private hands...or feet. Over five million people visit the Smithsonian display annually.

In Omaha, Nebraska, it's illegal to burp or sneeze in church.

WORLD-CLASS LOSERS

Have you ever dreamed about having a "sure thing"? It's not always that simple. Here are four stories of people who "couldn't miss"...but did.

T he Losers: John Augustus Sutter & James Wilson Marshall
The Sure Thing: The largest gold strike in American history.

Background: In the 1840s, Sutter was one of Northern California's largest landowners. His headquarters was Sutter's Fort, a trading post near the Sacramento River—an important stopping-point for westward-bound immigrants. Sutter welcomed them all.

One settler, a carpenter named James Marshall, became friends with Sutter. In 1847 they started a sawmill together on the South Fork of the American River at Coloma. Sutter put up the money, Marshall ran the mill, and they split the profits.

Good Luck: In January 1848, Marshall had to deepen his mill stream to allow the wheel to turn freely. His digging turned up some bright metal that he realized, after consulting the *American Encyclopedia*, was gold.

It appeared that he and Sutter were rich beyond their wildest dreams.

Tough Luck: They kept the secret for a few months. Then word leaked out, and the Gold Rush was on.

First, all of Marshall's workers left to pan for gold. With no laborers, the mill failed.

Then thousands of gold-crazy '49ers flocked to Sutter's land. They slaughtered his livestock for food, trampled his fields and staked claims on his property. He was ruined. The land was legally his, but he couldn't afford the cost of litigation to recover it.

Marshall "became despondent and misanthropic." When he died some 35 years later, he was working as a gardener in Coloma. Sutter died broke in 1880, still petitioning Congress for compensation for his losses.

On average, Americans spend 40% of their leisure time watching TV.

The Loser: Eli Whitney

The Sure Thing: Control of the South's cotton industry.

Background: After the Revolutionary War, the outlook for agriculture in the South was pretty grim. The only thing farmers could grow easily was green-seed cotton—an unprofitable crop because it took an entire day for one person to separate a single pound of cotton from the seeds.

In 1793, a young inventor named Eli Whitney overheard several South Carolina planters discussing the possibility of a machine that could clean cotton easily. If someone could invent one, they said, it would "save the South"…and make its inventor a fortune.

Good Luck: Whitney was intrigued by the challenge. After only a few days of experimenting, he came up with a working model of a "cotton gin." He received a patent for it in 1794.

Tough Luck. Unfortunately, Whitney couldn't cash in on his own creation. The machine was so efficient and amazingly simple that "any country handy man could copy it—and they did." He sued companies that pirated his design, but the courts kept ruling against him. In fact, it took 13 years for Whitney to get even one favorable judgment…and by then the patent had nearly expired.

The cotton gin revolutionized Southern agriculture. In 1792 the U.S. exported about 140,000 lbs. of cotton; by 1800, with the help of Whitney's machine, almost 18 *million* lbs. were being exported annually. However, Whitney never benefitted from it.

The Loser: Charles Goodyear

The Sure Thing: Control of the "vulcanizing" process that makes rubber useful in manufactured products.

Background: Goodyear's hardware store went broke in 1830, and over the next decade he spent a lot of time in debtor's prison. When he wasn't in jail, he was inventing things.

In 1834, he designed a rubber inner tube. He took it to the Roxbury India Rubber company, hoping they'd manufacture it. The company's owners admired his work, but couldn't buy anything; they were broke.

Rubber products, it turned out, were essentially worthless; rubber melted in heat and cracked in cold. "The individual who could unlock the secret to India rubber," the owners assured Goodyear, "stood to make a fortune."

"To someone forever in debt," recounts *Yankee* magazine, "these words were like throwing a life preserver to a drowning man. The raw material was cheap, and the necessary equipment for cooking rubber could be found in his wife's kitchen: a rolling pin, a marble slab, and a few pots and pans. Vulcanizing rubber became Goodyear's mission in life."

Good Luck: After five years of dire poverty, during which he experimented constantly, Goodyear accidentally dropped a batch of rubber and sulphur mixture on a hot stove. When it didn't melt, as he expected it would, he realized he had finally discovered vulcanization.

Tough Luck: He had lived off people's charity—and dreams—for so long that none of his family or friends believed in him any more. In fact, it took him three years to find someone who was willing to invest in his discovery.

Finally, in 1854, he perfected the process enough to receive a valuable patent. But he still never made a cent from it. Other companies stole the process and challenged his rights to it. He was forced to spend all the money he could get his hands on defending himself. He died a pauper in 1860, hounded by collection agents.

The Loser: Josh J. Evans
Sure Thing: A district judgeship in Oklahoma.
Background: Frank Ogden had been a popular judge in rural northwest Oklahoma for thirteen years. He normally ran for reelection unopposed, but just before the deadline for filing to run in 1990, it was announced that he had cancer. Doctors speculated that Ogden could last another term. However, Josh Evans decided to run against him. He even tried, unsuccessfully, to get Ogden removed from the ballot.

Good Luck: On August ninth, Ogden died. Since write-ins aren't allowed in Okalhoma, Evans looked like a shoo-in.

Tough Luck: Evans couldn't even beat a dead man. The local Bar Association endorsed the deceased judge, and the electorate gave him 91% of the vote. The final tally: 9,377 for Ogden; 959 for Evans.

PRIME-TIME RELIGION

If God is everywhere, why not on Gilligan's Island? *TV quotes from the book* Primetime Proverbs, *by Jack Mingo and John Javna.*

ON RELIGION

"I'm going to take the moment to contemplate most Western religions. I'm looking for something soft on morality, generous with holidays, and with a very short initiation period."
—**David Addison,**
Moonlighting

"The pilgrims who drink the water of the Ganges shall trot all the way to the Mosque."
—**Henry Gibson,**
Laugh-In

THE RULES OF HEAVEN

"There's no plea bargaining in heaven."
—**Mark McCormick,**
Hardcastle & McCormack

"You don't have to be homely to get into heaven."
—**Hattie Denton,**
The Rifleman

Jean-Paul Sartre [arriving in heaven]: "It's not what I expected."
God: "What did you expect?"
Sartre: "Nothing."
—*SCTV*

ABOUT GOD

"When I was dead I saw God. She looks just like Toody from *The Facts of Life*."
—**Larry,**
Newhart

"God don't make no mistakes—that's how He got to be God."
—**Archie Bunker,**
All in the Family

Gabe Kotter: "I think God is everywhere."
Arnold Horschack: "Even in liver?"
—**Welcome Back, Kotter**

On FAITH

"All faith must have a little doubt thrown in. Otherwise it just becomes flabby sentimentality."
—**Dr. Loveless,**
The Wild, Wild West

"You have to believe in the gods to see them."
—**Hopi the Indian,**
Gumby

The Barbie Fan Club has 8,500 chapters.

THE MONSTER MASH

This Halloween classic swept across America in 1962—
and 1973—like a bat out of…Here's the inside story,
from Behind the Hits, *by Bob Shannon and John Javna.*

BACKGROUND
In the late '50s, Universal Studios syndicated a package of its greatest monster movies—including *Dracula*, The *Mummy*, and *Frankenstein*, featuring Boris Karloff—to television stations around the country. That's how baby boom kids got their first look at classic horror films. It was love at first sight; by the early '60s, a monster craze was under way. There were monster models, monster trading cards, monster wallets, monster posters…and a monster song: "The Monster Mash," by Bobby "Boris" Pickett.

KARLOFF DOO-WOP
Bobby was an aspiring actor who made his living singing with a Hollywood rock 'n' roll group called the Cordials at night, while he went on casting calls during the day. He'd always done impressions, and Karloff was one of his best. So one night just for the hell of it, while the Cordials doo-wopped their way thorugh a classic tune called "Little Darlin'," Bobby did a monologue in the middle with a Karloff voice. The crowds loved it. A member of the band suggested that Bobby do more with the Karloff imitation—write an original song, perhaps.

Pickett resisted for a while, but finally he and a friend wrote a monster take-off of Dee Dee Sharp's hit, "Mashed Potato Time." They recorded it at a studio on Hollywood Boulevard, for Gary Paxton's Garpax Records.

SOUND EFFECTS
Paxton, who'd had his own hit with "Alley Oop" a few years earlier, came up with some clever low-budget techniques to produce the background noises that made the rock 'n' roll's ultimate Halloween party so effective.

In 1865, an estimated 10,000 hogs roamed wild in New York City.

For example:

- "The sound of the coffin opening was actually a rusty nail being drawn out of a two-by-four."
- The cauldron bubbling was really water being bubbled through a straw.
- The chains rattling was just the sound of chains being dropped on a tile floor.

"Boris" Pickett thought of "Monster Mash" as a cute novelty tune. But he didn't understand the power of the monster mania that was sweeping America. The song sold a million copies and became a #1 hit in October—just in time for Halloween. One of its fans, who recieved free copies from Pickett, was Boris Karloff.

RETURN FROM THE DEAD

Pickett followed "Monster Mash" with "Monster's Holiday," and with an album of monster rock 'n' roll. But he had no more monster hits until 1970, when "Monster Mash" was re-released. It was released again in 1973, and it really hit big, reaching the Top 10. Pickett, by then a cabdriver in New York City, attributed its 1973 success, in part, to Nixon's Watergate scandal. "At this point in time, with what's coming down with Watergate, people need some relief from the tension that's building up," he explained.

ROCKIN' MONSTERS

Before "Monster Mash," the most popular monster tune in rock history was "Purple People Eater," recorded in 1958 by Sheb Wooley. Here's how Wooley came up with it:

- A friend of Wooley's told him a riddle he'd heard from his kid: "What flies, has one horn, has one eye, and eats people?" The answer: "A one-eyed, one-horned flying purple people eater." Wooley thought it was amusing, and wrote a song based on it.
- A short time later, Wooley met with the president of MGM Records to decide on his next single. Wooley played every song he'd written, but still couldn't come up with one the guy liked. "You got anything else?" the president asked. "Well, yeah, one more thing, but it's nothing you'd wanna hear." "Let's hear it."
- It was "Purple People Eater." Wooley recorded it, and three weeks later it was the #1 single in the U.S.

THE REAL PURITANS

According to American folklore, the Puritans were stern martinets who wore dark clothes, burned witches and never had sex. That's only partly true.

W**ere the Puritans "puritanical"?**
In many ways, yes. They had little tolerance for differences of opinion. They didn't think much of the concept of democracy, either—John Winthrop, first governor of the Massachusetts Bay Colony, called it "the meanest and worst of all forms of government." The religious freedom they left Europe to find was denied in their own settlements, where religious dissenters were expelled.

Colonial Christmas.
They didn't celebrate Christmas—in fact, they made it illegal to do so. A law passed in 1659 levied a 5-shilling fine against anyone "found observing, by abstinence from labor, feasting or any other way, any such days as Christmas day."

On the other hand, the Puritans' reputation for shyness about sex was a fabrication by 19th century historians who were trying to give their Colonial ancestors a moral makeover. In reality, the Puritans considered sex a public concern and regularly discussed it during meetings. They valued sexual intercourse inside marriage to such an extent that, after lengthy public discussion, they expelled a husband from the church community because he had refused to sleep with his wife for over two years. Furthermore, parents and children all slept in close proximity, so youngsters got plenty of sexual education at an early age, with visual aids.

Animal Husbandry
Still, deviations from the norm were severely dealt with. In 1647, a 16-year-old from Plymouth, Mass. was "detected of buggery with a mare, a cowe, two goats, five sheep, two calves and a turkey," as Governor Bradford put it. The boy was put to death. "A very sade spectakle it was; for first the mare, and them the cowe, and the rest of the lesser catle, were kild before his face, according to the law, Levitticus 20:15, and then he him selfe was executed."

One of the three original Barbies was a brunette — the rest were blonde.

OTHER PRESIDENTIAL FIRSTS

We all know the first president (Washington), the first to resign (Nixon), the first Catholic president (Kennedy), and so on. But who was the first to be interviewed in the nude? Here's the BRI's list of other presidential firsts.

THE PRESIDENT: Theodore Roosevelt (1901-1909)
NOTABLE FIRST: First president to coin an advertising slogan.
BACKGROUND: While he was visiting Andrew Jackson's home in Nashville, Tennessee, Roosevelt was offered a cup of the coffee sold at the nearby Maxwell House hotel. When someone asked if he'd like another cup, Roosevelt replied: "Will I have another cup? Delighted! *It's good to the last drop!*" His words were eventually used by Maxwell House in their ad campaigns.
Note: Teddy was also the first president to be blinded while in office. He liked to box, and during one White House bout was hit so hard he became permanently blind in one eye.

THE PRESIDENT: James Madison (1809-1817)
NOTABLE FIRST: First commander-in-chief to actually command a military unit while in office.
BACKGROUND: When the British attacked Washington, D.C., during the War of 1812, President Madison personally took charge of an artillery battery. But that didn't last long; when the Americans started to lose, Madison fled the city.

THE PRESIDENT: Benjamin Harrison (1889-1893)
NOTABLE FIRST: First president with a fear of electricity.
BACKGROUND: President Harrison knew two things about electricity: The White House had just been wired for it; and it could kill people (the electric chair was becoming a common form of execution). That was all he needed to know—he didn't want anything more to do with it. Throughout his entire term, he and his wife refused to turn the lights on and off themselves. They either had the servants do it or left the lights on all night.

An estimated 70% of all Americans visit shopping malls at least once a week.

THE PRESIDENT: Andrew Jackson (1829-1837)
ACCOMPLISHMENT: First president to be born in more than one place.
BACKGROUND: The following places claim themselves as Andrew Jackson's birthplace: Union County, North Carolina; Berkeley County, West Virginia; Augusta County, West Virginia; York County, Pennsylvania; as well as England, Ireland, and the Atlantic Ocean (he may have been born at sea). His "official" birthplace: Waxhaw, South Carolina.

THE PRESIDENT: John Quincy Adams (1825-1829)
ACCOMPLISHMENT: First president interviewed in the nude.
BACKGROUND: President Adams loved to skinny-dip. In hot weather he'd sneak out for a swim in the Potomac. One morning Anne Royall—a reporter who had been trying to interview him for months—sneaked up while he was swimming, sat on his clothes, and refused to leave until he granted her an interview. He did.

THE PRESIDENT: Martin Van Buren (1837-1841)
ACCOMPLISHMENT: First president to forget about his wife.
BACKGROUND: In his autobiography, Van Buren did not mention his wife Hannah even once.

THE PRESIDENT: Warren G. Harding (1921-1923)
ACCOMPLISHMENT: First president to pardon a dog.
BACKGROUND: One morning Harding read a newspaper article about Pennsylvania dog that had been ordered destroyed because it had been brought into the country illegally. Harding—who loved animals—wrote a letter to the Governor of Pennsylvania. The governor saw to it that the dog's life was spared.

THE PRESIDENT: David Rice Atchison (1849-1849)
ACCOMPLISHMENT: First president to serve for one day.
BACKGROUND: Zachary Taylor was so religious that he refused to take the oath of office on a Sunday. So Atchison, President Pro Tempore of the U.S. Senate, stood in for him until he could be sworn in the next day.

SMART COOKIES

Cookies keep the Girl Scouts in the green. That box of Thin Mints or Do-Si-Does you order every season is part of a tradition that's nearly 60 years old.

FOUNDING MOTHERS

After Juliette Low founded the Girl Scouts in 1912, the local troops raised money by selling knitted clothes, baked goods and chickens. Then in 1934, Philadelphia press agent Bella Spewack (who later co-wrote *Kiss Me Kate)* came up with an idea she thought would make fund-raising easier: a vanilla cookie in the shape of the Girl Scout seal. She contracted with a local bakery to make them. One day she heard that reporters were going to interview actresses at a local flower show. Figuring her Girl Scout troop would get free publicity if they showed up selling cookies, she sent a contingent of green-clad cookie-mongers. They got so much publicity and sold so many cookies that within three years, more than a hundred local councils were selling the same professionally-baked cookies. It was the beginning of an American institution.

NOW IT'S BIG BUSINESS

• In 1990 the Girl Scouts sold 130 million boxes of cookies, grossing $225 million. That's 13 cookies for every person in the U.S. Average sale per scout? About 100 boxes.

• Some troops now offer "cookie seminars" and toll-free ordering numbers to boost sales. When asked about nutritional value, scouts are coached to respond: "Our cookies contain no preservatives and no artificial colors, and are made of 100% vegetable shortening."

• The *Girl Scout Manual* offers sales tips like this: "Your words and tone of voice must generate the image of someone people trust."

• The greatest cookie seller of all time was Markita Andrews, who sold 60,000 boxes in her twelve years of Girl Scouting. She was so successful that she was hired to make motivational speeches to big companies and appear in a 12-minute sales motivational film, *The Cookie Kid*, produced by Disney.

• Most popular cookies: Thin Mint, followed by Shortbread and Peanut Butter Sandwiches. Least popular: cheese-flavored crackers.

Nice place to visit: 24% of all Iowans have some sort of ornament on their lawns.

YOU SEND ME

*Here are the origins of some of the nation's
largest people and package movers.*

GREYHOUND BUSES

In 1914 Carl Eric Wickman opened a Hupmobile car dealership in Minnesota. When business was slow, he used one of the Hupmobiles to drive miners the 4 miles between the towns of Alice and Hibbing, charging 15¢ per trip (25¢ round trip). This enterprise turned out to be very profitable (he made $2.25 the first day), and by 1916 Wickman had expanded it to include long distance routes. He painted the Hupmobiles gray to hide the dust during long journeys…which prompted a hotel owner along one route to comment that they looked like greyhound dogs. Wickman liked the idea. He adopted the slogan "Ride the Greyhounds."

FEDERAL EXPRESS

When Fred Smith was a student at Yale University, he wrote a term paper outlining his idea for a nationwide overnight delivery service. His Professor gave him a C for the effort….but Smith (who'd inherited a fortune) invested $4 million to start the company anyway. He named it Federal Express because he thought his first major customer would be the Federal Reserve Bank. (Ironically, it wasn't).

UNITED PARCEL SERVICE

Jim Casey was 19 years old in 1907, when he started the American Messenger company in Seattle. His business consisted of only six messengers, two bicycles, and a telephone…but within a year he added 6 motorcycles and a Model T Ford. By 1918 he was handling the deliveries of 3 of Seattle's major department stores. By the end of World War I, Casey had changed the name of the business to the United Parcel Service, and focused exclusively on delivering for department stores. In 1953 UPS expanded service to 16 metropolitan areas and started expanding its service. Today UPS owns more than 300 aircraft and delivers 600,000 packages every day.

Ounce for ounce, a bumblebee is 150 times stronger than an elephant.

THE HARDER THEY FALL

The bigger they are, the harder they fall?
Sadly, that was true for these stars.

THE STAR: Veronica Lake, sultry actress known for her "peek-a-boo" hair-style (combed over one eye—in fact, practically covering one whole side of her face).

ACCOMPLISHMENTS: A leading box-office attraction of the early 1940s. Made 26 films, including *I Married a Witch* (the inspiration for the TV show, "Bewitched").

AT HER PEAK: Her hair-style was so popular that it hampered the war effort. Women working in factories kept getting their "peek-a-boo" hair caught in the machinery. U.S. government officials asked Lake to cut her hair. She did.

THE FALL: Without the hair, Lake wasn't special anymore. By the early '50s, her movie career was over. Though she found intermittent work in stage roles, she was reduced at one point to working as a barmaid in Manhattan. She died of acute hepatitis at age 53, on July 7, 1973.

THE STAR: D.W. Griffith, the genius regarded as "the father of modern cinema."

ACCOMPLISHMENTS: Griffith produced and directed nearly 500 films. The cinematic genres he created—from the epic to the psychological drama—influenced generations of directors. He launched the careers of Hollywood legends Mary Pickford, Douglas Fairbanks, Lionel Barrymore, and many others.

AT HIS PEAK: His films had such impact that Woodrow Wilson remarked, when he saw Griffith's *The Birth of a Nation* (the first film shown at the White House), that it was "like writing history with lightning."

THE FALL: Griffith's bouts with the bottle inspired him to make *The Struggle*, a 1931 exploration of alchoholism. It bombed. Griffith's own struggle with booze worsened, and his production company folded. Suddenly, he was unable to find work; in the last 17 years of his life, no one in Hollywood would give him a job.

Japan recycles more than half its household and commercial waste.

Although his films had earned tens of millions of dollars, he left an estate of only $30,000 when he died in 1948, at the age of 73.

THE STAR: "Shoeless Joe" Jackson, one of the greatest players in baseball history. Played for the Philadelphia Athletics (1908-09), Cleveland Indians (1910-15) and Chicago White Sox (1915-20).

ACCOMPLISHMENTS: Compiled the third-highest lifetime batting average of all time: .356. Only Ty Cobb, at .367, and Rogers Hornsby, at .358, are higher. In his first full year he hit .408 (but lost the batting title to Cobb, who hit .420).

AT HIS PEAK: Between 1910 and 1915, Jackson batted no lower than .331. Cobb called Jackson the greatest natural hitter who ever lived, adding, "He never figured anything out or studied anything with the same scientific approach I gave it. He just swung."

THE FALL: After the White Sox lost the 1919 World Series to the Cincinatti Reds, officials learned that eight Chicago players—including Jackson—had agreed to "throw" the Series in exchange for bribes from gangsters. They called it the "Black Sox" scandal.

The revelation outraged the country. A sensational investigation was launched and a grand jury was convened. Jackson, who had hit .375 in the Series (leading all batters), maintained he never accepted any money. He claimed he'd agreed to the plan only because the team's owner, notoriously stingy Charles Comiskey, was paying the players next to nothing. He was found innocent of any criminal wrongdoing, but baseball executives decided to make an example of him (and his teammates). He was banned from baseball for life.

Jackson resettled in his native South Carolina, where he ran a liquor store and played sandlot and textile-league baseball. He died of a heart attack on December 5, 1951, at the age of 63.

THE STAR: Joseph McCarthy, U.S. Senator (R-Wisc.) from 1947 to 1957.

ACCOMPLISHMENTS: Senator McCarthy did not create the Cold War, but he almost single-handedly fashioned the post-World War II anti-communist hysteria that swept through American society. His 1950 claim that more than 200 Communists had infiltrated the State Department launched a national witch hunt. It ruined hundreds of careers, led to infamous blacklists (especially in the motion picture industry), and, as one magazine put it, "convinced

---

Take a deep breath: 47% of smokers have tried to quit four or more times.

most Americans that their government was riddled with Reds bent on its destruction."

AT HIS PEAK: He could make or break careers and reputations. Polls showed that half of all Americans approved of his efforts, while less than one-third disapproved.

THE FALL: In April, 1954, a Senate committee began investigating his charge that the U.S. Army was "coddling Communists." Two-thirds of all TV sets in the country were tuned in. TV cameras captured his cruel sneer, his bullying manner, and America saw Army counsel Joseph Welch put McCarthy in his place with the famous words, "Have you no sense of decency, sir?" Welch got a standing ovation and McCarthy's colleagues in the Senate moved to censure him. His political career was effectively over. Always known as a two-fisted drinker, he hit the bottle harder and harder, and on May 2, 1957, he died of liver disease, at the age of 48.

THE STAR: Eliot Ness, legendary G-man whose 15-year law enforcement career was highlighted by his campaign against Chicago mob boss Al Capone.

ACCOMPLISHMENTS: In 1929, during Prohibition, Ness led the special ten-man Justice Department team known as "The Untouchables," targeting Capone. In 1935, at 32, Ness became Cleveland's youngest director of public safety. He went on to rid the police department of rampant corruption, brought dozens of mobsters to trial, and reduced juvenile crime by two-thirds.

AT HIS PEAK: In two years, Ness and his men did more to curtail organized crime in Chicago than federal, state, and local officials combined had in an entire decade. In its first six months alone, the "Untouchables" unit seized nineteen Capone distilleries and six breweries. By 1931 the team had effectively shut down Capone's alcohol-production operations.

THE FALL: In the spring of 1942, Ness drove his car, with its unmistakable "EN-1" license plates, into another vehicle—then left the scene. It was reported he'd been driving drunk. Ness denied it, but resigned under pressure two months later. Over the next 15 years, he spiralled downward through a series of failed business ventures, marriages, and an abortive political career. He managed to complete his memoirs, but didn't live to see them in print. When he died of a heart attack, on May 16, 1957, he was $8,000 in debt.

The bald eagle's nest can weigh as much as a ton.

BEAGLE, SHYSTER, & BEAGLE

This script from the first episode of a long-lost early radio show by the Marx Brothers was recently rediscovered. So close your ears, listen with your eyes, and travel back in time to Nov. 28. 1932, when the first episode of Five-Star Theater aired.

SCENE: *The offices of Beagle, Shyster, & Beagle, Attorneys at Law. Miss Dimple, the receptionist, is polishing her nails. Beagle (Groucho Marx) bursts in.*

MISS DIMPLE: Good morning, Mr. Beagle.

GROUCHO: Never mind that. Get President Hoover on the phone. There's a picture of me in the police station and it doesn't do me justice. It makes me look like my father. In fact, it *is* my father. Never mind calling the president. Just find out what the reward is.

MISS DIMPLE: Mr. Beagle, I've got some letters for you to sign.

GROUCHO: Not now, not now! I've had a big day in court.

MISS DIMPLE: What was the case?

GROUCHO: Disorderly conduct, but I think I'll get off. Why shouldn't I? She hit me first.

MISS DIMPLE: Mr. Beagle! You hit a woman?

GROUCHO: Well, she was my size. Even smaller. Besides, if it weren't for my own arrests, I'd never get a case. Any calls?

MISS DIMPLE: Yes, your creditors have been calling all morning. They said they're tired of phoning and that something will have to be done.

GROUCHO: All right. We'll do something. We'll have the phone taken out.

MISS DIMPLE: Okay.

GROUCHO: There's a good girl. Your salary is raised ten dollars.

MISS DIMPLE: Thank you, Mr. Beagle.

GROUCHO: It's nothing at all. Say, how about lending me that ten till payday?

MISS DIMPLE: But Mr. Beagle, I haven't been paid in weeks. Besides, you overlook the fact—

GROUCHO: I've overlooked plenty around here. A fine stenographer you are! What do you do with your time? The floors aren't washed, the windows aren't cleaned. and my pants aren't even pressed.

MISS DIMPLE: But Mr. Beagle—

GROUCHO: Enough of this small talk. Where's that ten dollars?

Groucho retires to his office. Soon after, Miss Dimple ushers in a client—a nervous, worried soul named Mr. Jones.

JONES: How do you do, Mr. Beagle. A friend of mine told me you were a good lawyer.

GROUCHO: You just *think* he's a friend of yours. Sit down. Have you got a couple of cigars?

JONES: Uh…no, I'm sorry.

GROUCHO: Well, why don't you send out for some? If you've got a quarter, I'll go myself.

JONES: Oh, no, no, Mr. Beagle.

GROUCHO: What's the matter? Don't you trust me?

JONES: Why—I'd like to talk to you. I'm having trouble with my wife.

GROUCHO: You are! Well, I'm having trouble with my wife, too, but I don't go around bragging about it. Hmm. You oughta be ashamed of yourself. Miss Dimple, show this gentleman the door. On second thought, never mind. He saw it when he came in.

JONES: But, Mr. Beagle—I came to you for advice. Let me tell you a story. My wife is in love with two men, and—

GROUCHO: Ha, ha, ha! Not a bad story. The boys are all repeating it around the club. Now let me tell you one. There were two

Two out of every three American boys own G.I. Joe dolls.

traveling men named Pat and Mike—

JONES: No, no, Mr. Beagle. I came here with a problem. I'm looking for evidence against my wife.

GROUCHO: What you really want is someone to shadow your wife. I've got just the man for you—my new assistant, Emmanuel Ravelli. He looks like an idiot and talks like an idiot. But don't let that fool you. He really is an idiot. You and Ravelli will have a lot in common.

JONES: Mr. Beagle, my time is valuable. Let me give you the facts. I married my wife secretly.

GROUCHO: You married her secretly? You mean you haven't told her about it? No wonder she runs around with other men.

JONES: Mr. Beagle, we must get this divorce—I want your assistant, Mr. Ravelli, to follow my wife.

GROUCHO: One thing at a time. Let's get the divorce first and then we can all follow your wife.

CHICO: Here I am, boss. You callin' Ravelli?

GROUCHO: See here. I don't like your sleeping on the company's time.

CHICO: I don't like sleeping on it it, either. Why don't you buy me a bed?

JONES: Mr. Ravelli, I've just been telling Mr. Beagle that, much as I regret to say it, my wife is going around with other men.

CHICO: She's going around with other men? 'At'sa fine. Hey! You think she like me?

JONES: Well, Mr. Ravelli, as long as you're going to trail my wife, I think I ought to describe her to you. She's of medium height and...but never mind, I've got a photograph.

CHICO: Hey, 'at'sa fine. Awright. I'll take a dozen.

JONES: I'm not selling them

CHICO: You mean, I get it for nothing?

JONES: Of course.

CHICO: Awright. Then I take two dozen.

In 1985, astronauts flew a paper plane in space, it worked just like on earth, only verrry slowwwly.

JONES: One picture ought to be enough for the present. There's one man my wife has been paying particular attention to. I'm counting on you to find out who he is. Do you think you can do it?

CHICO: Sure, you leave 'im to me. I find out who the man was with your wife. And I find out quick.

JONES: Really? How you going to do it?

CHICO: Well, first I put on a disguise ...

JONES: Yes?

CHICO: Then I get a bloodhound ...

JONES: Yes??

CHICO: Then I go to your house ...

JONES: Yes???

CHICO: Then I ask your wife.

(*Applause, commercial break*)

Two weeks later at the offices of Beagle, Shyster, & Beagle.

MISS DIMPLE: Law offices of Beagle, Shyster, and Beagle ...Oh, hello, Mr. Jones. I didn't recognize your voice...Yes, Mr. Ravelli is still trailing your wife ...but it hasn't been long ...just two weeks. We expect Mr. Ravelli in the office this morning. He says he has some news ...Okay, I'll tell Mr. Beagle you'll be in ...Goodbye.

(*Groucho comes in*).

MISS DIMPLE: Good morning, Mr. Beagle—

GROUCHO: Miss Dimple, before I forget—call Ravelli and tell him to be sure and oversleep.

MISS DIMPLE: But he phoned and said he was coming right in.

GROUCHO: In that case, I'm going right back to the poolroom (*he heads for the door*).

MISS DIMPLE: But Mr. Jones is on his way here to talk to you about his divorce.

GROUCHO: That's all he ever talks to me about. I'm getting pretty sick of it, too.

MISS DIMPLE: But Mr. Beagle, that's your business.

Each year, Americans consume 19 billion franks—an average of 87 per person.

GROUCHO: Well, I wish he'd keep his nose out of my business. (*Door opens.*)

MISS DIMPLE: Shh! Someone's coming in. I think it's Mr. Jones. How do you do, Mr. Jones?

JONES: How do you do, Miss Dimple? Morning, Mr. Beagle. About my divorce—

GROUCHO: Divorce! You going to start that again? Listen, Jones, can I sell you a ticket to the Firemen's Ball? It's a five-dollar ticket, and it's yours for a buck and a half.

JONES: Why, this is last year's ticket.

GROUCHO: I know it is, but they had a better show last year.

JONES: Mr. Beagle, when will I find out about my divorce case?

GROUCHO: See here, Jones, don't change the subject. What about that ticket?

JONES: I don't like to appear impatient, Mr. Beagle, but your assistant was supposed to bring in some evidence against my wife. Where is Mr. Ravelli?

CHICO: Hey! Who'sa calling Ravelli? Here I am.

JONES: Ah, Mr. Ravelli, I'd like to get the results of your investigation. Have you been trailing my wife?

CHICO: Sure, I shadow her all day.

JONES: What day was that?

CHICO: That was Shadowday. I went right to your house—

JONES: What did you find out?

CHICO: I find your wife out.

JONES: Then you wasted the entire two weeks?

CHICO: No. Monday, I shadow your wife. Tuesday, I go to the ball game—she don't show up. Wednesday, she go to the ball game—I don't show up. Thursday was a doubleheader. We both no show up. Friday it rain all day—there's a no ball game, so I go fishing.

JONES: Well, what's that got to do with my wife?

CHICO: Well, I no catcha no fish, but I catch your wife.

The state with the most outhouses is Alaska.

JONES: You caught my wife—with a man? Who was he?

CHICO: I don't wanna say.

JONES: I insist that you tell me the man's name.

CHICO: I don't wanna tell.

GROUCHO: Listen, Jones, my assistant isn't the type of fellow who'd bandy a man's good name in public—

JONES: For the last time, gentlemen—who was the man?

GROUCHO: Come clean, Ravelli, who was the man with his wife?

CHICO: Awright, awright. You maka me tell, I tell you. Mr. Jones, the man with your wife was my boss, Mr. Beagle.

JONES: This is an outrage. My attorney going out with my wife!

GROUCHO: What do you mean, outrage? Don't you think I'm good enough for her?

JONES: I'm going to get a new attorney.

GROUCHO: Hmm! I suppose you think we can't get a new client?

JONES: Good day! (*He stomps out and slams the door.*)

GROUCHO: Ravelli, you did noble work. You can have the rest of the year off. And if you never come back, I'll give you a bonus.

CHICO: Well, boss, there's something I wanna tell you.

GROUCHO: Go right ahead. I'm not listening.

CHICO: You want I should never come back?

GROUCHO: In a word, yes.

CHICO: Awright, boss, I make you a proposition. If you want I should never come back, I gotta have more money.

GROUCHO: Ravelli, it's worth it. (*Applause, theme music*)

ANNOUNCER: The crowd in the studio is giving the Marx Brothers a great ovation. We hope you in the radio audience enjoyed them as much as we did. Groucho and Chico will be back again next Monday at this same time.

The first "streamlined swimsuits" of the early 1900s were made of wool and weighed as much as 20 lbs.

PICASSO ORIGINALS

Pablo Picasso was known for his skill with lines.
Here are some you won't see in a museum.

"We know that art is not truth. Art is a lie that makes us realize truth."

"When I was a child my mother said to me, 'If you become a soldier you'll be a general. If you become a monk you'll become the pope.' Instead I became a painter and wound up as Picasso."

"I am only a public entertainer who has understood his time."

"There are only two kinds of women—goddesses and doormats."

"There are painters who transform the sun into a yellow spot, but there are others who, thanks to their art and intelligence, transform a yellow spot into the sun."

"One starts to get young at the age of sixty and then it is too late."

"There's nothing so similar to one poodle dog as another poodle dog and that goes for women, too."

"You never see anything very great which is not, at the same time, horrible in some respect. The genius of Einstein leads to Hiroshima."

"God is really only another artist. He invented the giraffe, the elephant, and the cat. He has no real style, he just goes on trying other things."

"Ah, good taste! What a dreadful thing! Taste is the enemy of creativeness."

"An artist must know how to convince others of the truth of his lies."

"If only we could pull out our brains and use only our eyes."

"If I like it, I say it's mine. If I don't, I say it's a fake."

"Work is a necessity for man. Man invented the alarm clock."

"You invent something, and then someone comes along and does it pretty."

Arachibutyrophobia: the fear of peanut butter sticking to the roof of your mouth.

LATIN 101

So you thought Latin was dead? Latin For All Occasions, *by Henry Beard, brings it back to life. Here are some excerpts:*

Useful phrase: "Amicule, deliciæ, num is sum qui mentiar tibi?"
Meaning: "Baby, sweetheart, would I lie to you?"

Useful phrase: "Perscriptio in manibus tabellariorum est."
Meaning: "The check is in the mail."

Useful phrase: "Braccæ tuæ aperiuntur."
Meaning: "Your fly is open."

Useful phrase: "Da mihi sis bubulæ frustum assæ, solana tuberosa in modo Gallico fricta ac quassum lactatum coagulatum crassum."
Meaning: "I'll have a hamburger, French fries, and a thick shake."

Useful phrase: "Cur non isti mictum ex occasione?"
Meaning: "Why didn't you go when you had the chance?"

Useful phrase: "In rivo fimi sine rivo sum."
Meaning: "I'm up the creek without a paddle."

Useful phrase: "Est mihi nulluus nummus superfluus."
Meaning: "I do not have any spare change."

Useful phrase: "Lex clavatoris designati rescindenda est."
Meaning: "The designated-hitter rule has got to go."

Useful phrase: "Observa quo vadis, cinaede!"
Meaning: "Watch where you're going, you jerk!"

Useful phrase: "Tractatorne in Germania Orinetali doctus est?"
Meaning: "Was your masseur trained in East Germany?"

Useful phrase: "Visne scire quod credam? Credo Elvem ipsum etiam vivere."
Meaning: "You know what I think? I think that Elvis is still alive."

Useful phrase: "Di! Ecce hora! Uxor mea necabit!"
Meaning: "God, look at the time! My wife will kill me!"

Hitler's favorite movie was *King Kong*.

THE TAJ MAHAL

*On the banks of the Jumna River, at Agra, India is a structure consid-
ered by many to be the most beautiful edifice ever built—the Taj Mahal.*

BACKGROUND

B In 1628, Shah Jahan became the fifth Mogul emperor of India. Of his four wives, his favorite was one he called *Mumtaz
Mahal* (which means "Ornament of the Palace").

• Shah Jahan was known as a benevolent, fatherly ruler. One ritu-
al he—and his subjects—especially enjoyed was "Tula Dan." He
would sit on a scale forty feet high, and was weighed against gold
coins. When an amount equal to his weight was measured out, the
coins were distributed to the poor.

• Mumtaz Mahal, on the other hand, was a bloodthirsty religious
zealot and a committed foe of Christianity. She goaded her husband into destroying a Christian colony at Hooghly, on the northeast coast of India. The entire colony was razed. The survivors were
marched 1,200 miles from Hooghly to Agra. There, the priests were
thrown beneath elephants; the rest were sold as slaves.

THE MONUMENT

• When Mumtaz Mahal died in 1631, Shah Jahan was so grief-
stricken that he disappeared into his quarters for eight days, "refus-
ing food or wine"; all that could be heard coming from his room
was a low moan.

• On the ninth day he emerged, determined to build a magnificent
tomb as a monument to his beloved. Mumtaz herself, on her deathbed, supposedly whispered into Shah Jahan's ear that he should
build " monument of perfect proportions" to symbolize and im-
mortalize their perfect love.

• The project took 22 years. More than 20,000 jewelers, builders,
masons and calligraphers worked on it day and night. When they
finished, they had created the wondrous white mausoleum which is
still regarded—nearly 340 years later—as the most remarkable

It is illegal to fly an airplane over the Taj Mahal.

piece of architecture in the world.

• The main building of the Taj Mahal is on a 186-foot square whose sides have been cut to form an octagon. This rests on a platform 2,000 feet long and 1,000 feet wide. At each of its four corners is a minaret—an Islamic prayer tower—three stories tall.

• Hundreds of tons of imported white marble were used.

• The Taj is adorned with Tibetan turquoise, Chinese jade, Arabian carnelian, and other precious metals.

• According to one account, Shah Jahan showed his appreciation for this masterpiece by ordering the hands of the master builders—and the head of the architect—to be chopped off, so the perfection of the Taj could never be duplicated.

LATER ON...

• In first centuries after it was built, the Taj Mahal wasn't a tourist attraction. Until the British Raj (occupation of India), any non-Moslem who entered it was put to death.

• Shah Jahan planned to build a second Taj Mahal, made of black marble, on the opposite bank of the Jumna. (He planned to make it his own tomb.) The two structures were to have been connected by a bridge of solid silver. Construction on this "Black Taj" supposedly was begun in the 1650s, but no traces of its foundation have ever been found. The project was halted when Shah Jahan was deposed by his sons.

• The Mogul spent his last years confined to a suite in Agra's famous Red Fort, where he was imprisoned by his son Aurangzeb, Agra's new ruler. From his window, Jahan could see his monument to Mumtaz—to whom he remained devoted (even though his entire harem was with him). Every day for eight years he sat gazing across the river.

• Jahan finally died at the age of 74, when he took an overdose of aphrodisiacs in an effort to prove his virility.

• Jahan was buried with Mumtaz in the Taj, but their actual remains are not in the main structure. The tombs upstairs are empty; the real ones are in the basement.

HOTEL

QUEEN MARY

MODERN TIMES

• The domes and minarets of the Taj are so reflective—even in moonlight—that, during the India-Pakistan War, large sections were covered in burlap so that Pakistani aircraft could not use it as a beacon.

• Today, the Taj is threatened by pollution. The river valley where it sits tends to trap corrosive air pollutants, including coal dust and sulfur dioxide, for days at a time. Only about 1% of its surface has been affected, but formerly bright-white marble is now streaked, pitted and yellow. Some of the red sandstone of auxiliary buildings is flaking. Most of the pollution is said to come from two coal-fired power plants, a railroad switching yard and many small coal-burning foundries.

• The Indian government has installed pollution-monitoring gear and promises to relocate the power stations and foundries, but these are long-term propositions. Meanwhile, the race to save the Taj is already being run by frantic workmen who are repairing and replacing slabs of marble as fast as possible.

THE OTHER TAJ

• Taj Mahal is one of the foremost modern American bluesmen.

• His real name: Henry St. Clair Fredericks.

• Our favorite of his albums: "Natch'l Blues" and "Giant Step." Both are recommended for your bathroom CD player.

• • •

GOTTA FILL THIS SPACE

Random quotes about greatness:

• "A small man can be just as exhausted as a great man." (Arthur Miller)

• "Behind every great man is a woman with nothing to wear." (L. Grant Glickman)

• "Calvin Coolidge—the greatest man ever to come out of Plymouth Corner, Vermont." (Clarence Darrow)

• "The privilege of the great is to see catastrophes from a terrace." (Jean Giraudoux).

On average, there are more than 1,800 thunder storms on Earth at any given time.

THE PLANE TRUTH

Occasionally, we get a letter from a reader who confesses he or she has read a Bathroom Reader on an airplane. Well, that's okay with us. To prove it, here's a bit of practical airplane advice from the Airline Passenger's Guerrilla Handbook, *by George Brown.*

Belive it or not, specialists have actually discovered a medical complaint called "economy class syndrome" (ECS). According to the British medical journal, *The Lancet*, the symptoms can appear several weeks after flights as short as three hours. The syndrome can result in anything from minor body pains and shortness of breath to heart attacks and strokes.

Doctors suspect that cramped legroom in economy class combined with dehydration interrupts the blood flow which causes clots, cutting off the supply of oxygen to various parts of the body. This may account for the results of one study which showed that 18 percent of sudden deaths on airplanes are due to blood clots in the lungs.

The medical specialists reported that the syndrome most often affects smokers, heavy drinkers, those whose feet don't reach the floor (because the seat puts more pressure on the backs of their legs), the elderly and those with a predisposition to coronary heart disease. But it also can affect normally healthy people, in some recorded cases causing them to develop pneumonia-like symptons due to blood clots in the lungs.

The best ways to fight ECS: drink nonalcoholic beverages, don't smoke, take aspirin to thin your blood and exercise on the plane.

How to Exercise on the Plane

The best type of exercise on a long flight is to get out of your seat, go to the back of the plane (or, if you're shy, into a toilet cubicle) and engage in traditional calisthenics, such as touching your toes, reaching for the sky and running in place. Avoid doing jumping jacks if you're in the lavatory.

If you can't or don't want to get up, there are certain sets of exercis-

---

Thomas Jefferson was the first president to wear long pants.

es you can do in your seat. Before you start, be sure to inform your seatmate of what you intend to do. This will prevent him from thinking you're having some sort of seizure, which could lead to his attempting to wrestle a pencil sideways into your mouth to keep you from choking on your tongue—always an embarrassing mistake for both parties.

The exercises are as follows:

1. Tighten and release, one group at a time, the muscles in your shoulders, back, buttocks and thighs.

2. By raising your thighs, lift both feet six inches off the floor and rotate them first in one direction and then in the other.

3. Reach up repeatedly toward your overhead light with one arm and then with the other as though trying to block out the light.

4. Bend forward with all your weight, press your crossed forearms onto your knees and, keeping your toes on the floor, repeatedly lift your heels as high as possible.

5. Sitting up, arching your back, repeatedly roll both shoulders forward and then back, first together and then one at a time.

6. Pretending you are on skis, push your knees to the right and your heels and hands to the left. Lift your feet off the floor, and swing your knees to the left and heels and hands to the right. Repeat twenty times.

7. Sitting back, lower your head as far forward as you can. Then, still facing forward, lower it to the left. Then, to the right. Repeat several times.

8. Lay your head back, with your mouth hanging open, and, arching your back, look as far back on the ceiling as you can.

9. With your right hand grab the back of your left armrest and pull your upper body around until you are looking behind you. Hold for ten seconds. Repeat in the other direction.

10. Place your right hand on your left shoulder and your left hand on your right shoulder, and hug yourself. Lean forward as though giving someone a Latin lover kiss. Repeat several times.

11. Sit up slowly, turn towards the aisle and tell the crowd looking at you that you've finished your exercises, so they can all go back to their seats.

In your lifetime, you'll sleep about 220,000 hours.

EXPERT OPINIONS

Being an expert means never having to admit you're wrong. Here are some memorable examples of "expert opinion," quoted in a great book called The Experts Speak, *by Christopher Cerf & Victor Navasky.*

O**N HEALTH:**
If excessive smoking actually plays a role in the production of lung cancer, it seems to be a minor one."
> **—The National Cancer Institute, 1954**

"How do we know? Fallout may be good for us."
> **—Edward Teller, 1950**

"A nuclear power plant is infinitely safer than eating, because 300 people choke to death on food every day."
> **—Dixie Lee Ray, Washington Governor, 1977**

...ON MILITARY STRATEGY:
"I tell you Wellington is a bad general, the English are bad soldiers; we will settle the matter by lunch time."
> **—Napoleon Bonaparte at the Battle of Waterloo, 1815**

"I guess we'll get through with them in a day."
> **—General George Custer at Little Big Horn, 1876**

...ON FILM
"The cinema is little more than a fad. It's canned drama. I'm going to get out of this business. It's too much for me. It'll never catch on."
> **—Charlie Chaplin, 1914**

"*Gone With the Wind* is going to be the biggest flop in the history of Hollywood. I'm just glad it'll be Clark Gable who's falling flat on his face and not Gary Cooper."
> **—Gary Cooper, 1938**

"You'd better learn secretarial work or else get married."
> **—Emmeline Snively (modeling agent) to Marilyn Monroe, 1944**

Bud Abbott, of Abbott & Costello, was born in a circus tent.

...ON TECHNOLOGY

"Rail travel at high speed is not possible, because passengers, unable to breathe, would die of asphyxiation."

—Dr. Dionysus Lardener, 1845

"Heavier-than-air flying machines are impossible."

—William Thomson, President of the Royal Society, 1890

"Nuclear powered vacuum cleaners will probably be a reality within 10 years."

—Alex Lewyt, President, Lewyt Vacuum Cleaner Co., 1955

"My invention...can be exploited for a certain time as a scientific curiosity, but apart from that it has no commercial value whatsoever."

—Auguste Lumiere (inventor of the movie camera), 1895.

...ON COMPUTERS

"While a calculator now is equipped with 18,000 vacuum tubes and weighs 30 tons, computers in the future may have only 1,000 vacuum tubes and only weigh 1 1/2 tons."

—*Popular Mechanics*, 1949

"I think there is a world market for about five computers."

—Thomas J. Watson, Chairman of IBM, 1943

"There is no reason for any individual to have a computer in their home."

—Ken Olson, President, Digital Equipment Corporation, 1977

...ON POLITICS

"If Richard Nixon is impeached, there will be mass suicides, mass nervous breakdowns, and total demoralization of the country."

—Helen Buffington, Committee to Re-Elect the President, 1974

"Dwight D. Eisenhower is a dedicated, conscious agent of the Communist conspiracy."

—Robert Welch, President, John Birch Society, 1963

A typical "lawn" in Austria is planted with cabbages and kohlrabi.

LUCKY STRIKES

Here's proof that the BRI appreciates other kinds of "bowling," too.

BIRTH OF BOWLING

• Bowling originated in German monasteries around 300 A.D. The monks had churchgoers knock down a bottle-shaped object called a *kegel* from a distance to prove their devotion to God. The kegel represented the devil, and upsetting it meant complete absolution from sin.

• Gradually, more kegels (pins) were added and it turned into a secular game. By the 1600s, a version called "nine-pin" had become popular throughout Europe.

• Ninepins was popular in the U.S. in the early 1800s. But because many lanes were located in saloons, the game became associated with drinking. Many states banned it. Bowlers got around the laws by adding a *tenth* pin to the set. Eventually ten-pins became more popular than Ninepins.

BOWLING LINGO

Apple: a bowling ball

Barmaid: a pin that's "hiding" behind another pin.

Bedposts, Snake eyes, Mule ears, Goal posts: 7-10 split.

Body English: using body contortions to change the course of an already thrown ball.

Cherry: downing only the front pins when going for a spare.

Christmas Tree: 3-7-10 or 2-7-10 splits.

Cincinnati: an 8-10 split

Creeper, powder puff: a sluggish ball.

Dead Apple: a ball with no power when it reaches the pins.

Golden Gate: A 4-6-7-10 split.

Grasshopper: a ball that sends the pins leaping

Grandma's Teeth: a random, gap-filled group of pins left standing.

Mother-In-Law: the 7 pin

Poodle: a roll right into the gutter.

Schleifer: a suspenseful, domino-like strike.

Woolworth, Dime Store: 5-10 ("five and dime") split.

Norman Rockwell started painting Saturday Evening Post covers at the age of 21.

TEA TIME

*Some things you probably never knew about
one of the world's most popular beverages.*

According to Chinese legend, tea was discovered in 2737 B.C. by Emperor Shen Nung, when leaves from a nearby plant fell into a pot of boiling water.

Japanese legend differs—it attributes the discovery of tea to Daruma, founder of Zen Buddhism. After nine years of meditating without sleep, it says, Daruma became groggy. This made him mad, so he cut off his eyelids. Blood from his eyes spilled to the ground, and a plant grew from that spot. The drink Daruma made from the plant cured his grogginess.

All teas (except herbal teas) come from the same plant—*Camellia Sinensis.* The only things that distinguish one variety of tea from another are blending, added flavors, and the length of time the leaves are allowed to dry, or "ferment."

Tea grows naturally in only one part of the world: the forested region shared by China, India, Burma, and Tibet.

Before the 1700s, the English considered tea a "man's" drink—and sold it only in coffee houses, places considered too rough for women. Thomas Twining changed this in 1706 when he opened London's first tea shop for ladies.

Thomas Lipton, founder of the Lipton Tea Co., owes his success to pigs. Lipton owned a general store in Glasgow, Scotland. To promote it, he dressed up pigs and led them in parades. The pigs, called "Lipton's Orphans," helped Lipton make enough money to buy a tea plantation, and get his start in the tea business.

The tea bag was invented in 1908, by accident. A New York tea importer mailed his customers free samples of his tea, which he packaged in tiny silk bags. When the customers wrote back asking for more of the bags, the importer realized they were using them to steep tea…and began packaging all of his tea that way.

♦

Watch how tea leaves unfold in boiling water. Experts call this "the agony of the leaves."

DEATH OF A CLOWN

Abbie Hoffman loved to make political points by making Americans laugh. Did somebody take him too seriously? Here's information from a new book, It's a Conspiracy, *by the American Paranoid Society.*

B**ACKGROUND**
Rabble-Rouser
Abbie Hoffman was best known for co-founding the Yippies, a band of hairy anti-war freaks who assembled outside the Democratic Convention in Chicago to nominate a pig ("Pigasus") for President of the United States in 1968.

• The riots that followed were later blamed on the police, but Hoffman and seven other activists were hauled into court on "conspiracy" charges. They were known as the Chicago 8. After one of the most publicized trials of the '60s, the case was eventually thrown out of court.

Counterculture King of Satire.
His social satire (he called it "street theater") always attracted attention:

• When he fluttered three hundred crisp dollar bills down onto the floor of the New York Stock Exchange, there was pandemonium as brokers fought for the money.

• His plan to levitate the Pentagon made the front page.

• He called his second book *Steal This Book!* When no publisher would touch it (because of the title), he published it himself, sold 200,000 copies, and gave most of the money away.

The Fugitive
After getting busted for selling cocaine to an undercover policeman, he jumped bail, had plastic surgery and emerged shortly as Barry Freed, an environmental activist in upstate New York.

• Though he was "wanted" by the law, he regularly played softball with the New York State Police, testified to a congressional committee, and was commended by New York's Governor Cuomo for his work.

• As *Newsweek* wrote, "Hoffman may have been the first fugitive

---

The state of Pennsylvania is not named after William Penn. It's named after his father.

surrender with a press agent and a business manager. Before giving up, he summoned ABC's Barbara Walters...for a taping session."

• After a brief sentence, he went back to protest. His next book, *Steal This Urine Test* was an attack on "Reagan's repressive policy." And in 1987 he was back on the streets, getting arrested—along with Amy Carter—in an anti-CIA protest.

GOING FOR BUSH

• Abbie next took on George Bush, then running for President. In an October, 1988, *Playboy* article he co-authored, Hoffman broke the story of the "October Surprise." He alleged that Reagan supporters had made a deal with Iran to postpone the release of the hostages and keep President Carter from getting re-elected. In his version of the story, Bush had a key role in the conspiracy.

• Presumably, Amy Carter is the person who told Hoffman of her father's suspicions. With his nose for publicity, Hoffman knew it was an explosive story.

• There were rumors Hoffman was assembling a book on the subject. If he was as effective in presenting the story as he was in championing the counterculture during the '60s—and in getting publicity for it—he could have created real headaches for the Republicans...and potentially, the CIA.

WHAT HAPPENED

On April 12, 1989, when he was unable to contact Hoffman by phone, his landlord entered his house and found him in bed, dead.

OFFICIAL EXPLANATION

Coroner Thomas J. Rosko reportedly found the residue of about 150 pills and alcohol in Abbie's system. He said, "There is no way to take that amount of phenobarbital without intent. It was intentional and self-inflicted."

SUSPICIOUS FACTS

• **Hard to swallow:** Hoffman supposedly took 150 pills. One-tenth that number would have been enough to kill anyone.

• **Bad Brakes:** According to conspiracy theorist John Judge in

Alternative Perspectives on American Democracy, "When he went to deliver the manuscript to *Playboy* Abbie had an automobile accident....He told his friend and long-time fellow activist David Dellinger, that his brakes had been tampered with."

• **That's Incredible:** The *New York Times* quoted Dellinger as saying: "I don't believe for one moment the suicide thing." The reason: He had spoken with Hoffman recently and reported that Abbie had "numerous plans for the future."

• **No Glory:** His family didn't believe it either. In fact, almost all of Abbie Hoffman's friends were puzzled by the lack of a suicide note—he had a compelling need to express himself. As one of Hoffman's sons said, "Abbie was the kind of guy who, if he was going to do it, would wrap himself in a flag and jump off the top of the ITT building."

WAS THERE A CONSPIRACY?

THEORY #1:

YES. Somebody was afraid he knew too much and he was sure to create problems for the"Establishment" in the future. A number of journalists think he was able to break the "October Surprise" story with information received from President Jimmy Carter. Moreover, he had made a lot of powerful enemies during the '60s. He was an easy target, given his history of drug use.

THEORY #2

NO. Abbie generated a lot of strong feelings, and the people who loved him had a hard time accepting a suicide verdict. Abbie Hoffman was also a long-time manic-depressive, and was taking medication for it. He was very depressed by the Eighties. One night, he may have hit bottom.

PARTING SHOTS

"It's hard to believe that Abbie committed suicide—especially so late in the day that he missed The *New York Times*'s deadline."

—Paul Krassner (Abbie's fellow prankster),
in *The Nation*

SONGWRITER STORIES

Songwriters often have fascinating stories to tell about their compositions. Unfortunately, we rarely get to hear those tales. Fortunately, there's a great book called Behind the Hits, *by Bob Shannon and John Javna, full of entertaining stories like these.*

LOLA, The Kinks

As songwriter Ray Davies recounts it, he was spending the evening with record producer Robert Wace at a nightclub; Wace was having a bit of luck with a particular young lady. "I'm really onto a good thing here," Wace told Davies, indicating the sultry black woman he was dancing with. But as the night wore on, Davies got a little suspicious. He noticed stubble on the chin of Wace's new girlfriend. Davies decided "she" was a man. Presumably, Wace was so smashed he couldn't tell the difference.

Davies recalls: "I had a few dances with it…him. It became kind of obvious. It's that thrust in the pelvic region when they're on the dance floor. It's never quite the same with a woman."

Davies wrote "Lola" about that incident. But he kept the language deliberately ambiguous ("I'm glad that I'm a man / And so is Lola"), so listeners would never be able to decide whether Lola was a man, a woman…or what.

HONOLULU LULU, Jan and Dean

In the early '60s, Roger Christian was one of the top deejays in L.A. He sometimes did live shows at high schools, and his friends, Jan and Dean, often performed with him. One graduation night after a grueling schedule of personal appearances, the exhausted Christian and Jan Berry decided to go to The Copper Penny, an all-night L.A. diner, for something to eat. The two of them co-wrote many of Jan and Dean's hits and this night, as they sat at the table, they started writing another one. They based it on a title that a record company executive had suggested—"Honolulu Lulu."

Christian scribbled the lyrics down on a napkin, and then they paid and left the restaurant. Out front, they said good night. "Give me the napkin," Jan said, "and I'll take it to the studio and write out the arrangements." "I don't have it—you do," Christian replied. "No I don't—you do." "Not me." Suddenly they realized that they'd left it on the table in the restaurant.

They bolted inside to retrieve it, but it was too late. The waitress had already cleared their dishes and everything had been thrown away. Roger and Jan sat down and tried to reconstruct the song, but they just couldn't get the lyrics to work like they had the first time. There was only one thing left to do. They went out to the back of the diner and started sorting through the contents of the dumpster, looking for their napkin in the dark. At about 4:00 A.M., they finally found it. The reward for their treasure hunt? "Honolulu Lulu" hit #11 on the national charts.

THEY'RE COMING TO TAKE ME AWAY, HA-HAAA!, Napoleon XIV

In 1966, a 28-year-old New York recording engineer named Jerry Samuels went into the studio to record a song that had no melody and needed almost no instruments. It was recited, not sung, and he used only drums and a tambourine to back himself up. The total cost for studio time was $15.

But if the production of the song was a little unusual, that was nothing compared to the content. Essentially, the "singer" went insane while he was reciting the lyrics. His voice began in a normal tone, and slowly went up until it was as high-pitched as the Chipmunks. What was making him crazy? His dog had run away.

The whole thing was completely bizarre…and very funny.

The first record company Samuels played it for, Warner Brothers, snapped it up. Within a week after releasing the record, more than 500,000 copies had been sold, making it the fastest-selling record in Warner's history.

Although it went on to sell over a million copies, "They're Coming To Take Me Away" was taken off the radio almost immediately. Mental health organizations protested that the record made fun of the mentally ill…and shouldn't receive airplay. That was Napoleon XIV's Waterloo; we never heard from him again.

Note: Samuels didn't have any money—or a song—to put on the flip side, so he just reversed the tape. He called it "Aaah-Ah Yawa Em Ekat Ot Gnimoc Er-Yeht."

I PUT A SPELL ON YOU, Screamin' Jay Hawkins

In the summer of 1954, Screamin' Jay Hawkins, a blues singer with seven records—all bombs—under his belt, was performing at a joint in Atlantic City called Herman's. In the middle of his set, his live-in girlfriend walked in, marched right up to the stage and tossed his house keys at him. Then she disappeared. It looked bad...and it was. Jay went home to find "Good-bye, my love" scrawled in lipstick on the bathroom mirror.

He plopped down on the bed and let out "the most painful" scream of his life. Then he began writing a "sweet ballad" that he hoped would get her back—"I Put a Spell on You."

Hawkins recorded it for the tiny Grand Records in Philadelphia, and it, too, took a dive. He couldn't get his lover back with that record—she never heard it.

It wasn't a total loss, though. In the meantime, Jay incorporated the song into his act and the head of Columbia Records, Arnold Matson, happened to see him perform it in a typically wild manner. Matson loved it. He signed Hawkins to the Okeh label (primarily Columbia's R&B label), and they went into the studio to do a version. But something was wrong. They tried take after take, and Matson still wasn't happy with it. It just wasn't as powerful as when Jay did it live. Why? "Is there something you do when you perform that you're not doing here?" Matson asked. "Well," Jay told him, "I usually drink a bit when I'm on stage."

As Hawkins tells it: "So he brought in a case of Italian Swiss Colony muscatel and we all got our heads bent...We all got blind drunk." Hawkins couldn't even remember the session when it was over. "Ten days later the record came out. I listened to it and heard all those drunken groans and screams and yells. I thought, 'Oh, my god!'" It ended in a series of sexual moans, so many radio stations refused to play it. Even after Columbia remastered it to cut out the controversial ending, they couldn't get it on the air. So it never made the charts. But it did become a cult favorite, especially in live performances when Hawkins was carried out in a coffin, wore Dracula capes, and played with snakes. It has also been recorded dozens of times by artists like Creedence Clearwater Revival, and was the theme music for the 1984 cult film, *Stranger Than Paradise*.

Note: Jay got his girlfriend back. Not, ironically, because of "Spell," but because she liked the flip side, "Little Demon."

Humans are the only animals that cry.

ROYAL PAINS

Gossip about some famous kings and a queen.

K ING WENCESLAS
Was the Christmas carol about "Good King Wenceslas" accurate? Apparently not. The real Wenceslas was King of Bohemia and Holy Roman Emperor in the latter part of the 14th century. According to one source, he was a tyrant who "prowled the street with his cronies at night, breaking into houses, molesting his female subjects, and generally venting his feelings in a riot of cruelty."

He did love his hunting dogs, though; he even slept with them, over the objections of his wife, Johanna. (Even after one of the dogs attacked and killed her while she slept.)

MACBETH

There really was a Scottish king named Macbeth; he ruled from 1040 to 1057. But according to David Randall in *Royal Misbehavior*, "Although little is known about him, there is no evidence that he was the henpecked social climber portrayed by Shakespeare....[In fact], he was a good and strong enough ruler to survive on the throne for 17 years—which is more than 25 other occupants of that precarious hot spot can claim." Lady Macbeth, granddaughter of King Kenneth III, was known in her time as a "patron of the church"—not as the Shakespearean "royal bitch."

RICHARD THE LIONHEARTED

Maybe it's because of the legend of Robin Hood that Richard I is remembered as a righteous hero. But according to *Royal Misbehavior*: "He was in reality an absentee monarch who spent no more than ten months of a ten-year reign in England, left the country to the vagaries of his brother John and failed to produce an heir or even, it is said, consummate his marriage. Indeed, his sexual proclivities meant that Robin Hood and his chums were not the only young men...who followed the king with expectations."

The average dollar bill has a life span of 18 months.

IVAN THE TERRIBLE

Monarchs aren't often as fearsome as their nicknames imply. But Ivan IV, Czar of Russia in the mid-1500s, was worse. "As a child," writes one historian, "he amused himself by throwing cats and dogs from the [200-foot-high] towers of the Kremlin. As Czar, when a group of seventy citizens complained to him of injustices in their town, he ordered hot wine poured over their heads and had them lie naked in the snow. When it was rumored that the city of Novogorod was conspiring to defect to neighboring Lithuania, Ivan exterminated the city, torturing its citizens for five weeks and killing 60,000 people."

He was so terrifying that he could actually scare people to death. In 1569 the girl he'd picked to be his third wife had a heart attack and died when she heard the news.

CATHERINE THE GREAT

From *They Went That-A-Way*, by Malcolm Forbes: "What you've probably heard about the death of Russian Empress Catherine the Great is wrong. The poor maligned woman, insatiable lover that she was, did not die *in flagrante delicto* with a horse that, according to the famous rumor, crushed her when the truss broke. No, the 67-year-old ruler was alone when she collapsed, having dismissed her lover—a 27-year-old man—earlier that morning."

Apparently Catherine had a stroke in her dressing room and was found on the floor, unconscious. She died the following night without ever coming to.

KING FAROUK

The last king of Egypt was so corrupt that he once freed a pickpocket from jail just so the prisoner could teach him how to steal. Farouk became as adept at it. "At receptions and parties," says David Randall, "he would move among the company, brushing against dignitaries and their ladies and then slipping off into an ante-room [to] empty his pockets of watches, wallets, lighters, and powder compacts. Eventually an entire warehouse was filled with these items, which even included the ceremonial sword, belt, and medals stolen from the body of the Shah of Persia as the funeral procession passed through Egypt in 1944."

Salt is the only rock humans can eat.

A FOOD IS BORN

Those brand names on your supermarket shelf had to come from somewhere, right? Here's the inside scoop on a few famous food products.

ANIMAL COOKIES. Cookies shaped like animals were introduced in England in the 1890s, but in 1902 Nabisco added something new. Recognizing the popularity of P.T. Barnum's "Greatest Show on Earth," they designed a box that looked like a circus cage, labeling it "Barnum's Animals." And to increase sales during the holiday season, they added a string handle that would allow parents to hang the boxes on Christmas trees.

TABASCO SAUCE. When Union troops in Louisiana occupied Avery Island and seized Edmund McIhenny's salt mines in 1862, he and his wife fled to Texas. They returned after the war to find that everything they owned had been destroyed—except for a crop of capsicum hot peppers. Desperate, McIhenny decided to try to make a sauce that he could sell to raise money. He aged a concoction of salt, vinegar and peppers in wooden barrels, and poured it into tiny old cologne bottles. He called his creation "tabasco sauce," after Mexico's Tabasco river, because he liked the name.

WORCESTERSHIRE SAUCE. When Sir Marcus Sandys, a British nobleman, returned to England from Bengal in the mid-1800s, he brought with him a recipe for a spicy sauce he had tasted in the Orient. He showed it to some chemists he knew in his home county of Worcestershire—John Lea and William Perrins—and asked them to reproduce the sauce exclusively for his use. Lea and Perrins agreed, but over time the sauce became so popular that Sandys gave them permission to sell it to other customers—and eventually sold them the recipe—which the Lea & Perrins Company uses to this day.

DUNCAN HINES. Duncan Hines was a traveling restaurant critic in the 1930s. His book *Adventures in Good Eating*—a guide to restaurants along major highways—was so popular that his name became a household word. Hines' notoriety attracted the attention of Roy Park, a New York businessman who was looking for a way to promote his new line of baked goods. He asked Hines to become a partner in the company, and Hines agreed. Together they formed Hines-Park Foods, Inc. in 1948. Their line of cake mixes captured 48% of the American cake mix market in less than *three weeks.*

YUBAN COFFEE. John Arbuckle, a turn-of-the-century Brooklyn merchant, sold his own popular blend of coffee. He needed a brand name for it, and decided to make one up using the letters that appeared on the shipments of coffee beans he received:

A B
N Y

(Arbuckle Brothers, New York) The combination he liked best was Yban. But it still wasn't quite right—so he added the letter u.

LOG CABIN SYRUP. P.J. Towle, a St. Paul, Minnesota grocer, was the first person to blend expensive maple syrup with other, more affordable syrups without losing the maple taste. A big fan of Abraham Lincoln, Towle decided to name the syrup Log Cabin in his honor—and sold it in cabin-shaped tin containers.

ORVILLE REDENBACHER'S POPCORN. In the 1950s an agronomist named Orville Redenbacher developed a hybrid strain of popcorn with a higher moisture content than regular corn—resulting in fluffier kernels and fewer "old maids" per batch. But popcorn companies refused to buy it—they insisted the public wanted *cheap* popcorn, not *good* popcorn. Redenbacher disagreed. He began selling to the public directly. Today Orville Redenbacher's is the best selling popcorn in the U.S.

• • •

WEIGHTING FOR A TRAIN
U.S. President William Taft weighed over 300 pounds. He used it to his advantage: once while stranded at a train station in the country, he was told that the express only stopped for "large parties." He sent a wire to the conductor saying "Stop at Hicksville. Large party waiting to catch train." Once on board, he explained: "You can go ahead. I am the large party."

TV OR NOT TV?

What's a Bathroom Reader without a little TV trivia?

THE PARTRIDGE FAMILY
Love them or hate them, *The Partridge Family* made money. Their show, records, and licensed merchandise reportedly earned $11 million a year. In addition, more than 200,000 people paid $2 each for membership in their fan club—and the *Partridge Family Magazine* sold 400,000 copies a month. They even had 7 hit singles—in spite of the fact that none of them played on the records, and only David Cassidy and Shirley Jones sang on them.

THE LOVE BOAT. This show was based on *The Love Boats:* a novel written by a former cruise hostess. She based it on her own experiences.
• The show was always filmed on a real cruise ship, with passengers acting as extras. But before the show's success, it was difficult to get passengers to cooperate; they complained that the film crew was in their way.

THE BRADY BUNCH. Executive producer Sherwood Schwartz interviewed 464 girls and boys to find the right Brady kids. He hadn't picked the adult leads yet, but he knew he wanted the kids to have the same color hair as their "parents." His solution: he picked two sets of Brady boys, and two sets of Brady girls (blonde and brunette). When Robert Reed and Florence Henderson were chosen to play the parents, he dumped the kids he didn't need.

I DREAM OF JEANNIE. Although network censors had no objection to Barbara Eden's sexy costume or the fact that Jeannie was living with a man for whom she would do anything (anything?), they *did* object to her navel showing. The solution: she had to put a cloth plug in it so it wouldn't show on film.
• Scripts were written by novelist Sidney Sheldon, who was writing scripts for "The Patty Duke Show" at the same time.

The only Hitchcock film to win the Oscar for best film of the year was *Rebecca,* in 1940.

TWO THUMBS DOWN

Are book reviews believable? When they're good reviews of Uncle John's Bathroom Reader *they are, of course. But consider these true-life comments, quoted in* Rotten Reviews *by Bill Henderson*

Subject: *Wuthering Heights,* by Emily Brönte
Reviewer's Comment: "The only consolation we have in reflecting upon it is that it will never be generally read."
—James Lorimer, *North British Review*

Subject: *Gulliver's Travels,* by Jonathan Swift
Reviewer's Comment: "Evidence of a diseased mind and lacerated heart." —John Dunlop, *The History of Fiction*

Subject: *Romeo & Juliet,* by William Shakespeare:
Reviewer's Comment: "March 1 [1662]. Saw *Romeo and Juliet,* the first time it was ever acted; but it is a play of itself the worst that ever I heard in my life, and the worst acted that ever I saw these people do." —Samuel Pepys, *Diary*

Subject: *Alice in Wonderland,* by Lewis Carroll
Reviewer's Comment: "We fancy that any real child might be more puzzled than enchanted by this stiff, overwrought story." —*Children's Books.*

Subject: *A Tale of Two Cities,* by Charles Dickens
Reviewer's Comment: "It was a sheer dead pull from start to finish. It all seemed so insincere, such a transparent make-believe, a mere piece of acting."—John Burroughs, *Century* magazine

Subject: *Anna Karenina,* by Leo Tolstoy
Reviewer's Comment: " Sentimental rubbish ...Show me one page that contains an idea." —*The Odessa Courier*

Subject: *A Doll's House,* by Henrik Ibsen
Reviewer's Comment: "It is as though someone had dramatized the cooking of a sunday dinner."—Clement Scott, *Sporting & Dramatic News*

Subject: *Moby Dick*, by Herman Melville
Reviewer's Comment: "A huge dose of hyperbolic slang, maudlin sentimentalism and tragic-comic bubble and squeak."—Willima Harrison Ainsworth, *New Monthly Magazine*

Subject: *The Great Gatsby*, by F. Scott Fitzgerald
Reviewer's Comment: "A little slack, a little soft, more than a little artificial, *The Great Gatsby* falls into the class of negligible novels."—*The Springfield Republican*

Subject: *The Sun Also Rises*, by Ernest Hemingway
Reviewer's Comment: "His characters are as shallow as the saucers in which they stack their daily emotions, and instead of interpreting his material—or even challenging it—he has been content merely to make a carbon copy of a not particularly significant surface life of Paris."—*The Dial*

Subject: *From Here to Eternity*, by James Jones
Reviewer's Comment: "Certainly America has something better to offer the world, along with its arms and armies, than such a confession of spiritual vacuum as this."—*Christian Science Monitor*

Subject: *Babbitt*, by Sinclair Lewis
Reviewer's Comment: "As a humorist, Mr. Lewis makes valiant attempts to be funny; he merely succeeds in being silly. In fact it is as yellow a novel as novel can be."—*Boston Evening Transcript*

AND THE MOTHER OF ALL "ROTTEN REVIEWS"

Subject: *Lady Chatterly's Lover*, by D. H. Lawrence:
Reviewer's Comments: "This pictorial account of the day-by-day life of an English gamekeeper is full of considerable interest to outdoor minded readers, as it contains many passages on pheasant-raising, the apprehending of poachers, ways to control vermin, and other chores and duties of the professional gamekeeper. Unfortunately, one is obliged to wade through many pages of extraneous material in order to discover and savor these sidelights on the management of a midland shooting estate, and in this reviewer's opinion the book cannot take the place of J. R. Miller's *Practical Gamekeeping*." —Ed Zern, *Field & Stream*

If you live in Kentucky, you're required by law to bathe at least once a year.

KENNEDY QUOTES

Robert Kennedy's legacy is his idealism...and his fatalism.
A few of the comments he left for us:

"One-fifth of the people are against everything all the time."

"I should like to love my country and still love justice."

"Some men see things as they are and ask, 'Why?' I dream of things that could be and ask, 'Why not?' "

"My views on birth control are distorted by the fact that I was seventh of nine children."

"Who knows if any of us will still be alive in 1972? Existence is so fickle, fate is so fickle."

"We give our money and go back to our homes and...our swimming pools and wonder, 'Why don't they keep quiet, why don't they go away?' "

"A revolution is coming—a revolution which will be peaceful if we are wise enough; compassionate if we care enough; successful if we are fortunate enough—but a revolution is coming whether we will it or not. We can affect its character; we cannot alter its inevitability."

"[Freedom] proposes ends, but it does not propose means."

"Every society gets the kind of criminal it deserves."

"What is dangerous about extremists is not that they are extreme, but that they are intolerant. The evil is not what they say about their cause, but what they say about their opponents."

(On learning of his brother's assassination). "I thought they'd get one of us, but Jack, after all he's been through, never worried about it...I thought it would be me."

"Did the CIA kill my brother?"

"With all the violence and killings we've had in the United States, I think you will agree that we must keep firearms from people who have no business with guns." (5 days later, he was assassinated.)

The emperor penguin can dive to depths of 870 ft. for as long as 18 minutes.

REMEMBER THE MAINE!

In 1898, America declared war against Spain. But was it caused by Spanish atrocities or newspaper profits? Here's information from a new book, It's a Conspiracy, *by the American Paranoid Society.*

B
ACKGROUND
Itching for a Fight

In the late 1890s, America was bursting at the seams. Having reached the end of its frontier, the nation now looked for new lands to conquer and causes to fight for. As young Teddy Roosevelt, put it, "I should welcome almost any war, for I think this country needs one."

The Newspaper Wars

• Had Roosevelt worked for a New York City newspaper, he would have found all the fighting he wanted. The city's dailies were locked in a fierce struggle for circulation.

• With seemingly endless millions to spend, young William Randolph Hearst from California bought the *New York Journal* and took on the city's largest daily, the *World*. He started by cutting the paper's price to a penny, though he lost money doing it. Then, to further outrage the *World's* publisher, Joseph Pulitzer, Hearst lured away his most talented people with strapping raises.

• But the real war was on the front pages, and its biggest casualty was the truth. Both papers favored "crime, underwear and indignation." So when Cuban separatists tried to overthrow the rotting empire of Spain, the dailies fought to make each dispatch more lurid than the last.

Extra! Extra!

• Sample from the *World*: "No man's life, no man's property is safe. American citizens are imprisoned or slain without cause...Blood on the roadsides, blood in the fields, blood on the doorsteps, blood, blood, blood!"

• Sample headline from the *Journal*, responding to a Spanish diplomat's remark—in a private letter—that President McKinley was "a low politician":

"THE WORST INSULT TO THE UNITED STATES IN ITS HISTORY!"

DATELINE, CUBA

• Offended by press attacks against them, Spanish authorities in Cuba restricted U.S. reporters to Havana. In response, the U.S.S. *Maine* was sent to Havana harbor, "to protect American interests." A quiet three weeks passed. Then, on February 15, 1898, the *Maine* was sunk by a mysterious explosion; 260 men died.

• The *Maine*'s Captain Sigsbee, cabled Washington, "Many killed and wounded...Don't send war vessels...Public opinion should be suspended until further report."

• When Spain's captain-general in charge of Cuba heard the news, he "burst into tears...and sent officers to express regret and organize assistance." The Spanish, joined by a U.S. Navy team, began investigating the cause of the explosion immediately. Their findings were eventually released on March 17.

JUMPING THE GUN

The papers couldn't wait, though. Hearst's *Journal* led the cry for war with headlines like:

"The Warship Maine Was Split In Two By An Enemy's Secret Infernal Machine" (Feb. 17)

"The Whole Country Thrills With The War Fever" (Feb. 18)

"Havana...insults The Memory Of The Maine Victims" (Feb. 23)

"War! Sure!" (March 1)

• Although the Spanish government finally met the United States' demands about freedom for Cuba—and President McKinley urged restraint—most Americans were howling for war. For example, "Frank James, ex-bandit brother of the legendary Jesse, offered to lead a company of cowboys."

• Ultimately, though, the decision rested on the Navy's findings.

Napoleon conquered Italy at the age of twenty-six.

OFFICIAL EXPLANATION

The Naval Court of Inquiry found that "the *Maine* was destroyed by the explosion of a submarine mine"; however, it was "unable to obtain evidence fixing the responsibility...upon any person or persons." America went to war.

SUSPICIOUS FACTS

• In addition to Captain Sigsbee's plea to withhold judgment, the *Journal*'s first dispatch from Cuba was also uncertain: "The injured do not know what caused the explosion. There is some doubt as to whether the explosion took place on the *Maine*."

• According to *The Yellow Kids*, "The Navy's new coal-powered warships...like the Maine [had] coal bunkers located near the ship's [gunpowder] magazines. There had been at least a dozen reported incidents on American ships in the previous year, and during one fire...sparks actually ignited wooden ammunition crates before the blaze was brought under control."

• The Navy Secretary "publicly announced his opinion that an explosion in the *Maine*'s magazine had caused the accident," and McKinley himself thought "the catastrophe had resulted from an internal explosion."

• Two days after the explosion, the navy's leading expert on explosives told a reporter that "no torpedo [or mine] as is known to modern warfare can of itself cause an explosion as powerful as that which destroyed the *Maine*."

WAS THERE A CONSPIRACY?

Theory #1: YES. William Randolph Hearst started a war with Spain to boost circulation. His quote to artist Frederick Remington is well-known: "You supply the pictures, I'll supply the war."

• On either side of the *Journal*'s front-page masthead ran the blurb, "How Do You Like The *Journal*'s War?"—until even Hearst saw its tastelessness and removed it.

• If it was a conspiracy, it worked: For the first week after the explosion, the *Journal* averaged 8-1/2 pages on the *Maine*. And the paper's circulation "soared from 416,885 copies on January 9th to 1,036,140 on February 18th."

Theory #2: YES. But the navy was also complicit. Unless the Naval Court of Inquiry found that Spain was guilty, it would have had to admit the Navy had been negligent.

• In August, 1897, a bunker fire interrupted a dinner party Captain Sigsbee was hosting on the *Maine*. As he helped his guests down the gangplank he said, "Gentlemen, you have had a narrow escape tonight."

• During the inquiry, Sigsbee likely perjured himself. Although he was vague and "unfamiliar with the ship," he claimed that the day of the explosion he had personally inspected the bunker wall and found it cool. Nobody on the panel believed him.

• Although the navy report was supposed to be delivered to the White House under the strictest confidentiality, its findings were published in the *Journal* before President McKinley even opened the secret document.

Theory #3: NO. American industrialists needed a war to distract the public; Hearst was just a bit player, albeit a noisy one.

• A depression had begun in 1893 and showed no signs of ending soon. This was causing widespread strikes, farm revolts and a dramatic growth of the Populist movement.

• As one industrialist put it, "A little war will knock the pus out of Populism." Another noted that "it will take men's minds off domestic concerns."

• With the American frontier used up, untouched lands overseas would give businesses new lands to exploit.

• The American people were undoubtedly whipped up by Hearst and his ilk, but they overwhelmingly supported the war, at least as a fight for Cuban liberty.

RANDOM QUOTE:
"The last thing I could imagine is moving in with three other friends, no matter how much I liked them."
                    —Betty White, star of "Golden Girls."

The White House's first telephone was installed by Alexander Graham Bell.

GOING THROUGH A PHRASE

Here are some well-known phrases and the stories behind them.

TURN A BLIND EYE
Meaning: To ignore something.

Background: Captain Horatio Nelson of the British Navy was blind in one eye. In 1801, he was part of a force attacking French troops in Copenhagen, Denmark. As the tide of battle turned, the command ship signaled for Nelson to withdraw, but Nelson wanted to continue fighting. When he was told that his commander was signalling, Nelson held his telescope up to his sightless eye and declared that he could not see any signal. He continued his attack ...and won.

CHARLEY HORSE
Meaning: A muscle cramp.

Background: In 1640 Charles I of England expanded the London police force. The new recruits were nicknamed "Charleys." There wasn't enough money to provide the new police with horses, so they patrolled on foot. They joked that their sore feet and legs came from riding "Charley's horse."

BURY THE HATCHET
Meaning: To make peace with an enemy.

Background: Some Native American tribes declared peace by literally burying a tomahawk in the ground.

SPEAK OF THE DEVIL
Meaning: Someone appears after you mention him or her.

Background: People believed that you could actually summon the devil by saying his name (to be safe, they used nicknames and euphemisms like "the Deuce"). Over time, the expression was used to jokingly imply that your friend was "Old Nick" himself.

AT THE END OF YOUR ROPE

Meaning: Exhausted all possibilities; out of options.

Background: Horsemen tied their horses to trees with long lengths of rope so they could graze a large area of land. But when the horse ate all the grass within its reach, it was out of luck, literally "at the end of its rope." An alternate but equally plausible explanation for the phrase has to do with being strung up on the gallows.

SOW WILD OATS

Meaning: Commit youthfully foolish acts.

Background: In the 11th century, when England was in the midst of its perpetual war against invaders, many farms were left to go fallow for years, even decades. Many of the grains which had been domesticated over generations reverted to their wild strains. When things settled down on the war front, a lot of the younger men had no experience farming and—eager to get on with it—collected seeds from the wild strains of oats, which grew great leaves and trunks, but few of the "heads" which contain the edible seeds. The plants weren't even worth harvesting.

WHITE ELEPHANT

Meaning: A costly but unwanted object.

Background: When the kings of ancient Siam didn't like someone, they sometimes "honored" them with a rare, sacred White Elephant. The beasts cost a fortune to feed and keep in style befitting their high station—but because they were considered sacred, they couldn't be expected to work like normal elephants.

TO BE AT LOOSE ENDS

Meaning: Frazzled and disorganized

Background: On old sailing ships, hundreds of ropes went everywhere. If they were allowed to unravel, they quickly became a tangled, disorganized mess. A mark of a good sea captain became the condition of his neatly taped "ends"; you could tell an inefficient and disorganized ship by its number of loose ends.

Random Quote: "People don't have much of a sense of humor when they themselves are victimized." —William F. Buckley

The first electric toothbrush was developed and tested on dogs. They reportedly enjoyed it.

PASS THE KETCHUP

Can you imagine life without ketchup? One BRI member tells the story of a French visitor who automatically started to pour ketchup on pancakes. When the host stopped him, the surprised visitor asked "Don't Americans put ketchup on everything?" Here's a little ketchup history.

ORIGIN. The Chinese invented *ke-tsiap*—a concoction of pickled fish and spices (but no tomatoes)—in the 1690s. By the early 1700s its popularity had spread to Malaysia, where British explorers first encountered it. By 1740 the sauce—renamed *ketchup*—was an English staple, and was becoming popular in the American colonies.

A BAD APPLE

Tomato ketchup wasn't invented until the 1790s, when New England colonists first mixed tomatoes into the sauce. Why did it take so long to add tomatoes? People were afraid to eat them. The tomato is a close relative of the toxic belladonna and nightshade plants; most people assumed the tomato was also poisonous. Thomas Jefferson helped dispel the myth; his highly publicized love of tomatoes helped popularize them.

KETCHUP FACTS

• Homemade tomato ketchup starts out as a watery gruel that has to be boiled down into a thick sauce—an all-day project that requires hours of stirring. Housewives of the 1870s loved the sauce, but they hated making it. So when Henry J. Heinz began selling bottled ketchup in 1875, he promoted it as a labor-saving device. He used the slogan "blessed relief for Mother and the other women of the household." Today more than half the ketchup sold in the U.S. is made by the H.J. Heinz Co.

• Note: Have you ever poured ketchup on something, wrapped it in aluminum foil, and then noticed later that there were holes in the foil? The ketchup is to blame; it's highly acidic and can actually dissolve small amounts of aluminum if it remains in contact with the metal long enough.

The average American uses two pine trees' worth of paper products each year.

GLASSIFIED INFORMATION

You don't have to throw glass bottles and containers out with the trash; they're recyclable. Here are more recycling tips from The Recycler's Handbook, *by the EarthWorks Group*

I t's interesting to listen to people talk about why they like glass. The appeal is more than just being able to recycle it easily— they like the way it looks and feels, too.

It's an ancient attraction. Glass bottles and jars have been a part of human culture for more than 3,000 years. We've been recycling them just about that long, too. In fact, it's conceivable that some of the glass you'll use today was once part of a bottle used by Richard the Lion-Hearted or Catherine the Great.

Of course it's not likely, but so what? The point is that recycling glass is a time-honored tradition. It's up to us to keep it going for the next 3,000 years.

A TOUCH OF GLASS

• Before recycled glass is shipped to manufacturers, it's broken so it'll take up less space. This broken glass is called "cullet."

• When it arrives at the glass factory, the cullet is run through a device which removes metal rings from bottles. A vacuum process removes plastic coatings and paper labels.

• When it's "clean," the cullet is added to raw materials and melt-ed down with them. Most bottles and jars contain at least 25% re-cycled glass.

• Glass never wears out—it can be recycled forever.

WHY RECYCLE?

• We save over a ton of resources for every ton of glass recycled. (If you want specifics, it's 1,330 pounds of sand, 433 pounds of soda ash, 433 pounds of limestone, and 151 pounds of feldspar.)

• A ton of glass produced from raw materials creates 384 pounds of mining waste. Using 50% recycled glass cuts it by about 75%.

• We get 27.8 pounds of air pollution for every ton of new glass produced. Recycling glass reduces that pollution by 14-20%.

• Recycling glass saves 25-32% of the energy used to make glass.

• Glass makes up about 8% of America's municipal garbage.

SIMPLE THINGS YOU CAN DO

1. Precycle

• Look for refillable bottles. They're the most energy and material efficient; they can be sterilized and reused up to seven times before recycling.

• Refillables aren't easy to find any more. But if enough consumers speak up at local supermarkets, they'll reappear on shelves. Case in point: Washington's Rainier Brewery, citing its customers' environmental concerns, has recently returned to using refillables for all its single serving bottles.

• An easy way to manage refillables: Get one of the sturdy crates they come in, and store "empties" in it. When the crates are full, take them to the store and exchange the empties for full bottles.

• In some areas of the Midwest and Mountain states, glass is not accepted because there's no market for it. In these areas, consider buying aluminum cans, which are recycled virtually everywhere.

2. Store It

• It's safer to pack bottles in boxes or bins than in bags.

• Don't leave the bottles in six-pack carriers; that makes extra processing work for recyclers (they have to remove the bottles).

• If you're selling your glass at a buyback center or dropping it off, you'll probably have to separate it into brown, green and clear glass. The reason: To make recycling profitable, glass factories need to turn brown glass into brown bottles, etc. If colors are mixed, the end product is an unpredictable hue. Glass factories don't like it because their orders are for specific colors.

• If you have any blue or other colored glass containers, recycle them with the brown or green glass—but only in small amounts.

- If the glass is even slightly tinted, sort as colored, not as clear.
- Broken bottles can be recycled, but not everyone accepts them.
- Curbside programs generally accept all colors mixed together; sorting occurs later. Keep glass unbroken if possible—it's easier for the recycling crew to handle.

3. Recycle

- Remove lids and caps. You can recycle steel caps with steel cans. (Plastic cap liners are no problem). For aluminum caps, check with the recycling center before including them with aluminum cans.
- It's okay to leave on neck rings, paper and plastic labels—they burn or blow off in the recycling process.
- Dump out food residue and lightly rinse bottles. Old food attracts animals, it's a mess for recyclers, and it stinks. Be sure to empty beer bottles. A drop of beer can turn into a slimy mold.
- Remove rocks and dirt from bottles found in parks, beaches, etc. Even a little stone can ruin a whole load of glass.

4. Absolutely Don't Include...

- Windows, drinking glasses, mirrors, Pyrex (baking dishes, coffee pots, etc.), or other glass. Any of these can ruin an entire batch of glass if they slip through at the factory. The reason: They don't melt at the same temperature as bottles.
- Ceramics (coffee mugs, mustard jars, plates, etc.). They don't melt down with the glass, so they contaminate it.

IF YOUR STATE HAS A "BOTTLE BILL..."

- Not all states accept the same bottles for redemption. Some take only beer and soft drink bottles; others include juice or liquor bottles. Check with stores or recycling centers.
- General Rules: Empty bottles; you may need to sort them by brand to get your deposit back. Broken bottles aren't redeemable.

SOURCES

"Glass Recycling: Why? How?" The Glass Packaging Institute, 1801 K St. N.W., Suite 1105-L, Washington, D.C. 20006.

If tin cans were really made of tin, you could crush them with your hand.

ELVIS TRIVIA

It's become a Bathroom Reader tradition to include a few sections on The King in every book. Here are bits of Elvis gossip.

Elvis didn't sing well enough to make his high school glee club.

Although he has received many co-writing credits, Elvis never wrote a song. His manager (Col. Tom Parker) simply told songwriters that Elvis wouldn't record their songs unless he got credit—and half the royalties.

Over the years, Elvis bought more than 100 Cadillacs and gave away around 20 of them. The first one he bought was a pink one for his mom.

There are 50 dogs named Elvis registered in Los Angeles county.

Elvis's favorite sandwich: grilled peanut butter and banana.

★

Elvis's 1956 two-sided hit, "Hound Dog"/"Don't Be Cruel," is the most popular jukebox selection of all time.

Every day the U.S. Postal Service receives at least one letter on the advisability of issuing an Elvis stamp. Mail is currently running 6 to 1 in favor.

According to one author, in 1960 Elvis began secretly dating Frank Sinatra's girlfriend, Juliet Prowse. Sinatra found out and one night showed up at Elvis's dressing room with two "unpleasant companions." Frank and friends "discussed Presley's continued good health." Elvis refused to return Prowse's calls after that.

If it wasn't for Colonel Parker torpedoing the offers, Elvis could have starred in *Midnight Cowboy* and opposite Barbra Streisand in *A Star is Born*.

Elvis' autopsy revealed that he had at least 10 different drugs in his system at the time of death. Official cause of death: heart failure brought on by "straining at stool." Translation: he died on the pot.

Rule of thumb: Widowed, divorced, and separated people smoke more than other people.

UNCLE JOHN'S BATHROOM CATALOG

*Looking for some "singing" toilet paper? How about "tinkle time targets"?
No bathroom reader's bathroom is complete without them. Here are
a few key bathroom items you can order by mail.*

The Little Plastic Cup

"Everybody's had to do it. The nurse tells you to go into the bathroom at the end of the hall and 'give us a sample.' And how many times have you sat in there until they had to come looking for you and you had to confess, sheepishly, that you 'just couldn't.' Now you can practice at home, and train yourself to avoid the embarrassment (or relive the thrill, if that's your thing)."

Specimen cup,
Item No. 20120

5 oz. Jerryco Inc.
601 Linden Place
Evanston, IL 60202

Tinkle Targets

"Teaching your little boys to aim properly when they're being toilet trained (and after) can be a trying chore. This'll turn boys of any age into sharpshooters. Each pack contains 45 colorful, flushable, non-staining targets. Just float one in the bowl and fire away."

Tinkle Targets
Item # G225

The Right Start Catalog
Right Start Plaza
5334 Sterling Center Drive
Westlake Village, CA 91361

Pink Flamingo Toilet Paper

"Flamingo toilet tissue can help you with any impossible bathroom decorating task. This is an exclusive "The Cat's Pyjamas" design; order their catalog and check out some of their other great flamingo bathroom items like shower curtains, toothbrush holders and towel bars."

Flamingo Toilet Paper
Item # CP756

The Cat's Pyjamas
20 Church Street
Montclair, NJ 07042

There are 35 pet-death support groups in the U.S.

Gag Black-Hands Soap

"Looks like regular designer soap, the manufacturers claim. But nobody would guess that when they wash their hands, the black color comes off the soap and stays on them. Easy way to tell which of your friends habitually 'forgets' to wash hands after using the bathroom."

Black Soap   Johnson Smith Company
Item # 2419   4514 19th Court East
                            PO Box 25500
                            Bradenton, FL 34206-5500

Toity Tunes

"'A musical novelty! Makes your toilet paper sing!' reads the colorful hang tag. And the battery is INCLUDED! This ingenious, maddening, little electronic device slips inside the toilet paper roll. When the tissue is pulled, what sounds like a mosquito orchestra starts loudly playing one of these old favorites: Christmas Medley, Happy Birthday, My Favorite Things, Home Sweet Home, Wedding March, Love Me Tender, Yesterday, Twinkle Twinkle Little Star, It's a Small World, Over the Rainbow, You Are My Sunshine, When the Saints Go Marching In, and our favorite: The Star Spangled Banner, since true patriots will leap to attention when this starts to play…"

Toity Tunes   Funny Side Up.
                            25 Stump Rd.
                            N. Wales, PA 19454

• • •

FROM OUR MUHAMMAD ALI FILES:

Just before takeoff on a commercial flight, a stewardess asked Ali to make sure his seat belt was fastened. "Superman don't need no seat belt," he protested. She answered: "Superman don't need no airplane, either." He fastened it.

DRIVE-IN MOVIES

*Although they've all but disappeared from the American landscape,
drive-in movies were once the coolest thing around.*

THE BIRTH OF THE DRIVE-IN

Richard M. Hollingshead Jr. had friends over one summer night in the late 1920s to see his home movies. It was a hot night, and the projector just made it hotter. Seeing his guests' discomfort, the inventor and businessman had an idea—why not show his movies outside?

He put his projector on the hood of the family's model T and projected image onto the white wall of his garage. His guests—and eventually the whole neighborhood—lounged on his car seats and lawn furniture.

Hollingshead knew he had a hit when his guests asked to see more of his home movies. While the picture flickered in front of his eyes, he started thinking about business possibilities.

COMMERCIAL POTENTIAL

His first idea was that gas stations could keep their patrons amused with short comedies or nature films while filling their tanks. That idea went nowhere. Then one night, he had a vision of an all-car outdoor movie theater where people could watch in the privacy and comfort of their own cars. He started tinkering with the idea, even watching films with his lawn sprinkler going to see if it was possible to watch a movie during a rain storm.

THE REAL THING

"The World's First Automobile Movie Theater" opened on May 6, 1933 at 2601 Admiral Wilson Boulevard in Camden, New Jersey. It was primitive, yet brilliant—room for 400 cars in seven rows of parking spots tilted at a 5% grade for better reclining and visibility. The site was provided by V. V. Smith, an early investor who happened to have made his fortune in parking lots. On opening night some 600 customers paid 25¢ per car plus 25¢ per person ($1.00 tops) to see *Wife Beware* starring Adolph Menjou.

George Washington, Thomas Jefferson, and John Adams played marbles even as adults.

Hollingshead had some trouble with sound. At first he embedded speakers in the ground under each car space, but the floorboards muffled the sounds. Next, he tried huge speakers on either side of the screen. Now everybody in cars could hear every word perfectly—but so could the unhappy neighbors and the freeloaders who watched from just outside the theatre boundary. He abandoned that, too, and next tried individual car speakers hanging on the car windows. Perfect.

Unfortunately, Hollingshead was ahead of his time. Film distributors, seeing the drive-in as a threat to indoor theatres, charged exorbitantly high rental prices and withheld their best first-runs. In 1935, a disgusted Hollingshead sold his theater.

RISE & FALL

But soon after, drive-in movies caught on. The baby boom of the late 1940s was also an automobile boom. People quickly discovered they could dress casually, bring their own food, smoke, talk, steam up the windows, and bring the kids without paying for a sitter. For teens, roomy back seats provided an arena for love's wrestling matches. The marriage of car and movie seemed perfect.

But not for long. Encroaching suburbia drove up cheap rural land prices, cars got smaller, TV became popular, the opportunities for sexual ecounters expanded, and the quality of the drive-in film fare declined from first run to B-minus. Drive-ins began disappearing from across the landscape, including Hollingshead's original one—its former site is now occupied by a fur store.

DRIVE-IN FACTS

• Some drive-in theatres even offered drive-in church services on Sunday morning. You didn't have to dress up and you said "Amen!" by honking your horn.

• In the late 1950s and early 1960s, over 4,000 drive-ins operated across the U.S.

• There are only about 1,000 operational drive-ins now. The National Association of Drive-In Operators is defunct.

Alaska does not have a state motto.

NAME THAT TOWN

*The origins of the names of cities and towns are
sometimes more interesting than the places themselves.*

Place: Anaconda, Montana
Background: In Copperopolis, Montana during the Civil
War, owners of the local copper mine were strong supporters
of the Union cause. Late in the war, word reached them that
General Grant's troops were circling Genreral Lee's troops "like an
anaconda"—the large snake that wraps itself around its prey and
squeezes it to death. To celebrate, they changed the mine's name to
Anaconda, and the town eventually followed suit.

Places: Bushong and Latham, Kansas
Background: In the 1880s, workers for the Missouri Pacific railroad
were building a new line through Kansas. To celebrate the success
of their hometown baseball team, the St. Louis Browns (who were
in the middle of a winning streak) they named 14 stations on the
line for their favorite players. Twelve of the stations have been
renamed, but Arlie Latham (shortstop) and Doc Bushong (pitcher)
are still on the map in Kansas.

Place: Pullman, Washington
Background: The citizens of this community decided to name their
town after George M. Pullman, the rich manufacturer of the
Pullman Car...hoping he would shower his namesake with new
libraries and other civic gifts. When they invited him to the
ceremonies, he sent his regrets, a nice thank you note and a check
for $50. That was the last the town heard from him.

Place: Eighty Eight, Kentucky
Background: Dabney Nunnally was the postmaster of a village 8.8
miles from Glasgow, KY. His handwriting was unreadable, but he
could scrawl legible numbers. "Let's call our place 88," he proposed.
"I can write that so anybody can read it." Unfortunately for
Nunnally, the government insisted that the name be spelled out.

A company in Australia makes coffins out of recycled newspapers.

Place: Old Glory, Texas
Background: Before World War I, this town was called Brandenburg. But anti-German sentiment ran so high during the war that no one wanted to live in a place that sounded German.

Place: Naughty Girl Meadow, Arizona
Background: The US Board of Geographic Names wouldn't allow them to use the real name—Whorehouse Meadow.

Place: Lufkin, Texas
Background: Surveyor E. P. Lufkin was laying out a railroad route, and some of his workers were jailed in nearby Homer, Texas for drunkenness. In retaliation, Luflkin rerouted the tracks to miss Homer completely. The newly located station, which he named for himself, flourished; Homer disappeared.

Place: Modesto, California
Background: Named because the founders were too "modest" to name it after themselves.

Place: Truth or Consequences, New Mexico
Background: In 1950, the hit radio show *Truth or Consequences* offered free publicity and valuable prizes to any town that would change its name. Hot Springs, NM quickly volunteered and even named the park in the center of town Ralph Edwards Park, after the game show's host

Place: Titusville, Florida
Background: In 1873, Henry Titus and Charles Rice decided to play a game of dominoes to decide who to name the town after.

Place: Tarzana, California
Background: Named after Tarzan to honor his creator, Edgar Rice Burroughs, who lived there for many years.

The only known meteorite fatality was a dog hit in Egypt in 1922.

THE PRESS & THE PREZ

Presidents and the press have a peculiar love-hate relationship.
Here are some anecdotes from If No News, Send Rumors,
a great bathroom reader by Stephen Bates.

When Paul Hume of the *Washington Post* wrote a harsh critique of Margaret Truman's singing debut, her father Harry wrote back, " I have just read your lousy review buried in the back pages. You sound like a frustrated old man who never made a success, an eight-ulcer man on a four-ulcer job and all four ulcers working. I never met you, but if I do you'll need a new nose and a supporter below."

President Franklin Roosevelt inscribed a photo of himself for the White House press room: "From their victim."

During a trip to India, President Jimmy Carter was shown a pit filled with cow manure, which generated methane gas for energy. ABC's Sam Donaldson said, "If I fell in, you'd pull me out, wouldn't you, Mr. President?" Carter replied, "Certainly—after a suitable interval."

Reporters covering the Kennedys once submitted a detailed questionnaire inquiring about the family's new dog. The First Lady filled it out. When she reached the question, "What do you feed the dog," she wrote: "Reporters."

On his desk President Reagan's press secretary, Larry Speakes, posted a sign: "You don't tell us how to stage the news, and we don't tell you how to cover it."

After the Apollo 11 astronauts returned to earth, President Nixon arranged to send fragments of moon rocks to world leaders. He remarked privately that he hoped to find some "contaminated" pieces to send to reporters.

When he was angry at reporters, Pres. [Franklin] Roosevelt sometimes punished them directly. Once, for example, he ordered Robert Post of

---

It took Noah Webster 20 years to write his dictionary.

the *New York Times* to wear a dunce cap and stand in the corner.

During his 1983 visit to Japan, President Reagan gave a speech praising freedom of the press. At his request, the entire speech was off the record.

After Washington Post reporter Judith Martin described Tricia Nixon as a "24-year-old woman dressed like an ice cream cone who can give neatness and cleanliness a bad name," the White House told Martin she would not be allowed to cover Tricia's wedding.

On Richard Nixon's post-resignation flight to San Clemente, he wandered back through Air Force One. The rear section had previously held reporters; now it held the Secret Service contingent. "Well," Nixon said, "it certainly smells better back here."

When President Johnson was angry with the columnists Evans and Novak, he referred to them as "Errors and Nofacts."

NIXON ON THE PRESS

• "For sixteen years, ever since the Hiss case, you've had a lot of fun....[J]ust think of how much you're going to be missing. You won't have Nixon to kick around anymore, because , gentlemen, this is my last press conference."—*News conference, 1962*

• "Don't take it personally, but I'm not going to pay that much attention to you." —*To reporters, 1969*

• "The press is the enemy."—*To aides, 1969*

• If we treat the press with a little more contempt we'll probably get better treatment."—*To aides, 1969*

• "Kicking the press is an art."—*To aides, 1972*

• " I have never heard or seen such outrageous, vicious, distorted reporting in 27 years of public life. I am not blaming anyone for that." —*News conference, 1973*

• "Don't get the impression that you arouse my anger...You see, one can only be angry with those he respects."—*News conference, 1973*

• "I have no enemies in the press whatsoever." —*To the Society of Newspaper Editors, 1984.*

The moon vibrated for 55 minutes after the Apollo 12 astronauts landed on it.

TRY, TRY AGAIN

Many products we take for granted today were flops when they were first introduced; it took a second—or even a third—effort to find a way to make them successful. Here are a few examples.

THE PRODUCT: Timex watches

Background: In 1942, the Waterbury Watch Company stopped making pocket watches and started making fuses for the U.S. military. Sales went up to $70 million, but plummeted to $300,000 after the war. To avoid bankruptcy, the company went back to manufacturing watches. They developed a line of cheap, durable timepieces anyone could afford—"Timex watches."

First Try: Salesmen took samples to jewelry stores (where watches were normally sold), expecting quick sales. But at $7.00 each, Timexes turned out to be too cheap and low-class for jewelers. They were used to a fancier product and a bigger profit margin; they refused to stock the watches.

Second Try: The company was forced to look for another place to sell its product. They sent salesmen out again, and to everyone's surprise, they found a market in drug stores. Whereas Timex products looked low-class in jewelry stores, they seemed ritzy next to aspirin and cough syrup. Within about a decade, one-third of all watches sold in the U.S. were Timexes.

THE PRODUCT: Tupperware

First Try: Earl Tupper invented Tupperware in the 1940s. Unlike glass or tin containers, Tupperware's plastic body and innovative airtight seal (based on a paint can design) made it ideal for keeping leftovers fresh. But consumers rejected it—they didn't understand how to use the plastic containers properly, and retailers rarely took the time to demonstrate them. By 1951 Tupper had given up.

Second Try: Mrs. Brownie Humphrey Wise, a "house party" saleswoman, came to Tupper's rescue. She was already selling Tupperware alongside other products at house parties, and pointed out to Tupper that the relaxed environment of a house party made it easy to demonstrate its advantages. Tupper agreed—and formed Tupperware Home Parties, Inc., in 1951. The parties worked—Tupperware was a hit. And it still is—today more than 75,000 Tupperware parties are held *every day*.

THE PRODUCT: Wisk Liquid Detergent

First Try: Unilever introduced Wisk, the first liquid laundry detergent ever, in 1956. It received a lot of publicity, but since it cost more than dry detergents, it wasn't a major success.

Second Try: A decade later, Unilever's market research revealed that housewives hated cleaning shirt collars more than any other laundry chore. So the company devised a new strategy for Wisk: They began running commercials that showed "ring around the collar" as the source of lost job promotions, husband-and-wife spats, etc. Their suggested solution: "Wisk around the collar." By 1974 sales of Wisk had tripled, and "ring around the collar" was a household phrase.

THE PRODUCT: Marlboro Cigarettes

First Try: Philip Morris introduced Marlboro in 1924 with upper-class women in mind—the cigarettes were longer and higher priced than standard brands. They also came with a "beauty tip"—an unfiltered mouthpiece that kept the smoker's lips from touching the cigarette paper. The gimmicks didn't work—Marlboro flopped. As late as 1954, it had less than 1% of the cigarette market.

Second Try: When filtered cigarettes were introduced in 1953, Philip Morris decided to dump the "beauty tip" and reintroduce Marlboro with a filter tip. (It was their worst-selling cigarette, and had the least to lose if it bombed). The company also replaced the brand's soft packaging with a new red and white "flip top" box. But women still ignored them, and the brand flopped again.

Third Try: In 1954, after 30 years of failures, Phillip Morris decided to forget about women. To attract male smokers, they gave the brand a more "manly" image, running commercials of pilots, hunters, sailors, and cowboys smoking Marlboros. Sales took off immediately; within a year, Marlboro was the fourth most popular smoke in the country. By the 1970s, it had become the most popular cigarette on Earth.

THE PRODUCT: Vaseline

Background: In 1857 a Brooklyn chemist named Robert Chese-brough visited the site of the first oil strike in U.S. history in Titus-ville, Pennsylvania. The oil workers he chatted with kept mention-ing "rod wax" —a substance that collected on oil pumping machinery. They swore it healed their cuts and burns.

Chesebrough took a sample home to study and worked on refin-ing it into a jelly-like product. He deliberately cut and burned himself—and rubbed the Vaseline (a combination of the German word for water—*wasser*—and the Greek word for oil—*elaion*) on his wounds. He found that it did actually speed up healing.

First Try: In 1870, Chesebrough set up a Vaseline factory and be-gan mailing free samples to physicians and scientists. He expected to use their endorsements to convince drug stores to carry Vaseline. But they ignored him.

Second Try: He had no choice but to go directly to the public. He loaded his wagon with jars of Vaseline and rode around New York state, handing them out to everyone he met along the way. Soon these "customers" began asking local druggists to order refills, and Chesebrough's business took off. By 1912 Vaseline had been writ-ten up in medical journals all over the world.

• • •

AND NOW BACK TO THE SHOW

Worst sitcom of the '70s: *Sugar Time!* (From *The Best of TV Sit-coms* by John Javna)

"If this were a horror film, it might be called *The Attack of the Rock-and-Roll Jiggling Bombers. Sugar Time!*, starring Barbi Benton (Hugh Hefner's girlfriend), Didi Carr, and Marianne Black, was about a group of braless, spandex-clad rock-and-roll singers who dreamt of stardom, despite their precarious financial condition. The show served a dual purpose. Literally. The late '70s were the era of the jigglers, and producers were looking for any excuse to put both of the jiggling actresses' talents on display. If they could sing (or act), so much the better. Unfortunately in this case, they couldn't. The show was created by James Komack, producer of such classics as *Chico and the Man*, and *The Courtship of Eddie's Father*."

The Jesus Christ lizard actually walks on water.

WHAT'S IN A NAME?

Interesting facts about names, from The Best Baby Name Book in the Whole Wild World, *by Bruce Lansky*

UNUSUAL NAMES

U
• "Ann Landers wrote about a couple who has six children, all named Eugene Jerome Dupuis, Junior. The children answer to One, Two, Three, Four, Five and Six, respectively."

• "Tonsilitis Jackson has brothers and sisters named Meningitis, Appendicitis and Peritonitis."

• "A couple in Louisiana named their children after colleges: Stanford, Duke, T'Lane, Harvard, Princeton, Auburn and Cornell. The parents' names? Stanford, Sr., and Loyola."

• "In 1979, the Pennsylvania Health Department discovered these two first names among the 159,000 birth certificates issued in the state that year—Pepsi and Cola."

• "Zachary Zzzzra has been listed in the *Guinness Book of World Records* as making 'the most determined attempt to be the last personal name in a local telephone directory' in San Francisco. That happened before his place was challenged by one Vladimir Zzzzzzabakov. Zzzzra reports that he called Zzzzzzabakov and demanded to know his real name (Zzzzra's name is really his own, he says). Zzzzzzabakov told him it was none of his . . . business. At any rate... Zzzzra changed his name to regain his former position. When the new phone book appeared, he was relieved to find himself comfortably in the last place again, as Zachary Zzzzzzzzzzra. Unknown to him, the contender, Zzzzzzabakov, had disappeared."

• "One family which was not terribly successful in limiting its expansion has a series of children called, respectively, Finis, Addenda, Appendix, Supplement and (last but not least) Errata."

LETTER ALONE

• "Harry S Truman owed his middle name, the initial S with no period, to a compromise his parents worked out. By using only the initial, they were able to please both his grandfathers, whose names were Shippe and Solomon."

• "A new recruit in the U.S. Army had only letters for his first and middle names—R B Jones. To avoid problems upon recruitment, he helpfully listed his name as ' R (only) B (only) Jones.' You guessed it—from then on he was, as far as the Army was concerned, 'Ronly Bonly Jones,' and all his records, dogtags, assignment forms and even discharge papers were issued in that name."

WHAT IN GOD'S NAME?

• "The majority of people in the Western hemisphere have names based on biblical ones. Women outnumber men, yet there are 3,037 male names in the Bible and only 181 female names, with the New Testament a more popular source than the Old."

• "Popes traditionally choose a new name upon their election. The practice began in 844 A.D. when Boca de Porco (Pig's Mouth) was elected. He changed his name to Sergious II."

• "Praise-God Barebones had a brother named If-Christ-Had-Not-Died-For-Thee-Thou-Wouldst-Have-Been-Damned Barebones, who was called 'Damned Barebones' for short."

• "Terril William Clark is listed in the phone book under his new name—God. Now he's looking for someone to publish a book he's written. 'Let's face it,' he reportedly said. 'The last book with my name on it was a blockbuster.'

LIVING UP TO THE NAME

• "Researchers have found that boys with peculiar first names have a higher incidence of mental problems than boys with common ones; no similar correlation was found for girls."

•"A recent study suggests that about two-thirds of the population of the U.S. is named to honor somebody. Of the people who are namesakes, about 60 percent are named after a relative and 40 percent for someone outside the family."

• "Many people dislike their own names. The most common reasons given for this dislike are that the names "sound too ugly," that they're old-fashioned, too hard to pronounce, too common, too uncommon, too long, sound too foreign, are too easy for people to joke about, and that they sound too effeminate (for men) or too masculine (for women)."

Cloud Nine was used by the U.S. Weather Bureau to describe the highest, least dangerous clouds.

THE LEGEND OF THE YELLOW RIBBON

When American troops came home from the Mideast in 1991, people welcomed them with yellow ribbons...as if that was a perfectly natural thing to do. Where did this "tradition" start? With a pop song—which, in turn, came from a Readers Digest *article. Here's the whole weird story, from* Behind the Hits, *by Bob Shannon and John Javna.*

INSPIRATION

Songwriter Irwin Levine leaned back and opened the January, 1972 issue of *Reader's Digest*. He skimmed through the magazine and read a few of the articles. Eventually he flipped to the story on page 64. The title said in red letters, "Going Home." And underneath: "Condensed from the New York *Post*." The piece was by newspaper columnist Pete Hamill; it had originally appeared in the New York *Post* on Oct. 14, 1971.

"I first heard this story a few years ago, from a girl I had met in New York's Greenwich Village," Hamill wrote in the introduction. "The girl told me she had been one of the participants. Since then, others...have said that they have read a version of it in some forgotten book, or been told it by an acquaintance who said that it actually happened to a friend. Probably the story is one of those mysterious bits of folklore that emerge from the national subconscious every few years, to be told anew in one form or another."

THE STORY

The two-page article was about a guy named Vingo, whom six teenagers spotted on a bus headed from New York City to Florida. The kids were going to Fort Lauderdale. Vingo, who'd been in a New York jail for the last four years, was on his way home. But he didn't know if his wife and kids would be there waiting for him. He'd told his wife when he first went in that he'd understand if she couldn't wait. Then he'd told her not to write, and she hadn't.

"Last week," said Vingo in the story, "when I was sure the parole was coming through, I wrote her again. We used to live in Brunswick, just before Jacksonville, and there's a big oak tree just as you come into town. I told her that if she'd take me back, she should put a yellow handkerchief on the tree, and I'd get off and come home. If she didn't want me, forget it—no handkerchief, and I'd go on through."

This tale was big news in the bus, so as they got to Brunswick everyone watched out the window for the tree. When they saw it, there was a massive celebration—dancing, tears, screaming. The tree was covered with ribbons. Vingo could go home.

THE SONG

Levine told his partner, Larry Brown, about the article. They both thought it could be a great song, and quickly wrote "Tie a Yellow Ribbon" based on it.

Then they gave it to a record producer, who convinced Tony Orlando to sing it. Orlando, a rhythm and blues fan, thought it was silly. But he couldn't get it out of his head. "I kept singing it around the house...against my will," he recalls.

It affected other people the same way; "Tie a Yellow Ribbon" sold three million copies in two weeks, and became the #1 record of 1973. By now, over a thousand versions have been recorded around the world.

THE FOLKLORE

A 1991 wire service report: "A yellow ribbon made by the wife of former Iranian hostage L. Bruce Laingen was donated yesterday to the Library of Congress, which accepted the bow as a genuine piece of American folklore.

"Shortly after Laingen was captured on Nov. 4, 1979 (when Muslim revolutionaries seized the U.S. Embassy in Tehran), Penne Laingen made the bow from 12 feet of yellow vinyl upholstery material and tied it around an oak tree in the front yard of the Laingen home in Bethesda, MD. When the 52 embassy hostages were freed Jan. 20, 1981, Laingen, the embassy's senior diplomat, returned home and removed the ribbon that had become a national symbol of hope for the hostages' eventual release.

"Laingen's yellow ribbon will be put on permanent display in the reading room of the library's American Folklife Center."

BOX OFFICE WINNERS

Who are the real movie superstars? We were surprised by some of the stars on these lists, compliled using the annual info from Quigley Publications.

TOP 10 BOX OFFICE STARS

...OF THE 1930s
1. Clark Gable
2. Shirley Temple
3. Joan Crawford
4. Will Rogers
5. Wallace Beery
6. Fred Astaire and Ginger Rogers
7. Norma Shearer
8. Marie Dressler
9. Janet Gaynor
10. Sonja Henie

...OF THE 1940s
1. Bob Hope
2. Bing Crosby
3. Betty Grable
4. Humphrey Bogart
5. Clark Gable
6. Bud Abbott and Lou Costello
7. Gary Cooper
8. Spencer Tracy
9. Greer Garson
10. James Cagney

...OF THE 1950s
1. John Wayne
2. James Stewart
3. Gary Cooper
4. Bing Crosby
5. Dean Martin and Jerry Lewis
6. Bob Hope
7. Frank Sinatra
8. William Holden
9. Randolph Scott
10. Marilyn Monroe

...OF THE 1960s
1. John Wayne
2. Elizabeth Taylor
3. Doris Day
4. Paul Newman
5. Jack Lemmon
6. Elvis Presley
7. Rock Hudson
8. Julie Andrews
9. Richard Burton
10. Sandra Dee

...OF THE 1970s
1. Clint Eastwood
2. Steve McQueen
3. Paul Newman
4. Barbra Streisand
5. John Wayne
6. Robert Redford
7. Charles Bronson
8. Burt Reynolds
9. Woody Allen
10. Al Pacino

...OF THE 1980s
1. Clint Eastwood
2. Eddie Murphy
3. Burt Reynolds
4. Tom Cruise
5. Sylvester Stallone
6. Michael J. Fox
7. Arnold Schwarzenegger
8. Michael Douglas
9. Harrison Ford
10. Dudley Moore

Origin of the term "bigwig:" King Louis IV of France was a big fan of big wigs.

POLITICAL SYMBOLS

You know what they represent—but do you know where they come from?

The Republican Elephant: First appeared in *Harper's Weekly* in 1874, in a political cartoon drawn by Thomas Nast. Rumors were circulating that President Ulysses S. Grant, a Republican, was going to run for a third term. Fearful of what would happen if Grant were reelected, Nast drew a cartoon of the rumor, incorporating another news story: a false report that wild animals had escaped from the Central Park Zoo and were roaming the streets in search of prey. He drew the Republican Party as a stampeding elephant.

The Democratic Donkey: In the 1828 presidential elections, Andrew Jackson's opponents referred to him as a "stubborn jackass." Proud of his reputation for obstinacy, Jackson (a Democrat) began using donkeys in his campaign posters and flyers. Democrats have been doing it ever since.

The Peace Symbol: Created by Gerald Holtom, a British artist, in 1958. A member of the Campaign for Nuclear Disarmament, Holtom was looking for a symbol to promote the antinuclear group that could be easily reproduced on banners. He based it on letters in the semaphore (flag) alphabet that Navy ships use to communicate with each other. The circle stands for the word "total;" the two smaller lines represent the letter N (nuclear), and the long vertical line in the center stands for the letter D (disarmament)—"Total Nuclear Disarmament." It was first displayed at a 1958 peace march in England.

The Swastika: Originally a Hindu symbol that represented the sun's daily path across the sky—and that, ironically, was considered a "good luck" symbol before World War II. It has been found on religious artifacts all over the world, from the Middle East to Asia to North and South America. Its image was tarnished forever when Adolf Hitler adopted it as the symbol for the Nazi party.

UNSUNG HEROES

Everyone knows about Thomas Edison and Alexander Graham Bell. But the guy who invented the portable vacuum cleaner is anonymous. The folks at the BRI's Division of Practical Science think it's time this injustice is corrected. Here are some heroes we should all recognize.

HERO: Earl Richardson
WHAT HE DID: Designed the first practical electric iron.
THE STORY: In 1905 Richardson, a California utility worker, decided to improve the electric irons of the day. Existing models weighed as much as 15 lbs, and were warm only while they were sitting in their bases. Richardson's solution: design a lighter iron that stayed hot, even when in use. He succeeded, but still had a problem. Most power companies of the day generated power only in the evenings—their purpose was to provide power for lighting—but women liked to iron during the day. In 1906, Richardson convinced his local utility to generate electricity all day on Tuesdays... and housewives started buying his irons.

HEROINE: Josephine Cochrane
WHAT SHE DID: Invented the dishwasher.
THE STORY: Though she invented the dishwasher, Josephine never washed dishes herself. A wealthy woman of the 1890s, she invented the machine because she was tired of servants breaking her valuable china as they washed it. One afternoon, Cochrane went out into the woodshed alongside her house and began building wire compartments that would hold her dishes. She set these in a large copper boiler, and attached a motor to pump the water and rotate the dishes. Her friends convinced her to patent it; in 1893 one of her machines won top prize at the Chicago World's Fair.

HERO: James Murray Spengler
WHAT HE DID: Invented the portable vacuum cleaner
THE STORY: A failed inventor, Spengler hit rock-bottom in

1907 and had to take a job as a janitor in an Ohio department store. The mechanical carpet cleaner he used to clean the store's carpets kicked up dust and set off his allergies—so Spengler decided to build a better contraption. He made his first vacuum out of a pillow case, a soap box, an old fan, and some tape; he patented it in 1908. Later he sold the rights to his device to William Hoover, an Ohio businessman, and retired with the money he made.

HERO: Henry Alden Sherwin
WHAT HE DID: Developed ready-mixed paint.
THE STORY: You knew that Sherwin Williams sold ready-mixed paint, but did you know they invented it? The year was 1870, and Sherwin, co-owner of a paint company, wanted to sell pre-mixed colors, so homeowners wouldn't have to mix their own (a risky business). His partners hated the idea, and forced Sherwin out of the company. So he found a new partner, Edward Williams; together they formed Sherwin Williams in 1880.

HERO: Frederick Walton and Thomas Armstrong
WHAT THEY DID: Invented linoleum floors.
THE STORY: Frederick Walton, an Englishman, deserves the credit for inventing linoleum. But Thomas Armstrong, an American, deserves credit for making it what it is today. Walton patented his floor covering, a layer of linseed oil, resin, and cork dust with a woven backing, in 1860. When Thomas Armstrong, a cork maker, heard of Walton's invention, he developed his own cork-based floor covering. Unlike Walton, he experimented with coloring, patterns, and other ideas, giving linoleum the features that made it a fixture in American homes.

HERO: Edwin Budding
WHAT HE DID: Invented the lawn mower.
THE STORY: Edwin Budding was a foreman in an English textile plant in the late 1820s. He was obsessed with a new machine the plant used to shear excess fibers from cotton cloth. He thought a similar machine might help him keep his lawn trimmed, and he set out to make one. Today's mowers are direct descendents of the machine he invented.

Dentist's lament: An estimated 16% of U.S. women and 13% of U.S. men are toothless.

A TOY IS BORN

We all grew up with them: Raggedy Ann, Legos, Lionel Trains…

RAGGEDY ANN

In the early 1900s a little girl named Marcella Gruelle was rummaging through the attic of her parents' Connecticut home when she found a hand-made doll. It was dusty and torn, but Marcella liked it so much that her father repaired it for her. He even gave it a name: Raggedy Ann, (inspired by two poems by James Whitcomb Riley: "The Raggedy Man" and "Little Orphan Annie").

In fact, Marcella spent so much time with the doll that her father (Johnny Gruelle), a cartoonist, started writing and illustrating stories about it. His books—the original *Raggedy Ann* series—made Raggedy Ann one of the most popular dolls of the 20th Century.

MATCHBOX CARS

In 1952 John Odell and Leslie Smith, owners of a British industrial die-casting factory, started casting toys at night to make extra money. Their first toy: a tiny replica of Princess Elizabeth's Royal Coach. When Elizabeth became Queen in 1953, more than a million of them were sold.

So the partners went into toymaking full time. They created a line of tiny automobiles they called *Matchbox Toys* (because the cars were tiny enough to fit in a matchbox)…then they took it a step further and decided to sell their products in packages that actually *looked* like matchboxes.

LEGOS

One afternoon in 1954, a shopkeeper complained to Godtfred Kirk-Christiansen, a Danish toymaker, that most modern toys didn't challenge children to think. That night, Christiansen came up with an idea for a new toy: building blocks that locked together, enabling children to use their imagination and build interesting structures that weren't possible with standard blocks. He called his creation *Legos*, from the Danish words *leg godt*, which means "play well." Today they're sold in more than 125 countries.

LIONEL TRAINS

Joshua Lionel Cohen was an inventor in the late 1900s. His earliest creations included fuses for land mines, primitive versions of the electronic doorbell, and something he called a flowerpot light, (a small, battery-operated lamp which was intended to illuminate plants in hotel lobbies). He also invented a tiny electric motor, but couldn't figure out what to do with it. He finally stuffed one into a model train, named it Lionel (after himself), and sold it with 30 feet of track to a novelty store. Within a day or two the store asked for more. Cohen decided to go into train-making full time, and by 1903 his Lionel Train Company had an entire catalog of trains and accessories.

Note: Cohen's trains made him rich, but he never earned any money—or credit—for his most famous invention: the battery-operated flowerpot light. It was such a loser that he sold the design to his business partner. The partner started selling the lights *without* the flowerpots—under a new name—*The Eveready Flashlight*.

CABBAGE PATCH KIDS

Xavier Roberts, a Georgia folk artist, was selling his soft sculpture dolls at a craft fair when a customer walked up and asked him how much the dolls cost. Roberts had a splitting headache. He snapped back: "They're not for sale."—but quickly recovered and said: "They're up for adoption." The idea behind Cabbage Patch Kids was born.

Roberts carried the concept to extremes. He converted an old medical clinic into "Babyland General Hospital," where employees "delivered" his "babies" and gave them "birth certificates" with names like Bessie Sue or Billie Jo. His dolls were ugly, but they still became a national craze in 1983. Customers in one toy store rioted after waiting more than eight hours to buy the dolls. One woman broke her leg—and the store owner had to protect himself with a baseball bat.

Note: In 1980 Martha Nelson, a craft artist Roberts had worked with in the past, sued him, claiming he had stolen some of her soft sculpture techniques. The court ruled that Roberts *had* used some of Nelson's ideas, but since she never copyrighted the design, she wasn't entitled to any of the profits.

An ant can survive for 2 weeks underwater.

CHANDLER SAYS...

Raymond Chandler was a master of detective fiction.
Here's a sample of his style, from his books.

"When in doubt, have two guys come in through the doors with guns."

"He didn't know the right people. That's all a police record means."

"Guns never settle anything. They're just a fast curtain to a bad second act."

"It was a blonde. A blonde to make a bishop kick a hole in a stained glass window."

"She gave me a smile I could feel in my hip pocket."

"You could tell by his eyes that he was plastered to the hairline, but otherwise he looked like any other nice young guy in a dinner jacket who had been spending too much money in a joint that exists for that purpose and no other."

On marriage: "For two people in a hundred it's wonderful. The rest just work at it. After 20 years all the guy has left is a work bench in the garage."

"She had a pair of blue-gray eyes that looked at me as if I had said a dirty word."

"She lowered her lashes until they almost cuddled her cheeks and raised them again, like a theater curtain....That was supposed to make me roll over on my back with all four paws in the air."

"The [dying] General spoke again, slowly, using his strength as carefully as an out-of-work showgirl uses her last good pair of stockings."

"I lit the cigarette and blew a lungful at him and he sniffed at it like a terrier at a rathole."

"Alcohol is like love: the first kiss is magic, the second is intimate, the third is routine. After that you just take the girl's clothes off."

"Los Angeles is a city no worse than others, a city rich and vigorous and full of pride, a city lost and beaten and full of emptiness."

CN U RD THS?

*The cryptic messages on personalized license plates
can be fun...or maddening—as these examples.*

CAR BRAGGIN'
FSTRNU
IDSMOKU
2AHSUM
WOWZER
NUN BTR
I XLR8
UDLUUZ
WAY2BAD

CAR MODESTY
EYEZOR
HAZRDUS
JUS2LOUD
LOTECH
GASGUZ
H2OLOO
OK4NOW
SHLOMO

**AUTO
BIOGRAPHY**
JUSAHIK
NDCENT
I 4GET 2
FMNIST
GAY1
ERLEBRD
IMON2U
IMOKUOK
NVR2OLD
WELLRED
PHAQUE

AIRHED
H82BL8
KUNFUZD
PINHEAD
REDNEK
TRCULNT
XNTRIK
2CRAY Z
BEERFAT
IMNOZEE
CURMUJN
DESPOT
EZ HUMP
FLAKEY
KARMA
I ELVIS

IT'S A LIVING
RABBI
TUPRWR
ILSTR8TR
CME4OB
I FIX BAX
MDUC2P
OPNWDE
LITIG8R
ISUEM
SHYSTERR
I ADD4U
I CALQL8
KAR2NST
PNO2R
DCOR8

EDUKTR
GESTALT
MS DONUT
SOUL DR
2THFXR
2BY CME

JUST FOR FUN
POLKA
H2O SKE
ROC4EVR
N2HRSES
W8LIFTN
XRCIZE
AV8TR
ICESK8
HAIKU
HDBANGR
ILUV10S
K9SHOW
LV2PUN
PBS YES
SGTPEPR
W8N4SUN
2DA BCHS

GOOD ADVICE
BCRE8TV
BCOOL
DOITNOW
B LOGICL
10D 2IT
UBUKLUP

"If we ever needed a brain, now is the time."—Squiggy, "Laverne and Shirley"

I'M GAME

You can't play board games in the bathroom (not yet, anyway—someone may be developing one right now)...but you can still read about them.

START HERE

S • The earliest board game on record is the royal game of Ur, which was invented more than 4,000 years ago in Mesopotamia, the site of present-day Iraq. It was a "race" game; the first player to complete the course was the winner. Moves were governed by throwing dice-like objects. Archaeologists believe it is the forerunner of backgammon.

• The Egyptian game of Senet was a best-seller some 4,000 years ago. Even King Tut had one. He liked it so much he was buried with it.

• The first American board game, "The Mansion of Happiness," was produced in 1843. Its theme was Victorian: Players tried to avoid Passion, Idleness, Cruelty, Immodesty and Ingratitude. Drunkenness was punished by a trip to the stocks.

THE PLAYERS

• *Milton Bradley*: In 1860 he bought a lithographic press and began printing board games. His first game: The Checkered Game of Life. Object: Get to "happy old age" while avoiding "disgrace" and "ruin."

• *The Parker Brothers*: In 1883, about 50 years before Monopoly, George Parker went into the game business. His first product was a card game called Banking. Later, with the help of his brothers Charles and Edward, he revolutionized the toy industry by introducing mass-produced board games.

• *Mark Twain*: The great American author also invented a game. He called it "Mark Twain's Memory Builder: A Game for Acquiring and Retaining All Sorts of Facts and Dates." In the introduction to the rules he wrote: "Many public-school children seem to know only two dates—1492 and 4th of July; but as a rule they don't know what happened on either occasion. It is because they have not had a chance to play this game."

THE GAME BOARD

If you're going to go to Atlantic City to check out the properties that the Monopoly spaces are named after, be prepared for heartbreak. According to Nathan Cobb, a *Boston Globe* writer who made the pilgrimmage a few years ago:

• You can't take a ride on the Reading Railroad; it's out of business. The only railroad left is Conrail, which doesn't take passengers.

• Advance to St. Charles Place? Forget it. It's gone, replaced by a casino parking lot.

• Kentucky Avenue is a string of burger huts and seedy bars.

• Pacific Avenue is crawling with hookers.

• There's no longer a Community Chest…or the old Water Works.

• You won't find any Free Parking.

• Many of the nineteen other Monopoly streets that still exist are lined with buildings that are boarded up and run down. One wine-guzzling derelict sitting on Oriental Avenue, when told it could be had for $100 on the Monopoly board, declared, "Damn, it ain't worth that much."

TOKEN FACTS

• Parcheesi, the original male chauvinist game, was created in the 1500s in India by Akbar the Great. It was played in the palace courtyard with young women as game pawns. "Home" was originally the emperor's throne. What Akbar did with the women once he got them all "home" is not documented.

• Backgammon was once known as "Nero's Game."

• There are five legal Scrabble words using 'q' without 'u': faqir, qaid, qoph, qindar and qintar.

• In 1988, the 23rd foreign language version of Monopoly was manufactured—in the USSR. Among the changes: a Russian bear token, real estate names corresponding to Moscow locations (Broadway became the Arbat Mall) and rubles instead of dollars.

WHAT ALES YOU?

*Here's a bit of information you can use to impress
your friends next time you go out for a beer.*

In medieval times, taverns were rough and dangerous places. Glass-bottomed beer tankards were invented so a drinker could take a hefty bottoms-up gulp while still keeping a wary eye on fellow drinkers.

Beer steins were first seen in Europe in the 1500s. Covered containers protected the beer from flies, which were thought to carry the plague.

Eberhard Anheuser, a St. Louis soap maker, bought a failing brewery in 1860 and tried to turn it around. But within 2 years he owed so much money to the local brewer's supply store—owned by Aldophus Busch—that he had to take Busch on as a partner to cancel the debt. Busch married his daughter in 1860, and assumed control of the brewery when he died.

About one out of four beers consumed in the U. S. is a Budweiser. Next most popular domestic beers are Miller Lite, Coors Light, Bud Light, Busch, Miller High Life, Milwaukee's Best, Old Milwaukee, and Coors.

In the late 1860s Adolph Coors stowed away on a ship to America to avoid serving in the German Army. He and a partner founded the Golden brewery in Golden, Colorado in 1873—which he bought outright in 1880.

The reason you spend a lot of time in the john when you drink beer: besides the bulk of liquid that passes through you, the alcohol acts as a diuretic, taking the liquids out of your body and flushing them down the tubes. This dehydration causes a lot of the hangover the next morning. Best prevention? Drink a glass of water or two every time you visit the facilities.

Frederick Miller, royal brewmaster at Germany's Hohenzollern Castle, fled to Milwaukee in 1854 to escape the political strife consuming his country. He founded the Miller Brewing Company in 1855.

Northeasterners and westerners drink more imported beer than elsewhere—more than twice the national average.

Pigeons are the only birds that can drink water without raising their heads to swallow.

NUMBER, PLEASE

Think of all the numbers you know—your phone number, your address, etc. There's no explanation for most of them. But here are a few we can give you a reason for.

NUMBER: 5280 feet (a mile).
ORIGIN: The term *mile* comes from the Latin word *mille*—meaning 1,000. To the Romans it was the distance a soldier could cover in 1,000 paces—about 5,000 feet. But British farmers measured their fields in *furlongs*, which were 660 feet long, and they didn't want to change. So when the mile was introduced in England, it was changed to 5,280 feet—exactly eight furlongs.

NUMBER: 60 feet, 6 inches (the distance between the pitcher's mound and home plate in baseball).
ORIGIN: The pitching distance was 50 feet until 1893—when some baseball executives changed it to 60 feet. But the surveyor they hired to remap their infield misread their instructions—he thought 60 feet 0 inches was 60 feet 6 inches. The extra 6 inches have been there ever since.

NUMBER: Age 65 (when Americans qualify for Social Security).
ORIGIN: German Chancellor Otto von Bismarck established the world's first Social Security program in 1881 to undercut the popularity of the socialist movement. He set the retirement age at 65 because he knew he wouldn't have to pay out many benefits—in the 1880s living to age 65 was as likely as living to 105 today. When FDR set up Social Security in the U.S., he copied the German retirement age—not realizing why it had been chosen to begin with.

NUMBER: 26 miles, 385 yards (the length of a marathon).
ORIGIN: The distance of a marathon was first standardized at 25 miles in 1896. During the 1908 London Olympics, however, Queen Alexandra wanted her grandchildren to see the start of the race. So the starting line was moved back 1 mile and 385 yards—onto the front lawn of Windsor Castle. Marathons are still that length. today.

Studies show that churchgoers have lower blood pressure than others.

BEN FRANKLIN'S ALMANAC

*Here are more bits of wisdom from the man who thought
a penny saved is a penny earned.*

"A single man has not nearly the value he'd have in a state of union. He resembles the odd half of a pair of scissors."

"There are more old drunkards than old doctors."

"If a man empties a purse into his head, no man can take it away from him. An investment in knowledge always pays the best interest."

"None preaches better than the ant, and she says nothing."

"He that is good for making excuses is seldom good for anything else."

"In general, mankind, since the improvement of cookery, eats twice as much as nature requires."

"The heart of a fool is in his mouth; but the mouth of a wise man is in his heart."

"He that lives upon hope will die fasting."

"Where there's marriage without love, there will be love without marriage."

"He that falls in love with himself will have no rivals."

"God heals and the doctor takes the fee."

"He that is of the opinion that money will do everything may well be accused of doing everything for money."

"Plough deep while sluggards sleep."

"Three may keep a secret if two of them are dead."

"There was never a good war, or a bad peace."

"Nothing gives an author so much pleasure as to find his works quoted by other learned authors."

"Necessity never made a good bargain."

"At twenty years of age, the will reigns; at thirty, the wit; and at forty, the judgement."

"There are no ugly loves nor handsome prisons."

"Admiration is the daughter of ignorance."

The Roman Emperor Caligula's last words were: "I'm still alive!"

THE COLA WARS

Some competitors have friendly rivalries, but not Coke and Pepsi. These two have battled for most of this century, taking no prisoners. And the cola wars continue today.

BEFORE THE BATTLES

To understand the bitterness between Coke and Pepsi, you have to go back a hundred years to the two pharmacists (both veterans of the Confederate army) who formulated the sticky-sweet brown liquids.

COKE BEGINNINGS

John Pemberton, a pharmacist in Atlanta, created Coca-Cola as a non-alcoholic "nerve medicine" in 1886.

• He came up with the first Coke syrup by boiling a batch of herbs, coca leaves and kola nuts in his back yard.

• He mixed the syrup with tap water and sold it in his drug store.

• It wasn't until a customer with an upset stomach specifically asked him to mix the syrup with fizzy water that he realized Coke's potential as a soft drink.

• He didn't live to see Coca-Cola become a success. Shortly after he created the drink, Pemberton's health began to fail. He sold the rights to Coke to a group of druggists for about $350; he died in 1888.

THE NEW REGIME

Only one of Coca-Cola's new owners, Asa Candler, saw the drink's huge potential. By 1891, he had bought complete control of the company for $2,300, and registered *Coca-Cola* as a trademark a few years later. Candler plowed nearly all of the company's early profits back into the business, and kept costs to a minimum (one employee reported earning "$3.00 per week and lots of Coca-Cola").

He had an unmatched flair for promotion, and began the company's tradition of giving away Coca-Cola clocks, fans, calendars, urns, scales, thermometers, and other premiums to storekeepers that ordered Coke syrup.

By 1892 he was selling more than 35,000 gallons of syrup a year, and by the turn of the century, Coca-Cola had become the best known product in America.

EARLY COMPETITORS

Coca-Cola's meteoric rise had inspired scores of imitators. Coke sued dozens of them for trademark infringement, including the Koke Company, Kola Koke, Coke-Ola, Koko-Cola, Koko-Kola, Ko-Kola, and Coca & Cola. The case against the Koke Company went all the way to the Supreme Court, and Coca-Cola won.

HITTING THE BOTTLE

According to legend, a mystery man walked into Coca-Cola's offices one day in 1891. He told Candler he knew a way to double the company's sales overnight, and would share his idea for $5,000 (or, some say, $50,000). Candler paid him. The man handed Candler a slip of paper which said, "Bottle it."

Regardless of whether the story is true, Candler resisted bottling Coca-Cola for a long time, fearing that pressurized bottles might explode and expose the company to legal liability. Eventually, a Mississippi candy store owner started bottling the liquid on his own. He had enormous success (and no lawsuits), and five years later, Candler opened his first bottling plant.

At first, Coca-Cola's bottles were indistinguishable from those of other companies, but in 1915 Coke hired an Indiana glass company to design a bottle that customers would recognize "even in the dark." Loosely adapting sketches of a cola nut they found in the Encyclopedia Britannica, the glassworkers designed the distinctive bottle that is still in use today.

Candler ran Coca-Cola until 1916, when he turned over control of the company to his sons. His wife's death in 1919 sent him into a deep depression; he tried to shake it off by taking a trip to Europe. While he was away, his sons sold the company to Robert Woodruff, an Atlanta entrepreneur, for $25 million dollars.

PEPSI-COLA HITS THE SPOT

Meanwhile, back to 1893: In North Carolina, pharmacist Caleb Bradham decided he wanted to cash in on the success of Coke. At first, he called his imitation "Brad's Drink," but then decided to name it after *pepsin,*a digestive aid, hoping people would buy it as a stomach remedy. Like Pemberton, he didn't see Pepsi's potential as a soft drink until it became popular among people who *weren't* sick.

Bradham paid careful attention to advertising and sales grew to 100,000 gallons of syrup by 1898. Pepsi continued to grow until the end of World War I, when sugar prices shot up from 5 1/2¢ a pound to 22 1/2¢ a pound. To hedge against future shortages, Bradham stocked up on sugar at the higher price. But a few months later, sugar plummeted to 3 1/2¢ a pound, and the company went bankrupt. Bradham returned to his drug store, leaving the soda world.

Roy C. McGargel bought the rights to Pepsi-Cola in 1920 and tried to put the company back on its feet. But he couldn't afford a large advertising budget, and the company faltered. It went bankrupt in 1925, reorganized, and went bankrupt again in 1931.

SKIRMISH #1: LOFTY GOALS

The day after Pepsi-Cola went bankrupt in 1931, Charles Guth, the president the Loft Candy Store chain, bought it for $10,500. It didn't seem like a wise investment at the time, since Coca-Cola was already the industry giant and was getting bigger every year. But Guth wanted something more than mere money—he bought Pepsi to get *revenge*.

Guth hated the Coca-Cola Company. Even though Loft's 115 candy stores sold 4 million servings of Coke every year, the company had refused to give him a quantity discount. When Guth bought Pepsi for himself, it gave him the chance to dump Coke from Loft stores.

• Coca-Cola was furious: Guth was one of its largest customers, and losing his business hurt. It decided to fight back.

• It secretly sent its employees into Guth's stores to order "a Coke." On 620 occasions, they reported, they were served Pepsi instead. The company sued Guth, claiming he didn't have the right to serve Pepsi to customers asking for "a Coke." Coca-Cola fought the case for more than 10 years. It lost in 1942. The bitterness between the two companies was just beginning.

SKIRMISH #2: "12 FULL OUNCES, THAT'S A LOT"

Two years after buying Pepsi, Guth had had enough. He couldn't expand sales beyond his own stores, and wanted to sell out. The logical buyer was Coke. Guth offered them the company at a bargain price...and they refused.

Desperate to cut costs, Guth began bottling Pepsi in secondhand beer bottles, which held nearly twice as much soda as normal soft drink bottles. Guth saved money, and hoped the larger serving size would increase sales.

It didn't. Nearly bankrupt, Guth took one last gamble to save his company: He cut Pepsi's price from 10¢ to a nickel, offering twice as much cola as Coke for 1/2 the price. The gamble paid off. By 1938 Pepsi was making $4 million a year and growing fast.

PALACE COUP

Guth won the battle, but lost it all in an internal power play. By 1935 he had spent so much of his attention and energy building up Pepsi that Loft Candy Stores was on the verge of bankruptcy. Loft's board of directors forced him to resign and hired the Phoenix Security Company to nurse the candy company back to health.

Guth still owned Pepsi-Cola outright; he said he had bought it with his own money. But audits showed that he had bought it using Loft's funds. Upon discovering this, Phoenix Securities hatched a scheme to take control of Pepsi for itself. It bought up much of Loft's nearly worthless stock. Acting on behalf of the candy company, it then sued Guth for control of Pepsi. Phoenix won the suit in 1939. Their scheme had worked—for the bargain basement price of a nearly bankrupt chain of candy stores, Phoenix Securities had taken control of the second most successful soft drink company in the nation.

SKIRMISH #3: A SMOKING GUN

While Coca-Cola was still the undisputed leader of the cola companies, Pepsi-Cola's booming sales made it nervous. In 1934 it fired the next volley with a trademark infringement suit against Pepsi-

There are 120 drops of water in a teaspoon.

Cola to force it to drop the word "Cola" from its name. Coke had already won similar lawsuits against several companies, and Walter Mack, Pepsi's new president, actually expected to lose.

Everyone else thought Pepsi would lose, too. The widow of the president of Cleo-Cola, which lost a similar lawsuit, visited Mack to commiserate. "My husband thought he was right too," she said, "but they still put him out of business. And I still have a photograph of the check they gave him."

Check? What check? Purely by chance, she given Mack an important piece of evidence proving that Coca-Cola had been bribing soft drink executives to deliberately lose the lawsuits it filed against them, in order to strengthen its trademark position for future cases.

Mack asked the widow for a copy of the check, and introduced it as evidence in court. Caught red-handed, Coca-Cola asked for a two day recess. The next day Robert Woodruff, President of Coca-Cola, met with Mack in a New York hotel. He offered to withdraw the suit, and Mack agreed—but only after forcing Woodruff to sign a statement he had written out on the hotel's stationery: "I, Robert Woodruff, hereby agree that [Coca-Cola] will recognize the Pepsi-Cola trademark and never attack it in the United States."

Coke kept its word. It never again attacked Pepsi's trademark in this country. However, in other countries around the world Coke attacked Pepsi's trademark whenever and however possible.

SKIRMISH #3: BEG, BORROW & STEELE

By 1949 Pepsi was in trouble again. Coke had recaptured 84% of the U.S. soda market, and Pepsi was again near bankruptcy. The problem: Pepsi's image. Its huge bottles and low price had made it popular during the Great Depression—but they also gave the brand a reputation as a "cheap" drink for people who couldn't afford Coke. Affluent post-war America was returning to Coke.

Luckily for Pepsi, a Coca-Cola vice president named Alfred Steele jumped ship. A former circus showman, Steele's flamboyant antics had been unpopular at Coke, and his career with the company had bottomed out. He quit and become president of Pepsi-Cola, taking 15 other top executives with him. For the second time in its history, Pepsi was being run by a man bent on getting revenge on Coke.

Dinosaurs ranged from nearly 3 stories high to about the size of a small turkey.

Steele was just what Pepsi needed. He reworked Pepsi's image, updating the company's logo to the familiar circular one used for decades, and switching to fancy swirl bottles. He launched a massive advertising campaign which positioned Pepsi as a superior product, even a status symbol.

In 1955, he married actress Joan Crawford, a former Coca-Cola endorser, and she began appearing in Pepsi ads and publicity events. Her Hollywood glamour helped shake off the brand's "low class" image. Steele succeeded in breathing new life into Pepsi. By the time he died in 1959, he had cut Coke's lead in half.

SKIRMISH #5: ICE COLD WAR

During the '50s, Pepsi was active in conservative politics. It was a big supporter of Senator Joseph McCarthy and his anti-communist associate, Richard Nixon. In 1959, Vice President Nixon travelled to Moscow to attend an international trade show of American and Soviet products, including Pepsi-Cola. Soviet President Nikita Khrushchev was there, and while touring the Macy's kitchen exhibit the two men got into a heated argument over the merits of communism and capitalism.

Pepsi officials asked Nixon to bring Krushchev to their display to cool off after the debate. Nixon happily obliged, shoving a Pepsi into Krushchev's hand. Photos of the scene were a public relations bonanza for Pepsi: at the height of the cold war, the leader of the Communist world was photographed drinking a Pepsi In one stroke, Pepsi's worldwide image and prestige had finally caught up with Coca-Cola's, and Donald Kendall, Pepsi's overseas operations chief, never forgot Nixon's gesture. A few years late he got a chance to return the favor.

Nixon lost the presidential campaign in 1960, and the California gubernatorial race in 1962. Now unemployed, he was offered the presidency of several universities, considered for the chairmanship of Chrysler, and was even suggested as commissioner of baseball. But he decided to practice law so he could stay active in politics. His wife, Pat, was too embarrassed by his defeat to stay in California, so they moved to New York.

Nixon hadn't practiced law for a long time and wasn't exactly a prestigious figure any more, so he had a hard time finding a firm

---

In 1977 there were over 15,000 discos in the United States.

that would take him. Donald Kendall repaid the Moscow favor by presenting him with the Pepsi account, worth a considerable amount of money. And the job helped keep him in the public eye. He traveled around the world opening Pepsi bottling plants, stopping to meet world leaders. Coincidence: He was in Dallas making a Pepsi-related appearance on Nov. 22, 1963, when JFK was killed.

Even after Nixon was elected President in 1968, his relationship with the company remained close. During his years in office, Pepsi was the only soft drink served at the White House. In 1972, Pepsi won the right to begin selling soft drinks in the USSR after Nixon personally asked the Soviets to "look favorably" on Pepsi's request. Pepsi had pull even when Nixon didn't intervene directly: foreign governments knew that giving Pepsi favorable treatment would score points with the his administration.

SKIRMISH #6: COKE SHALL RISE AGAIN

In 1962, the same year Nixon became Pepsi's lawyer, a young Georgian named Jimmy Carter lost the Democratic nomination for the state senate. But he suspected election fraud, and hired King & Spalding, Atlanta's most prominent law firm, to challenge the results. They succeeded: Carter was declared the Democratic nominee, and went on to win the election.

The law firm got Carter together with officials from another of its clients: the Coca-Cola Company. Company officials saw immediately that he had potential as a national candidate. They introduced him to the inner circle of Georgia's corporate and industrial leaders, whose money and support would later prove crucial in Carter's campaigns for governor and president.

Carter remained close to Coca-Cola for the rest of his career. As governor he often used the company's jets on official trips, and when his 1976 presidential campaign started losing steam, he turned to Coke's image makers to film his campaign commercials.

As early as 1974 he admitted the company's role in developing his knowledge of foreign affairs: "We have our own built-in State Department in the Coca-Cola company. The provide me ahead of time with…penetrating analyses of what the country is, what its problems are, who its leaders are, and when I arrive there, provide me with an introduction to the leaders of that country."

Like Nixon, Carter returned the favor after being elected president. One of the first acts of his administration: removing the White House Pepsi-Cola machines and replacing them with Coke.

After Carter was elected, Portugal allowed Coke to be bottled and sold in the country—lifting a ban that was more than 50 years old. Not long afterward, U.S. government approved a $300 million emergency loan to the country. And when China opened its markets to American companies during Carter's term, Coke was the one that got the nod.

SKIRMISH #7: PEPSICO STRIKES BACK

In the mid-1960s, the Pepsi-Cola Company (renamed *Pepsico*) began diversifying into the snack-food and restaurant business eventually buying Kentucky Fried Chicken, Pizza Hut and other popular chains, in part so they could switch their soda fountains over to Pepsi-Cola. Pepsico's diversification strategy worked: by 1979 the company succeeded at the unthinkable—the company had grown larger than Coca-Cola. While undiversified Coke still sold more soft drinks and had higher profits, Pepsi was gaining even there. And now Coke's own surveys were showing that younger drinkers preferred the taste of Pepsi. Coke decided to act.

A SHOT TO THE FOOT: NEW COKE

In 1985, the Coke company announced it was replacing the old Coke formula with one a new one. Extensive marketing tests indicated that people preferred New Coke over both the old product *and* Pepsi.

But the marketing tests didn't anticipate the huge negative reaction to tinkering with a beloved old product. It was a major embarrassment for Coca-Cola. Pepsi declared victory, consumers revolted, and within two months old Coke was back—in the form of "Classic Coke." Today it outsells New Coke by a ratio of 4 to 1.

Today, the makers of the sweet liquids continue their bitter battle.

NOW AND ZEN

If all of the world can be seen in a grain of sand, as some Zen masters say, why not on TV? Cosmic quotes from the book Primetime Proverbs, *by Jack Mingo and John Javna.*

SELF KNOWLEDGE

"I am what I am and that's all that I am."

—**Popeye,**
The Popeye Show

"The blossom below the water knows not sunlight. And men, not knowing, will find me hard to understand."

—**Caine,**
Kung Fu

COSMIC THOUGHTS

"There's a time to be Daniel Boone, and there's a time to be a plumber."

—**MacGyver,**
MacGyver

"The butcher with the sharpest knife has the warmest heart."

—**Village saying,**
The Prisoner

"A day without grapes is like a day without apples."

—**Kelly Robinson,**
I Spy

"There's a big difference between making instant coffee and bringing a Rastafarian back from the dead."

—**Ricardo Tubbs,**
Miami Vice

EVERYTHING IS EVERYTHING

"I know they're blue berries, but they might not be blueberries. And while all blueberries are blue berries, not all blue berries are blueberries."

—**Alex Reiger,** *Taxi*"

RULES FOR LIVING

"No good deed goes unpunished."

—**B.J. Hunnicut,**
M*A*S*H

"Most people's lives are governed by telephone numbers."

—**Narrator,** *Hitchhiker's Guide to theGalaxy*

"No river is shallow to a man who cannot swim."

—**Paladin,**
Have Gun Will Travel

Wide load: the Earth weighs approximately 6,588,000,000,000,000,000,000,000 tons.

FIRST HITS

Here are the inside stories of the first hit records for three of the most successful music acts in history—the Beatles, Elvis, and Simon & Garfunkel—from Behind the Hits, *by Bob Shannon and John Javna.*

T HE BEATLES

First Hit: "Love Me Do," 1962

BACKGROUND: The tune was written by Paul McCartney, who called it "our greatest philosophical song." He skipped school and wrote it when he was sixteen years old.

By the time the Beatles went to London in 1962 to try to get a recording contract, it was one of their best numbers.

They played it at their audition…but the record executive assigned to work with them, George Martin, wasn't particularly impressed. Still, he agreed to give them a contract—and even make "Love Me Do" their first single—provided they got a new drummer.

THE SESSION: The recording session took place on September 11, 1962, at Abbey Road Studios. The Beatles arrived with a new drummer, Ringo Starr…But Martin didn't trust him and brought his own session drummer, Andy White, to make the record. Ringo was despondent, so Martin took pity on him; he recorded several versions with Ringo, and several with White. (In fact, Ringo played on the English hit, and White was the drummer on the single released in America.) It took seventeen takes to get the song right. By the time they were done, John Lennon's lips were numb from playing the harmonica so much.

IT'S A HIT. On October 4, 1962, "Love Me Do" was released in England on Parlophone Records. It surged into the Top 20 and established the Beatles as a viable commercial group. But behind the scenes was manager Brian Epstein, making sure that the Beatles succeeded. He bought 10,000 copies himself, knowing that was the minimum amount their record company had to sell to make a disc a best-seller. Epstein's gimmick worked. The record company was impressed and got behind the Beatles' next single, "Please Please Me," which reached #1 in Britain and started a chain of events that revolutionized popular music.

In America, in 1962, no one wanted any part of the silly "Love Me Do." Capitol Records, which owned the rights to the song, practically gave it to Vee Jay Records, which later issued it on an album called "Introducing the Beatles."

On May 2, 1964, about a year and a half after it was first re-leased, "Love Me Do" became the Beatles' fourth American #1 record.

ELVIS PRESLEY

First Hit: "Heartbreak Hotel," 1956

BACKGROUND: The headline on the front page of the *Miami Herald* read, "Do You Know This Man?" Below it was a photograph of a suicide victim. Who was he? The story explained that he'd left no clue about his identity behind—only a pathetic hand-written message that read, "I walk a lonely street." It asked the family—or anyone who recognized the photo—to get in touch with the police.

THE SONG: In Gainesville, Florida, a songwriter named Tommy Durden read the paper and was struck by the suicide note. Now *that* was a great line for a blues tune, he mused. The more he thought about it, the more he liked it...so he hopped in his car and drove over to Mae Axton's house to work on it. Mae was Tommy's col-laborator in songwriting; she was also a local TV and radio person-ality. When Elvis Presley had come to town earlier in the year, she'd befriended the young singer and reportedly assured him that she'd be the one to write his first million-seller.

Mae agreed that the suicide line might make a good song, but couldn't stop thinking about how the guy's family would suffer when they found out about him. He might have walked a lonely street, but at the end of it there was surely going to be heartbreak for the people who loved him. So Mae decided there should be a "heartbreak hotel" at the end of "lonely street." From there it took fifteen minutes to write the whole song.

IT'S A HIT: A friend of Mae's named Glen Reeves dropped by her house and agreed to tape a version of the song in a pseudo-Elvis style—so Elvis would be able to imagine how he'd sound on the tune. Then Mae, demo in hand, drove up to Tennessee to play it for Elvis. "Hot dog, Mae!" Presley is said to have exclaimed, "Play it again!" Legend has it that when he recorded the song, Elvis copied Reeves's version note-for-note.

In exchange for agreeing to make it his first RCA record, Elvis got an equal share of the writer's credit. "Heartbreak Hotel" went to the top of the charts, establishing Elvis as the most popular new singer in America.

SIMON & GARFUNKEL

First Hit: "Hey Schoolgirl," 1957

BACKGROUND: Paul Simon got to know Artie Garfunkel in P.S. 164 in Queens when they both appeared in their sixth-grade graduation play, *Alice In Wonderland*. Paul was the White Rabbit, Artie was the Cheshire Cat. Because of their mutual interest in music, they became close friends, and when they were fourteen, they began writing songs together.

THE SINGERS: According to Paul Simon: "We were fifteen years old when we signed a contract with Big Records as Tom and Jerry. 'Hey Schoolgirl' was the first song we recorded. To go along with the Tom and Jerry thing, I took on the stage name of Tom Landis and Artie took Jerry Graph. I picked Landis because I was going out with a girl named Sue Landis at the time and Artie picked Graph because he used to [keep track] of all the current hit records on big sheets of graph paper. 'Hey Schoolgirl' was sold in both 45 and 78 RPM; on the 45 it says by Landis-Graph, but on the 78 it's got P. Simon and A. Garfunkel."

IT'S A HIT: The song was released in 1957 and sold 120,000 copies, peaking at #54 after being on *Billboard's* "Top 100" for nine weeks. "You can't imagine," says Simon, "what it was like having a hit record behind you at the age of sixteen. One month Artie and I were watching 'American Bandstand' on television and the next month we were on the show." They had to follow Jerry Lee Lewis playing "Great Balls of Fire." It's one of the few "Bandstand" shows not preserved on tape.

"Hey Schoolgirl" was "Tom and Jerry's" only hit. Simon says he bought a red Impala convertible with the royalties.

IF THE SHOE FITS...

In ancient Inca weddings, the bride and groom weren't considered "officially" married until they had taken off their sandals and traded them with one another.

OH, MARILYN

Some little known facts about the life of the ultimate Hollywood icon.

Marilyn Monroe was born Norma Jean Mortenson, an illegitimate child, on June 1, 1926 in Los Angeles. Her mother, Gladys Pearl Baker, was a negative cutter in a Hollywood film studio. Her father, Edward Mortenson, was a baker.

Norma Jean's mother entered a sanitarium when she was three, and sent Norma Jean to live with her aunt. Her aunt later dumped her in a Los Angeles orphanage, where she was neglected and sexually abused.

Norma Jean spent much of her childhood in foster homes. She married an aircraft worker at age 16—to avoid getting sent to yet another foster home.

★

She was was discovered by an Army photographer whose boss had told him "to take some morale-building shots of pretty girls for *Yank* and *Stars and Stripes*." The photographer's boss: a soldier named Ronald Reagan.

She stuttered as a child: "It comes back sometimes," she said. "Once I had a small part with a scene in which I had to climb a staircase and I couldn't bring out my line. The director rushed over and shouted: 'You don't actually stutter?' 'Y-y-you th-think not?' I said to him."

Early in her career, Monroe was desperate for money. So she agreed to pose nude for a calendar, and was paid the standard modeling fee. To date more than 1 million copies of the photos have been sold, generating more than $750,000 in profits. Marilyn's share: $50.

Marilyn never understood why men were so attracted to her: "Why I was a siren, I hadn't the faintest idea. There were no thoughts of sex in my head…I had no thoughts of being seduced by a duke or a movie star. The truth was that with all my lipstick and mascara and precocious curves, I was as unsensual as a fossil. But I seemed to affect people otherwise."

Oops! One third of the U.S. population is reportedly the result of unwanted pregnancies.

TEARS IN THE SNOW

All's fair in love, war…and politics. But did somebody go just a little too far to win in '72? Here's information from a new book called It's a Conspiracy, *by the American Paranoid Society.*

BACKGROUND

As election year 1972 got underway, all eyes turned to New Hampshire, the nation's first primary. The Republican candidate would be President Richard Nixon, of course. But his re-election was not the foregone conclusion it seems in retrospect. Among other issues, his handling of the Vietnam war made him vulnerable.

• The Democrats' early favorite, Ted Kennedy, had been knocked out by Chappaquiddick. Of the eleven Democrats running, Senator Ed Muskie—Hubert Humphrey's 1968 running mate—looked like the strongest candidate. In the polls, a Muskie-Nixon race was dead even.

• Because Muskie was from Maine, he was expected to win the New Hampshire primary easily. But experts said a really impressive victory might clinch the nomination for him early.

WHAT HAPPENED

• William Loeb, owner and editor of New Hampshire's largest newspaper (the *Union Leader*)—and an arch-conservative—had been sniping at his liberal neighbor for years, nicknaming him "Moscow Muskie."

• Loeb also constantly repeated claims that Muskie had called French-Canadian descendants "Canucks," an unforgivable ethnic slur. This offended nearly half the state's voters.

• A little more than a week before the primary, Loeb ran a story about Mrs. Muskie headlined, "Big Daddy's Jane," slurring the candidate's wife as a heavy boozer with an itch for dirty stories.

A government study of U.S. eating habits turned up a man who drank 64 cups of coffee a day.

• It was a serious accusation in conservative New Hampshire. Muskie, terribly stung by the cheap shot at his wife, took the attack personally. He took the fight to Loeb the next day.

• Standing on a flatbed truck in a driving snowstorm outside *Union Leader* offices, the senator called Loeb ,"a gutless coward." Then Muskie, slump-shouldered and weary from campaigning, stood in the blizzard and wept.

• It was touching, but it killed him in the polls. Broadcast endlessly on the news, Muskie's emotional moment made him look like a basket case. As *Time* put it: "The moment of weakness left many voters wondering about Muskie's ability to stand up under stress."

• Muskie still won the primary, but with such a small margin that his campaign lost its momentum and soon collapsed.

THE OFFICIAL EXPLANATION

Since there were no allegations of a conspiracy at the time of the incident, there were no official explanations denying one.

SUSPICIOUS FACTS

• Loeb's source for the "Canuck" story was a letter from Paul Morrison in Deerfield Beach, Florida. However, when veteran reporter David Broder looked for Morrison, he could not be found.

• In fact, the Muskie camp was *plagued* with bizarre incidents. In March, 200 letters on *Citizens for Muskie* stationery were sent to supporters of Henry Jackson, a Muskie rival. The letters—which created tension between the Democratic camps—contended that Jackson had fathered an illegitimate child, and was later arrested on "homosexual charges."

• Some voters in largely white New Hampshire got calls at 2 or 3AM from representatives of the "Harlem for Muskie Committee" who promised "full justice for black people."

• Sometimes, the skulduggery was really intricate. "At a Muskie fund-raiser for 1300 people in Washington, D.C., several arrivals weren't planned: 200 pizzas nobody ordered, two magicians, and 16 ambassadors from African and Middle Eastern countries who, though entirely out of place, had to be treated courteously and fed."

It took 1,700 years to complete the Great Wall of China.

WAS THERE A CONSPIRACY?

Theory #1: YES. Ed Muskie was systematically harrassed and embarrassed to destroy his candidacy.

• The reporters who later broke the Watergate story said the "Canuck" letter and all the other tricks were part of a "massive campaign of political spying and sabotage conducted on behalf of the re-election effort by the White House and Nixon campaign officials."

• The "Canuck" letter was said to have been written by White House PR man Ken Clawson, but he denied it. According to Nixon's master of dirty tricks, Donald Segretti, Muskie's Washington fund raiser almost had one more guest: "We also made inquiries about renting an elephant, but were unable to make the arrangements."

• In time, all of Nixon's '72 adversaries were destroyed in one way or another. The Democrats' eventual nominee, George McGovern, was scuttled by leaks that his running mate had been in a mental hospital; George Wallace, whose strong appeal to conservatives might have drawn votes from Nixon, was shot in the stomach; and Ted Kennedy never ran because of Chappaquiddick. Coincidences?

Theory #2: NO. Loeb acted on his own.

• In light of the facts that came to light after Watergate, that's pretty hard to believe. The real question is, how far did the Nixon tricksters go in undermining the democratic process?

PARTING SHOTS

Muskie later said that though he was upset, he had not actually cried: it was melting snow running down his face. Whatever—it cost him the election. "It was," as he put it, "a bitch of a day."

Ringo Starr once claimed he wanted to get rich in order to open a chain of hairdressing salons.

SOLUTIONS

POP QUIZ, PAGE 18

1. Her eyes
2. Discovered by accident
3. Stearic acid from beef fat
4. At a picnic
5. Missionaries, because they were embarassed by all that bare skin
6. A crocodile
7. From his father's cowlick
8. Shirley Temple, W. C. Fields
9. Trick question—it *was* Bogart
10. Moe, Shemp, and Curley
11. Actually Vance was one year *younger*
12. Stabbed during a fight over a hunting dog
13. *Scrambled Eggs*
14. One
15. Two. Exactly the same. (There's one long groove on each side.)
16. Plastic
17. TV show
18. Money

HOW LONG, PAGE 58

1. B; 2. B; 3. A; 4. C; 5. C; 6. C; 7. B; 8. A; 9. B;
10. A; 11. B; 12. B; 13. A; 14. B; 15. B; 16. A; 17. A; 18. B.

PUNS:

1. "People who live in grass houses shouldn't stow thrones."
2. "Repaint, and thin no more."
3. "Let your pages do the walking through the yellow fingers."
4. "It takes two Wongs to make a white."
5. "I wouldn't send a knight out on a dog like this"
6. "A Benny shaved is a benny urned."
7. "The Czech is in the male."
8. "A weigh a day keeps the doctor an apple."

THE LAST PAGE

FELLOW BATHROOM READERS:

The fight for good bathroom reading should never be taken loosely—we must sit firmly for what we believe in, even while the rest of the world is taking pot shots at us.

Once we prove we're not simply a flush-in-the-pan, writers and publishers will find their resistance unrolling.

So we invite you to take the plunge: "Sit Down and Be Counted!" by joining The Bathroom Readers' Institute. Send a self-addressed, stamped envelope to: B.R.I., 1400 Shattuck Avenue, #25, Berkeley, CA 94709. You'll receive your attractive free membership card, a copy of the B.R.I. newsletter (if we ever get around to publishing one), and earn a permanent spot on the B.R.I. honor roll.

ⓒ⋗   ⓒ⋗   ⓒ⋗

UNCLE JOHN'S *FIFTH* BATHROOM READER IS IN THE WORKS

Don't fret—there's more good reading on its way. In fact, there are a few ways you can contribute to the next volume:

l) Is there a subject you'd like to see us cover? Write and let us know. We aim to please.

2) Got a neat idea for a couple of pages in the new Reader? If you're the first to suggest it, and we use it, we'll send you a free copy of the book.

3) Have you seen or read an article you'd recommend as quintessential bathroom reading? Or is there a passage in a book that you want to share with other B.R.I. members? Tell us where to find it, or send a copy. If you're the first to suggest it and we publish it in the next volume, there's a free book in it for you.

Well, we're out of space, and when you've gotta go, you've gotta go. Hope to hear from you soon. Meanwhile, remember:
Go With the Flow.